Mindful COUNSELLING and PSYCHOTHERAPY

SAGE has been part of the global academic community since 1965, supporting high quality research and learning that transforms society and our understanding of individuals, groups and cultures. SAGE is the independent, innovative, natural home for authors, editors and societies who share our commitment and passion for the social sciences.

Find out more at: **www.sagepublications.com**

Mindful COUNSELLING *and* PSYCHOTHERAPY

PRACTISING MINDFULLY ACROSS APPROACHES & ISSUES

MEG BARKER

Los Angeles | London | New Delhi
Singapore | Washington DC

Los Angeles | London | New Delhi
Singapore | Washington DC

SAGE Publications Ltd
1 Oliver's Yard
55 City Road
London EC1Y 1SP

SAGE Publications Inc.
2455 Teller Road
Thousand Oaks, California 91320

SAGE Publications India Pvt Ltd
B 1/I 1 Mohan Cooperative Industrial Area
Mathura Road
New Delhi 110 044

SAGE Publications Asia-Pacific Pte Ltd
3 Church Street
#10-04 Samsung Hub
Singapore 049483

Editor: Kate Wharton
Production editor: Rachel Burrows
Copyeditor: Solveig Gardner Servian
Proofreader: Anna Gilding
Marketing manager: Tamara Navaratnam
Cover design: Jennifer Crisp
Typeset by: C&M Digitals (P) Ltd, Chennai, India
Printed in India at Replika Press Pvt Ltd

Library of Congress Control Number: 2012955290

British Library Cataloguing in Publication data

A catalogue record for this book is available from the
British Library

ISBN 978–1–4462–1110–6
ISBN 978–1–4462–1111–3 (pbk)

Contents

About the author

Meg Barker is a senior lecturer in psychology at the Open University and a sexual and relationship therapist. Meg has researched and written extensively on relationships, gender and sexuality – particularly on bisexuality, BDSM and polyamory – and discusses these matters for a general audience on the Rewriting the Rules blog (www.rewriting-the-rules.com). Meg co-edits the journal *Psychology & Sexuality* and co-organises the Critical Sexology, Social Mindfulness, BiUK and Sense about Sex projects, as well as working closely with the College of Sexual and Relationship Therapists (COSRT). Meg is also the co-author of the Sage books *Understanding counselling and psychotherapy* (with Andreas Vossler and Darren Langdridge), and *Sexuality and gender for mental health professionals: A practical guide* (with Christina Richards).

Acknowledgements

Much gratitude to Christina Richards for all her expertise on mental health and counselling psychology, which this book would have been much weaker without, as well as for invaluable proofreading. Thanks so much to Steven Stanley for helping to forge the social mindfulness project and for being a fellow lone mindful voice in the wilderness of critical social psychology.

Thanks to all of my fellow mindful therapists, counsellors, psychologists and scientists as well as to all the Buddhist scholars and practitioners who are engaging in these important debates. I would particularly like to acknowledge Stephen and Martine Batchelor for setting me on this long and fruitful journey with their inspirational writing.

Introduction

Aims

This chapter aims to:

- invite you into a mindful engagement with this book,
- introduce mindfulness, and the various ways in which it can be understood,
- begin our exploration of how counsellors and therapists might engage with mindful ideas and practices,
- give you a sense of where we'll be going in the rest of the book.

An invitation to mindfulness

Martine Batchelor (2001) tells the story of a friend of hers who, after years in a Zen monastery, decided to return to the world. He took a job in PR in New York City, which is about as far from the life of a monk as it is possible to get. When he got there, he put a sign up above his front door which said 'Zendo' (meditation hall) so that he would see it every morning as he left for work.

The point he was making is that life is our meditation hall. As we will see, mindfulness is not something to be practised on a cushion and left behind as soon as we stand up; rather it is a way of being which we attempt to bring to everything we do. As the author of the classic book *The Miracle of Mindfulness*, Thich Nhat Hanh ([1975] 1991: 27) puts it: 'every day and every hour, one should practice mindfulness' (he also goes on to say that this is by no means an easy task!).

This has implications for the way in which we approach this book, you and I.

For me, the challenge is to write mindfully. That means bringing my attention to the task in hand rather than drifting off into panics about how many words I've written so far, or fantasies of seeing the completed book on the bookshelf. It is about a kind of focused attention: while I'm writing this sentence I attempt to be writing this sentence.

That attention operates within a wider, more spacious, awareness. I'm aware of the baggage I bring to this task: desires to make a book that is all things to all people, or fears of being exposed in the areas I'm less knowledgeable about. I'm aware of a tendency to distraction, perhaps in order to avoid these concerns: I could just check my email, or get another cup of coffee, or search for a reference to justify what I'm saying. Being mindful is about noticing when my attention drifts and gently bringing myself back to what I'm doing. Perhaps I notice tension in my shoulders, or the fact that I snap when I'm interrupted. I pause, take a breath, and remind myself of what it is that I'm doing here.

And what I am doing, fundamentally, is something social: I am communicating with you. Writing, like therapy, involves a constant awareness of the interconnections between us, rather than remaining stuck within myself and my own anxieties and cravings. For example, instead of trying to prove how much I know, I can imagine what you – as somebody who is perhaps new to this area – will want to find out about and how best to put this across. I am also in communication with all the authors, researchers and therapists whose work I am drawing upon in this book. How can I do them justice and interest you in further dialogue with others who are passionate about these ideas and practices?

For you, I invite you to read this book mindfully[1].

Pause for reflection

Before reading on, consider how you are approaching this book.

- What situations are you reading in? (e.g. Rushing to work? As part of a slow Sunday morning? Working towards a specific course or assignment?)
- What do you bring to the reading? (e.g. Your own therapeutic expertise? Certain associations with Buddhism or mindfulness therapy? Past experiences with meditation or similar practices?)
- What are you hoping for, and expecting from, the book? (To check it off your to-do list? To get a new technique to add to your toolkit? To help yourself with your own struggles? To make some new connections?)

---

[1]This is an idea that I developed from Christina Richards's (2011) work on reader reflexivity.

You could attempt to be present to what you are reading (or to do it another time if that's not where you're at). You might consider, for example, how much you read at one go; whether you pause at all to reflect on what you're reading; whether you engage with the practices I suggest now, or later, or not at all; and whether you make notes as you go along to connect what you read with your own thoughts and experiences, and other ideas that you've come across.

Just as I try to be mindful of you as I write, you could attempt to be mindful of the human being behind this writing. I'm somebody who has been reading about Buddhism for the past decade, and who brings mindful ideas and practices into my work having trained in other forms of therapy. My background in psychology means that I have a pretty good understanding of the social and cognitive psychological research in this area. However, I am not a Buddhist scholar, nor am I a neuroscientist, nor have I done the '8-week course' in mindfulness-based cognitive therapy (MBCT), which is often held up as the one legitimate approach to mindful counselling (NICE, 2000)[2].

It is my hope that the breadth of knowledge that I bring will be useful, particularly to a beginner in this area. I can give you a sense of where these mindful ideas come from and how they have influenced the various western therapeutic approaches (rather than focusing on one form of therapy, as many books do). I can give you my own thoughts on the aspects of mindful theory and practice which will be useful for the various forms of suffering that we encounter in the therapy room, drawing on research and writing in these areas.

As we will see, there is no one true version of mindfulness, and it has been understood in different ways by different people at different times. My own approach emphasises social, relational and ethical aspects, so there will be more on these than in some of the cognitive-behavioural therapy or neuroscientific books on the topic for example. However, like most western authors on this topic I will inevitably translate the original ideas around mindfulness into a form which makes sense in the world that I live in. And it will be a translation of a translation as I draw primarily on other authors and therapists who have already adapted these ideas into this context. I will attempt to be mindful myself of both the potentials and pitfalls of such adaptations (Williams & Kabat-Zinn, 2011b).

For a deeper understanding of the theories, practices or research which I touch upon, I invite you to follow up on the Further Reading suggestions at the end of each chapter which resonate with you.

---

[2]The '8 week course' is the basis of all major university accredited mindfulness trainings in the UK, but is only one 'way in' which you may want to consider alongside the other possibilities covered in this book.

What is mindfulness?

Mindful experience

Before we get into the various ways in which mindfulness can be defined, let's turn to the experience of being mindful so that you can get a sense of what it feels like to you.

Practice: Mindful haiku

This activity is based on the work of Nugent, Moss, Barnes and Wilks (2011). They wanted to understand the experience of being mindful, so they got a group of healthcare practitioners to take part in mindful practice and to write a list of words and phrases associated with it, which they then turned into a haiku (see below). It is up to you whether you do one, two or all three parts of this activity. If expressing the experience in writing doesn't work for you, you could always try drawing or speaking about it instead.

1. Mindful practice[3]:

Find somewhere quiet and sit comfortably, either on a cushion or in a chair, with your back upright but not tense. Rest your hands in your lap or on your knees.

Close your eyes and check for any parts of your body that feel tense: your face, your shoulders, your back. Relax these. Breathe in and out three times.

Now for 10 minutes focus your attention on your breath. Don't try to control its rhythm but just notice it happening. Become aware of the various sensations that accompany it entering and leaving your body: the warmth or coolness of the air, the feeling of your body against the floor or chair, the shifting of your clothes against your skin. Let your mind settle on the ebb and flow of the breath like a boat which is anchored, gently rising and falling with the waves. If you find yourself distracted by thoughts or physical sensations, don't judge them or try to stop them, just notice them and gently bring your attention back to the breath.

---

[3]Adapted from Batchelor (1997: 23). This is a meditative method which dates back to the earliest Buddhist scriptures and is prominent in most recent Buddhist and therapy texts on mindfulness. The way Buddha put it was 'just mindful he breathes in, mindful he breathes out ... When a monk breathes in long, he knows "I breathe in long"; and when he breathes out long, he knows, "I breathe out long" ... When he breathes in short, he knows "I breathe in short"; and when he breathes out short, he knows, "I breathe out short"'.

2. Word list

After opening your eyes and stretching, write down a list of all the words and phrases that you can think of to describe the experience.

3. Haiku

Once you have this list, write a haiku based on any of these words or phrases to capture something of this experience. A haiku is a Japanese poem. In English they tend to be written on three lines with five syllables in the first line, seven in the second, and five in the third (although you don't have to stick rigidly to that here, just three linked phrases is fine). For example, something I came up with was:

> Sat still, open arms
> Thoughts rush in to fill the space
> Still empty really.

Of course there might be many haiku you could write about the same experience, so don't worry about the task, just see what happens when you put your words and phrases into this form.

We'll come back to the specific value of therapists and counsellors practising mindfulness themselves in Chapter 2. For now, the kinds of things the practitioners in this study said about the experience were that mindfulness enabled space to pause in life; that it deepened their relationships with themselves (e.g. through tuning into how they felt); that it enabled them to observe things they wouldn't otherwise have noticed (such as how tense they were), opening up the potential of changing these things; and that it was a way of paying attention that they could bring to any experience (not just to specific meditations like this one).

Participants also said that being mindful often brought discomfort and uncertainty. This is something worth emphasising from the start, going back to what Thich Nhat Hanh said about mindfulness not being easy. Quietly attending to ourselves does not always bring peace. It can bring us face to face with things that we'd rather avoid. Also the ways in which being mindful invites us to engage with thoughts and feelings can be very challenging. For example, many practices suggest that we notice and let go of these, rather than avoiding them or following them and making stories out of them as we generally do.

Most autobiographical accounts of people's first attempts at mindful meditation include words like 'boredom', 'pain', 'frustration' and 'anger' more often than they do words like 'calm', 'peace' and 'wisdom' which we often associate with such practices. It is worth bearing this in mind when we decide to engage ourselves, or our clients, with mindfulness. We should be aware of the expectations that people tend to have, and the reality that most people experience. We'll come back to this in more detail in Chapter 1 when we explore mindful practices in depth.

Defining mindfulness

If you haven't previously read anything about mindful therapies or Buddhism, your definition of 'mindful' might be something like 'remembering something' or 'taking heed whilst doing something'. As therapists we might say 'I'm mindful of the cultural pressures around body image' when we don't want to assume that it will be easy for our client to stop obsessing about their appearance, for example. Mindfulness is a reminder to keep something in mind.

There is something of this sense of remembering in the Buddhist idea of mindfulness (Bodhi, 2011). We have to keep remembering to return our attention to what we are doing, as it inevitably drifts off (Analayo, 2003). Whether meditating or trying to be mindful in my everyday life I constantly forget and fall back into old habits. Part of being mindful is a continued commitment to remember to gently redirect our attention.

'Mindfulness' was the way in which one of the first people to translate Buddhist scriptures into English, Rhys-Davids ([1810] 2007), translated the Pali language word 'sati'. Sati originally connoted remembering, but the Buddha gave it a new meaning, referring to a state of wakeful awareness in which we purposefully, gently and spaciously attend to our whole experience, whatever we are doing. The Buddha described it as 'contemplating the body in the body ... feelings in feelings ... mind in mind ... phenomena in phenomena, ardent, clearly comprehending, mindful, having removed covetousness and displeasure in regard to the world' (Bodhi, 2011: 20). This is what I was trying to capture when I reflected on how we might mindfully read, or write, this book, and it is also what we were cultivating in the breathing practice.

The emphasis on attention and awareness is reflected in the word cloud (Figure 0.1) of current words associated with mindfulness.

Pause for reflection

Which of the words you came up with earlier appear in this cloud? Which are missing?

Figure 0.1 'What is mindfulness?' word cloud[4]

We might define mindfulness as something like giving open, curious attention to the way that things are, rather than attempting to avoid or grasp hold of any aspect of experience. There are, however, a few things to clarify about the concept of mindfulness which will echo through the rest of the book.

First, although it includes the word 'mind', mindfulness is certainly not about being 'full of mind' or focused on what is going on in our heads. Some have even suggested that 'heartfulness' and/or 'bodyfulness' might be more appropriate terms. Buddhism is 'non-dualistic' (Dunne, 2011), which means that it doesn't separate the mind from the body, or thoughts from emotions, or internal experiences from external ones. So when we are mindful we open our awareness to all experience that bubbles up (sensations, thoughts, feelings, sounds, etc.) and we may well begin to realise how tricky it is to draw distinctions between them (how is the feeling of stress separate from the sharp feeling in my throat? Which part of this shame is the thought and which is the feeling? Where does the sound end and my hearing of it begin? What is this 'me' that I'm referring to?).

Second, although 'mindfulness' is a noun, Rhys-Davids suggests that *sati* is a verb: it is not a thing or an object, but rather a practice or way of being: he talks of a 'presence of mind' and a 'wakefulness of heart' ([1890] 1963: 58). This has implications for researching mindfulness

---

[4]Adapted from www.wordle.net/show/wrdl/4709248/WhatIsMindfulness. The cloud was created by copying the first couple of pages of google hits for 'what is mindfulness' into wordle. The bigger the word, the more times it was mentioned.

(see Chapter 4): is mindfulness an object that we can study (Stanley, 2012c)? It also has implications for practice as it is not just a form of meditation, but a way of being in our whole life.

Third, you may well also have come across a definition of mindfulness which is something like 'non-judgemental attention to the present moment'[5]. This version owes a lot to the work of Jon Kabat-Zinn, who popularised mindfulness in western psychotherapy. Certainly *one version* of mindfulness does involve continually bringing our awareness back to the present moment and non-judgementally accepting any feelings, sensations or thoughts that arise. This is partly why breathing meditation is so popular, because our breath is always available to us and it grounds us in the here-and-now of what we are doing. However, neither the present moment nor being non-judgemental are intrinsic to mindfulness (Dreyfuss, 2011). As well as being mindful of the here-and-now, it is also possible to mindfully attend to a memory or to our plans for the future, for example, or to contemplate our death or other people in our lives in mindful meditation (when we cultivate awareness of the impermanence of life, or compassion). Regarding being non-judgemental (Gethin, 2011), if we attempt to bring mindfulness into our whole lives then we will also attempt to make judgements in a mindful manner, such as when we are deciding what the most ethical action is, for example, or whether to make an intervention in the therapy room. Also, some degree of discrimination is necessary in recognising and altering the habits that we notice when we are mindfully observing ourselves.

Fourth, as we will discover in Chapter 1, mindfulness was originally part of the path that Buddhists were encouraged to follow which advocated 'right mindfulness', not just 'mindfulness' alone. This means that it is intrinsically linked to ethics (Grossman, 2010). The purpose of being mindful was to transcend the cravings, ignorance and hatred that lead to suffering: that was why the aim was to cultivate attention and remembering as opposed to carelessness and forgetfulness.

These issues are worth continuing to reflect upon as we explore different ways in which mindfulness has been taken up therapeutically. Is mindfulness an individual, mental activity, or might it raise wider implications for us as social and embodied beings? Can we study a thing called mindfulness or apply it as one technique among many, or is it a whole way of being that pervades life? How might the non-judgemental, present-focused form of mindfulness be useful, and what

---

[5]Indeed, this is the definition I drew upon in my previous chapter on mindfulness in Barker, Vossler, & Langdridge (2010). I considered the key elements to be: awareness, (non-judgemental) acceptance and presence. Although exploration of the latter two is useful, we can now see that perhaps only the former (awareness) is really integral to the concept.

other forms of mindfulness are possible beyond this? Is mindfulness a form of attention that can be cultivated by anyone for any purpose (e.g. becoming more productive, or even military training), or is it inextricably linked to a specific ethical stance towards suffering?

Barnes, Moss and Stanley (in prep) apply an idea from systemic therapy to current understandings of mindfulness. In families and other groups, certain 'boastful' stories get told which become the dominant stories (e.g. of who does what in the family, or how they came to be this way). These stories often overwhelm and silence more 'shy' stories. Barnes et al. argue that scientific stories that involve measuring mindfulness and assessing its impact on symptoms have become the boastful stories, and we will return to these in more detail in Chapter 4 when we look at scientific research on mindfulness. However, in this book I will attempt to give room to some of the shyer stories of mindfulness, as well as the more boastful ones, and to highlight some places where these are in tension. For example, as we will see in Chapters 3 and 5, many recent versions of mindfulness are advocated to make people happier, which is in conflict with other versions of mindfulness that see the pursuit of happiness as part of the problem. It is up to you, of course, to reflect on such tensions and to find your own position in relation to them.

We may well find, as we go along, that it is more useful to focus on the experience of being mindful and to float between different understandings of the term rather than grasping after one fixed definition.

Mindful counselling and psychotherapy

Mindfulness therapies have been the fastest growing therapeutic approaches in recent years, with more and more professionals seeking training in this area and looking to complement their own approaches with mindfulness. Mindfulness is increasingly officially recognised as an effective treatment for a variety of 'common mental health problems', with positive outcomes in research evaluating its success (see Chapter 4). The number of research publications on mindfulness being produced worldwide increased exponentially in the late 1990s and continues to rise. There are many best-selling self-help books outlining mindfulness approaches for a general audience, so it is also increasingly likely that people will already be engaged in some form of mindfulness when they seek professional help.

Mark Williams and Jon Kabat-Zinn (2011b), along with many contributors to their recent edited collection on mindfulness, argue that the current time is a critical point at which to pause and take stock about this convergence of classical Buddhist teachings and western therapy and psychology.

They suggest that we need to reflect upon potential confluences and disjunctions and also to think about how we go forward from here. It is my hope that this book will be part of this process of reflection, and that it will enable readers new to this area to engage with mindfulness in a way that is informed by an awareness of both the potentials and limitations of integrating Buddhist philosophy and practice with western therapies.

In recent years mindfulness has become an umbrella term covering all engagements between psychology, psychotherapy and counselling on the one hand, and Buddhist theories and practices on the other. Perhaps this is partly due to the fact that the word 'mindfulness' doesn't have the religious connotations that the word 'Buddhism' holds, which may be off-putting to more secular western audiences. Whilst, as we have seen, mindfulness specifically refers to the cultivation of a certain form of attention, mindfulness therapies often include those that emphasise forms of acceptance or compassion, for example, as well as awareness and attention. This is, perhaps, appropriate because, as we will see in Chapter 1, mindfulness cannot really be extracted from the wider Buddhist theories in which it originates. Some have argued that mindfulness and other aspects (such as wisdom or loving-kindness) are intrinsically cultivated together: when you practise one, you practise the other (Salzberg, 2011).

For these reasons, this book will explore engagements between Buddhism and therapy beyond the very specific employment of mindful attention. However, the reader is encouraged to be aware that different writers use 'mindfulness' in very different ways. This ranges from a narrow definition of 'mindfulness meditation' as only practices where everything that emerges is attended to (in comparison to concentration meditations, like the breathing one, where we bring ourselves back to an object of concentration), to mindfulness encompassing various different meditation and everyday practices (as in Thich Nhat Hanh's approach), to mindfulness as an umbrella term for all engagements which draw on Buddhist theories or practices.

Figure 0.2 illustrates the three main sources that we will be drawing on in the book. Each source is multiple because there are many different forms of Buddhism, and these have been engaged with in even more diverse ways by the authors who have brought them to western audiences. Many forms of therapy have engaged with the various forms of Buddhism to produce diverse therapeutic concepts and practices, and mindfulness has been studied with a variety of methods and from diverse research perspectives.

The first four chapters of the book take us through each of these three sources. As Cohen (2010) neatly puts it, this is a journey from the Bodhi tree (where the Buddha found enlightenment), to the analyst's couch, to the MRI scanner. In Chapter 1 we focus on the main theories and practices of mindfulness, providing more background on the Buddhist

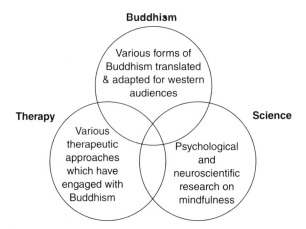

Figure 0.2 Three sources

understanding of suffering in which these originated, as well as further examples of mindful – and related – practices. In Chapters 2 and 3 we turn to counselling and psychotherapy, exploring the key ways in which we can apply mindfulness in our own work. In Chapter 2 we see that while mindfulness is often understood as something that we teach to clients, it can – and perhaps should – also be something that we practise ourselves as therapists, and a way of relating to clients. In Chapter 3 we consider how we might integrate mindfulness with our existing therapeutic approaches, exploring how cognitive-behavioural, humanistic, and psychodynamic therapists (in particular) have engaged with mindfulness. We cover the aspects of theory and practice that they have drawn upon, how this has impacted on their therapeutic practices, the research that has been conducted on the types of therapy that have emerged, and the meeting points and tensions that have emerged. In Chapter 4 we overview the research that has been conducted on these therapies to date, including the recent wave of neuroscientific studies on mindful brains, and outcome research about their effectiveness. We also cover less well known social psychological work on mindfulness and mindlessness as well as qualitative research on the mindful experience.

Once we have introduced mindful therapy and explored how we might work mindfully in general, we spend the rest of the book considering some of the most common difficulties that people present with in therapy, and how mindful ideas and practices might understand and work with these. In each case, we draw on Buddhist theory and practice, on specific mindfulness therapies that have addressed these issues, and on the research that has been conducted so far. In each chapter I offer examples to illustrate how we might usefully work with these issues in a mindful manner.

Finally, we conclude the book by considering what has been valuable about the ways in which western therapy has engaged with mindfulness so far, as well as exploring possible future directions. We turn our mindful attention on therapy itself, and I offer some thoughts on what my own preferred form of social mindfulness might have to offer.

Summary and conclusions

Mindfulness is a way of being that we can bring to everything we do, and which we might explicitly cultivate through meditation and through mindfully engaging in simple everyday activities. It can be defined, roughly, as giving open, curious attention to the way that things are, rather than attempting to avoid or grasp hold of any aspect of experience, although it is worth being aware of the different ways it is defined in different contexts and not grasping too tightly onto any of these.

Mindful therapies have become extremely popular in recent years. The rest of the book explores the ways in which Buddhist ideas and practices have been engaged with by western therapists and psychologists, and draws out implications of this work for the common issues that people bring to therapy.

Further reading

A great starting point, and a very accessible read, is Thich Nhat Hanh's classic book:
Nhat Hanh, T. ([1975] 1991). *The miracle of mindfulness.* London: Rider.

You can read more about Thich Nhat Hanh on his Plum Village website: www.plum village.org/thich-nhat-hanh.html.

If you are interested in going further into the various definitions and understandings of mindfulness, then the special issue of the journal *Contemporary Buddhism* which I mention in this chapter is very helpful:
Williams, J. M. G., & Kabat-Zinn, J. (Eds.). (2011). Special issue on mindfulness. *Contemporary Buddhism, 12* (1), 1–306.

A couple of very recent accessible self-help books on mindfulness are:
Williams, J. M., & Penman, D. (2011). *Mindfulness: A practical guide to finding peace in a frantic world.* London: Piatkus.

Heaversage, J., & Halliwell, E. (2012). *The mindful manifesto.* Carlsbad, CA: Hay House.

There are further resources on mindfulness listed at: http://socialmindfulness.word press.com/references/mindfulness.

PART ONE

Mindful therapies

ONE Mindful theory and practice

Aims

This chapter aims to:

- introduce the key theory behind mindfulness: the Buddhist understanding of human suffering and how to end it,
- briefly describe the history of Buddhism,
- consider how Buddhist ideas are relevant to the current western world and to therapy, covering two key ways in which they have been adapted to these contexts: secularisation and psychologisation,
- give a sense of the range of mindful practices that have emerged from the various forms of Buddhism and from more recent engagements with it, particularly focusing on forms of meditation.

Theory

While you read this chapter – as Keown (1996) suggests in his brief history of Buddhism – it is worth remembering the Buddhist tale of the difficulty of describing an elephant when you can't see it. Touching one part of the elephant will leave us with a poor perception of what the whole animal is like, and it is inevitable that such a short overview won't capture the entirety of Buddhism. Hopefully, though, I will give some sense of the parts I am emphasising and missing out so that you can access appropriate further reading if you'd like to gain a fuller picture.

The ideas and practices that we are drawing on in this book originated around the fifth century BCE in the foothills of the Himalayas with the man who became known as 'the Buddha'. Whilst he clearly drew on many of the ways of understanding and relating to the world that were around in that time and place (e.g. reincarnation and meditation), he also put forward a new way of making sense of suffering and proposed an alternative form of meditative practice that would explicitly address this.

Right from the start we can see why Buddhist ideas would be of such interest to counsellors and psychotherapists because the whole philosophy originated in an attempt to understand why people suffer, and – like psychotherapy – the solution that is proposed involves internal exploration to yield a deep understanding of our own nature (Watson, 2008).

The Buddha was born to a noble family and named Siddhattha Gotama[1] (he was only called the Buddha, or enlightened one, after his awakening). The story goes that he lived his early years in palaces surrounded by servants who attended to all his needs. His father attempted to ensure that he was never confronted by anything that would distress him. However, as he grew older, he became restless and dissatisfied and wanted to journey beyond the palace walls. His father tried to make it so that he would see nothing disturbing on these journeys. However, despite this, Siddhattha saw one person crippled by old age, one person wracked with illness, a corpse and a wandering monk. As a result of this he realised that life was transient and uncertain, and that it inevitably involved suffering.

Troubled by these realisations, Siddhattha left his home and family, including a wife and son, and became a homeless monk himself, seeking a spiritual answer to the human condition. He practised the religions of the day, including entering profound meditative states, denying himself pleasures, and controlling his breath and food intake, which left him weak and emaciated. These experiences, after the pampered life of the palaces, encouraged him to seek a middle way between extremes of indulgence and austerity. At this point he sat under a tree (which later became known as 'the Bhodi tree') for seven days. At the end of this time he had an awakening and understood the nature of suffering and how to end it. Although he realised how difficult it would be to communicate this realisation to others, he decided not to retreat into solitude and instead spent the rest of his life travelling and teaching.

It is unlikely that this account of the Buddha's life is historically accurate[2]. Rather this story itself is a way of communicating the key

---

[1] He is called Siddhattha Gotama in Pali, the language in which the earliest Buddhist scriptures were written, and Siddhartha Gautama, in Sanskrit.

[2] This is both because it was only a few centuries after he died that accounts of his life began to emerge, and because the concept of a narrative biography is a western invention (Keown, 1996).

ideas of the philosophy. We live our lives locked in 'palaces', often of our own creation, where we attempt to have all of the things that we desire and none of the things that we don't. We distract ourselves from the scary realities of ageing, pain and death. Despite our sense of security and safety in our 'palaces', these realities make their way into our awareness and we realise, on some level, that life involves suffering and that it ends. Recognition of this calls us to engage directly with suffering rather than trying to avoid it. This is also intrinsically linked (as in the Buddha's life) with the compassionate aim of ameliorating the suffering of others.

These elements of the story are captured in the main teachings of Buddhism (the Dharma). At the centre of this are the four 'noble truths'. As with mindfulness, rather than seeing these truths as objects or things to believe, it can be more useful to view them as actions to take.

The four noble truths as actions (adapted from Batchelor, 1997)

1 Attend to suffering.
2 Understand its roots in craving.
3 Let go of craving, in order to end suffering.
4 Cultivate the path (keep practising 1–3 and they will become more effortless).

Let's consider each of these 'noble truths' in a little more depth.

Suffering (or *dukkha*) is a broad term that encompasses the painful realities of life (the ageing, illness, pain and death of ourselves and others) as well as emotional and psychological forms of pain (such as grief, sorrow and despair) and the everyday dissatisfactions of not getting what we want and getting what we don't want[3]. The first part of the cessation of suffering is to face suffering head on rather than pretending that it isn't there or wishing that it didn't exist (which, in itself, is a form of craving). There is obviously a paradox here that suffering is ameliorated by facing up to the inevitability of suffering. Perhaps one useful way to understand this is that being with our pain as it is prevents the extra layers of suffering that we generally add to our experience.

---

[3]Some have misunderstood Buddhism as pessimistic due to this emphasis on suffering. It is important to realise that it is not saying that *all* life is suffering, just that there is suffering in life.

Because we tend to try desperately to prevent any suffering, when we do suffer we often feel bad about it. We become sad about being sad, tense about being in pain, guilty about feeling angry, scared about being afraid and so on. Attending to suffering prevents that additional layer of suffering, enabling us to see it more clearly as it is.

As we'll see later in the book, Buddhist understandings would not really separate out different kinds of suffering (as we frequently do with depression, anxiety, addiction, etc.) Rather these are all seen as part of general suffering, which is all rooted in the same thing: craving.

Craving, or thirst, is not the same thing as desire. Rather it is about a desire that is excessive or focused in problematic directions. So, for example, the desire to ease somebody else's suffering, or to stop doing something that is damaging you, would not be seen as craving[4]. Craving includes grasping hold of what is pleasant (attachment), hurling away what is unpleasant (aversion), and also delusion or ignorance (Olendzki, 2011) which we could understand as not recognising the complexity involved in determining what is good and bad[5]. This is something that is captured in that classic Rolling Stones song: you can't always get what you want but ... you might find you get what you need.

I find Martine Batchelor's metaphor for craving useful. She says that it is like having a precious object in our hand. We can grab hold of it so tight that we get cramp and can't see it, or we can hurl it away and lose it entirely. A middle way is to hold it firmly enough to protect it, but gently enough not to crush it, so that we can see it clearly and decide whether it is something to keep hold of or to put down (Batchelor, 2007). We can usefully apply this to many things beyond our possessions, for example aspects of ourselves, our identities, our relationships, our work and our feelings and thoughts.

Letting go of craving, as I'm sure you are aware, is easier said than done. This is where the practices of Buddhism – including mindfulness – come in, which we will explore in greater depth shortly. We attempt to slow down and to notice our tendencies to try to avoid suffering, to grasp what we want and to hurl away what we don't want, to distract ourselves, and to deny what is going on.

In observing these things we may realise some fundamental truths. For example, we see that everything – pleasant and unpleasant – passes away. At its most basic we find that the terrific itch we long to scratch

---

[4]Although they could be done in craving ways, for example if we are too invested in the role of rescuer or too perfectionist with ourselves, for example.

[5]The Taoist parable of the Chinese farmer is a useful one in relation to this. You can find it on p.132.

during meditation is not there a few minutes later. Recognising the impermanence of feelings, sensations, thoughts and so on brings us into a different relationship with them. We may also realise what it is that causes something to come into being. Instead of just finding ourselves in a rage or a panic, we begin to notice the combination of things that led to it, for example the way in which we followed a certain thought and turned it into a big story. We see how things come to be, and that they end (Bodhi, 2011).

We might also begin to question our conceptualisations of what is 'positive' and 'negative' anyway as we notice the strength that comes from difficult experiences, for example, or the way in which some-thing that feels good can be bad for us in various ways. Of particular significance in relation to letting go is our conceptualisation of our-selves. We may well notice that we cling to certain ideas of who we are and recoil from others. Letting go also involves putting down the sense of a fixed, static self. This can mean a relief from the suffering of trying to present a perfect self all the time and the fear that we are really lacking (Barker, 2012a).

Finally, *cultivating the path* involves committing to the first three 'noble truths' and practising them in meditation and in daily life. Stephen Batchelor (1997) uses the metaphor of a field of tall grass. Each time we walk a path through the field we flatten the grass and make it easier to walk the next time. Buddha proposed an 'eightfold path' of ways of being which would enable this cultivation. The path includes developing wisdom (through understanding the nature of suffering and resolving to let go of craving), developing morality (through communi-cating, acting and living in ways that will bring about the cessation of suffering in ourselves and others) and meditation (gaining control over our thoughts, and cultivating both mindful awareness and calm).

Pause for reflection

Does this understanding of suffering resonate with your own experience and/ or those of the clients you've worked with? Do you think they are relevant to the world in which you are working today? (See Teasdale & Chaskalson, 2011)

History

The Buddha appointed no successor and encouraged people to weigh up the Dharma for themselves, considering both the scriptures and their own experiences when deciding what to accept[6]. However, being a missionary religion, the Buddha's ideas and practices spread beyond the part of India where they began. Many different Buddhist schools and sects have developed over the centuries. One major separation is between the Theravāda school, which predominates in south Asian countries like Sri Lanka, Thailand and Burma, and the Māhāyana schools of North Asia.

Theravāda Buddhism emphasises the early teachings, whilst Māhā-yana forms of Buddhism adapted and developed these with further scriptures such as the Lotus Sūtra, which proposed that the original Dharma was a simplified version which Buddha created to be under-stood by the people at the time. Māhāyana Buddhisms include the Ch'an Buddhism of China (influenced by Taoism), and Japanese Zen which developed from this, as well as the Pure Land and Nichiren versions of Buddhism which flourished in Japan, and the Tibetan Vajrayāna (or tantra) school which is led by the Dalai Lama. Whilst there are commonalities between these schools, there are also impor-tant differences in both the ideas and practices that are considered to be key. It is worth being aware of which Buddhism/s are being drawn upon – and what their emphases are – when reading further around this area.

From this history we can see that the Dharma has adapted to fit each new culture it has entered; this isn't new to the current engage-ment between Buddhism and western thought. However, many would argue that this most recent leg of the journey of Buddhism is without parallel in relation to the cultural differences concerned (e.g. Bodhi, 2011).

In the nineteenth century, scholars began bringing Buddhism to western audiences through translations such as the one by Rhys-Davids which we encountered in the previous chapter. This began the process of western thinkers (such as the philosophers Schopenhauer and Nietzsche) drawing upon Buddhist ideas, and Buddhists from Asia bringing Buddhist ideas to western audiences (such as D. T. Suzuki and later the current Dalai Lama and Thich Nhat Hanh).

A particularly key moment occurred in the 1960s when many people who were disillusioned with western politics and ways of life went on 'the hippy trail'. Several people returned from Asia after engaging with forms of Buddhism, incorporating these in various ways into their own philosophy. This often involved a *secularisation* as religious aspects of

---

[6]From the Kalama Sutta, although Cohen (2010) warns that this Sutta is often taken out of context and over-emphasised because it resonates so well with a western liberal humanistic understanding of people as free agents.

Buddhism (such as the ideas of rebirth, karma and the presence of gods) were often stripped away or reinterpreted as metaphors.

It seems that we are currently going through a second key moment following the take-up of Buddhist ideas (as translated through the previous group of interpreters) by mainstream psychology and psychotherapy. This *psychologisation* leaves some people fearful that vital elements of Buddhist thought will be lost or diluted, and that it will be reduced to a mere therapy which may just make the cycle of craving and suffering more pleasant or bearable rather than actually liberating people from it (Bodhi, 2011; Cohen, 2010).

Commentators are split on the issues of both secularisation and psychologisation. On the one hand, both of these have opened up Buddhist ideas and practices to much wider audiences who might find them invaluable in their lives. Like the various directions that Mahāyana Buddhism has taken, perhaps we need to be open to 'skilful means'. This refers to any approach which makes these important ideas available to people. Talk of the Buddha or the four noble truths can be alienating to western audiences in a way that mindfulness is not, for example (Kabat-Zinn, 2011). On the other hand, with such adaptations, there is always a danger of exploitation or appropriation whereby vital ideas and practices are reduced to just another technique or become simply a passing fashion (Maex, 2011).

Personally, I tend to embrace the secularisation of authors such as Stephen Batchelor (2010) who have enabled me to engage with ideas that I have found immensely valuable, and I remain more sceptical of psychologisation as I notice a movement away from the political, ethical and social aspects of Buddhist thought which seem to be integral to me. My feelings on this matter will obviously influence the positions I take in this book, so I invite you to keep remembering that one could equally be critical of secularisation and embracing of psychologisation. Whatever the case, as Mark Williams and Jon Kabat-Zinn (2011b) (key figures in the current mindfulness movement) themselves highlight, it is important to retain respectfulness towards the original sources and a humility and gratitude as we develop our own thought and practice.

Returning to our pause for reflection, it is useful to wonder why Buddhist ideas have become so popular in the west in recent years. There are doubtless many reasons, but one possibility is that the kinds of cravings and sufferings that the Buddha highlighted are particularly endemic in the western world at the beginning of the twenty-first century. We seem hooked on wanting more of what we desire (e.g. possessions, success, the approval of others), comparing ourselves enviously to others who have these things, and desperately fearing the loss of them if we have them. Alain De Botton (2004) locates this pattern in a combination of secularism, democracy and consumer capitalism:

- *Secularism:* many of us no longer believe we will be rewarded in the next life, so we seek rewards in this one.
- *Democracy:* the idea that everyone can achieve success implies that if we don't succeed it is our own fault.
- *Consumer capitalism:* mass media and commerce relies on perpetuating the idea that we are lacking in some way that needs to be addressed (by watching this show or buying that product).

John Naish (2008) and others have related this to the ecological and economic difficulties that we now face. Oliver James (2007) suggests that, rather than leading to happiness, such a culture exacerbates suffering, as evidenced by our high rates of depression and anxiety.

Let's consider a case study to think through ways in which Buddhist teachings might be relevant to the lives of our clients today.

Case study: Erin

Erin is a 30-year-old woman who approaches you for help. In the first session she tells you her story. She says that she had a happy childhood. Her parents bought her nice things and encouraged her in school. She was popular and fitted in well, always enjoying the latest fashions in music and clothes. Pain and death were things she sometimes saw in crime shows or on the news but they never seemed real and she tended to switch channel to something more cheerful. She sometimes had a nagging sense that there was somehow 'more to it all' but tried not to dwell on that.

Then, in her late teens, a few things happened that jolted her sense of well-being. Once, after ignoring a homeless man's request for change, he shouted after her and she felt exposed and terrified although she couldn't explain why. At college she got together with a boyfriend who had recently lost his mother to cancer. She noticed that her friends didn't seem to want to be around them because he could be difficult. Eventually she broke up with him, but felt bad about it and drifted away from her friends anyway. Seeing what a dark place the world could be, she became withdrawn herself. She realised that even her family found her difficult to be around and began to wonder what was wrong with her.

At first she tried to get control back over her life by becoming attractive and fun again. She went on several diets and exercise regimes but nothing seemed to work and she felt even worse about herself. After bursting into tears at work one day she went to a counsellor. He seemed to suggest that there must have been something difficult in her childhood, but that didn't make sense to her and left her feeling that it must be her own fault that she was struggling. Her doctor then diagnosed depression and put her on some pills. It was a relief to think that there might be something wrong with her brain, but she's still not sure and says that she gets low and scared about the future despite the drugs.

Think about

- How would your current therapeutic approach make sense of Erin's distress? What would it suggest about how to work with her?
- How would the Buddhist approach to suffering understand Erin's experience?
- Are there any ideas from the book so far that might usefully be brought into your work with Erin?

One way forward

Here we can start to see some of the differences and similarities between the Buddhist approach and our current common-sense and therapeutic understandings of suffering. Whilst the western doctor might diagnose Erin, Buddhism would regard her recognition of the suffering in life as functional rather than dysfunctional. Instead of searching for something wrong in Erin that needed fixing, Buddhism would locate her struggles in the shared human experience of living in a world where there is pain.

So a starting point in therapy might be to acknowledge the understandable nature of Erin's distress, and to raise the possibility of a middle way between the avoidance of suffering during her childhood, and the self-punishing attempts to fix herself that characterise her adulthood so far. A compassionate therapist would look to decrease Erin's suffering, but by facing it rather than by denying it or offering some form of fix.

Seeing suffering as rooted in craving, we might explore what it is that Erin craves and consider – with her – the ways in which she relates to 'positive' and 'negative' aspects of everyday life. It is here where we might bring in some of the mindfulness practices that we'll cover in the remainder of this chapter.

Practice

As counsellors and therapists we can decide to what extent we engage with Buddhist theory, practice, or both. Some schools of Buddhism, such as Zen, put emphasis on experience rather than on reading texts. At the other extreme, some people find meditative practices so culturally unfamiliar that they focus on understanding the theories and applying them in their lives, rather than engaging with any traditional practices. However, we might be wary of attempting to separate mindful practice from 'the highly sophisticated and beautiful epistemological framework in which it is nested' (Williams & Kabat-Zinn, 2011b: 3) or of subscribing to Buddhist theory without tuning in, experientially, to the ways in which craving operates in our own thoughts and lives.

As we saw in the previous chapter there are two linked forms of Buddhist practice: the deliberate practice of meditation, and the practice of mindful ways of being in our everyday lives. We could see this as a continuum with individual meditation (of the kind we tried in the Introduction) at one end, attempts to bring mindfulness into every aspects of our everyday lives and relationships at the other end, and in the middle things like meditative forms of conversation, or deliberately doing housework tasks in a mindful manner.

We can see the central importance placed on meditation in Buddhism from the fact that it was through meditation that the Buddha found enlightenment. The point of meditation is both to understand the way suffering is rooted in craving experientially (the former part of the Dharma), and to practice letting go of craving in a way which cultivates the path (the latter part). However, western forms of Buddhism and mindfulness therapies have been criticised for putting too much emphasis on solitary meditation, which was generally only practised by monks and nuns in Buddhist countries. Hickey (2010) quotes the Dalai Lama as arguing for the value of sound sleep over meditation and emphasises the importance of community as well as solitary practice, which is often lost in the west (see Concluding Thoughts at the end of the book).

Here I will outline various kinds of meditative practices which can be used to cultivate mindfulness and related qualities (see Introduction). In the following chapters we will consider specific practices in more detail. However, throughout it is important to keep hold of the idea of a mindful approach to life as a whole (see Introduction) rather than grasping meditation and other practices too tightly.

There are several kinds of meditation. We can practise meditation just as a relaxation exercise in order to calm ourselves, for example if we lie on the floor and imagine a peaceful scene. Cultivating calmness is part of the Buddhist path so we could see such meditations as fitting with Buddhist thought, even though they are not directly related to understanding suffering or letting go of craving. Then there are two explicitly Buddhist forms of meditation: vipassanā aims to develop insight into experience, whilst samatha is about attaining concentration (Batchelor, 2011). Some liken vipassanā to a broad searchlight and samatha to a focused laser beam (Germer, 2005a): In vipassanā we attend to the whole of our experience in a wide, open, awareness, noticing what arises and that it passes away, whereas in samatha we focus on a particular experience, object or phrase, such as the feeling of the breath, or repeatedly asking 'What is this?' in Korean Zen, or contemplating a Japanese Zen Koan[7].

Bhikkhu Bodhi suggests that meditation can therefore be regarded as on a spectrum of conceptual content from zero (where we are open to everything), to light (e.g. focusing on breathing), to heavy (e.g. deliberately focusing on a difficult feeling, or the fact of our mortality) (Bodhi, 2011).

Some of the most popular subjects for more conceptual meditations are the four 'measureless states': loving-kindness, compassion, sympathetic joy and equanimity (see Chapter 2 for more on the latter three of these).

Practice: Loving-kindness meditation

The comic below illustrates the loving-kindness meditation: you start by wishing that you, yourself, will be happy, at peace and free from suffering. You then expand out to wish the same thing for somebody nearby, for those in your vicinity more broadly, for a loved one, a stranger, an enemy or somebody you find more difficult, and then for the whole world.

Figure 1.1   Loving-kindness meditation

(Continued)

---

[7]A list of these can be found here at the gateless gate website: www.ibiblio.org/zen/cgi-bin/koan-index.pl.

(Continued)

Try having a go at this more conceptual meditation for yourself. Sit as you were for the breathing practice in the Introduction, but this time take a few minutes to meditate on the loving-kindness phrase for each of these people or groups in turn, visualising them if that works for you[8].

When you have finished you might compare your experiences of the more and less conceptual styles of meditation. Did you find this or the breathing meditation easier? More satisfying? More relevant to the Buddhist theory we've covered?

Meditation does not have to be still. In Chapters 6 and 9 we'll mention more explicitly body-focused meditations such as slow walking, where the object of attention is the sensation of movement. We can similarly meditate during yoga, qigong or tai chi exercises.

Some people prefer to meditate in solitude (e.g. at home or outside) whilst others find meditation groups or retreats more conducive.

We might also find that different meditations are appropriate to different situations. For example, when I run a mindfulness workshop I tend to do a breathing meditation to focus everyone's attention at the beginning of the day. At the end of the session I do the listening meditation (outlined in Chapter 8), which tunes people back in to the world beyond the workshop.

Pause for reflection

What have you found difficult or challenging about the two meditations which we have tried so far (breathing and loving-kindness)?

It is worth remembering that, for many of us in the western world, meditation has not been part of our lives, and it can be challenging in many ways. We might usefully contemplate which parts of the original meditation forms are integral and which are not. For example, whilst the upright posture might be important for keeping us alert, many find that sitting cross-legged is very uncomfortable for a body that isn't used to it, and prefer sitting in a chair. Whilst it can be valuable to learn that

---

[8]You can find meditations on the other measureless states in Martine Batchelor's book in the further reading, and through the rest of this book.

pain comes and goes in meditation (see Chapter 9), we might question whether spending an entire meditation session in agony is worthwhile! We might also consider the length of time we meditate for, and where we do it. The specific technique of meditation is far less important than the motivation and sincerity we bring to the practice (Batchelor, 2011), and it may well be better to find a practice that works for us rather than forcing something we will find very difficult to keep going with.

The other thing that many of us are not used to is being so quiet with ourselves. In modern life it is easy to fill up every bit of one's time with interaction and distractions like television and email. I include the comic in Figure 1.2 (another one from my own experience on a meditation retreat) as a further reminder that meditation is not easy.

When first meditating, most people are convinced that they are 'doing it wrong' because they don't manage to have a blank mind or a wonderful of inner peace. These are really misconceptions of what meditation is about. The kind of meditation depicted in the comic could be regarded as exactly what it is about because I noticed both how my suffering is rooted in various habitual cravings (e.g. for approval and to feel better) and that the niggling feelings and thoughts that do bubble up also pass away again. Rather than seeing this experience as a stream of failures to remain present and criticising ourselves for it, we can remind ourselves that this *is* the practice: repeatedly being drawn away and returning back.

One final important point, highlighted by both Barry Magid (2008) and Pema Chödrön (2001), is that we easily fall into old ways of treating

Figure 1.2   The joys of meditation

ourselves when meditating. For example, if we suggested meditation to Erin (from our case study) she might well start doing it with the aim of fixing what was wrong with her, beating herself up if she lapsed or found it difficult. We need to be aware of our motivations for meditation and notice when we are trying to grasp at something (e.g. the idea of ourselves as a serene being) or hurl something away (e.g. all of the parts of ourselves that we hope to fix by meditating).

It can be extremely difficult to commit to regular meditation practice. For clients and therapists who wish to, it is worth exploring how they might fit meditative rituals into their daily lives, including times of day when they can make time for meditation, as well as existing rituals they might do in a more explicitly mindful way such as having a cup of tea, walking the dog or washing the dishes as Thich Nhat Hanh suggests:

> While washing the dishes one should only be washing the dishes, which means that while washing the dishes one should be completely aware of the fact that one is washing the dishes ... The fact that I am standing there and washing these bowls is a wondrous reality. I'm being completely myself, following my breath, conscious of my thoughts and actions. There's no way I can be tossed around mindlessly like a bottle slapped here and there on the waves. ([1975] 1991: 4–5)

As with the breathing meditation in the Introduction, everyday mindfulness involves attempting to be fully present to the task: just to be with the tea, the walking or the dishes, and to gently bring our attention back if it wanders.

Some of the mindfulness-based cognitive therapists suggest a 'three-minute breathing space' that can be done when feeling tired or stressed, or at regular points such as after going to the toilet.

Practice: Three minute breathing space

Step 1 – *Awareness:* Ask yourself where you are and what is going on, to bring yourself back to the present from whatever you were doing.

Step 2 – *Gathering:* Bring your attention to the breath, as in our breathing meditation.

Step 3 – *Expanding:* Expand your attention out to include a sense of your body as a whole and your surroundings.

You can also download applications to provide regular reminders to take a mindful break during the day, or to help you to time your meditations.

I am always wary when I hear somebody announce that a particular activity is intrinsically mindful or mindless. What for some people might be conducive to mindfulness, might well not be for others (Barker, 2011a). One person can sit for hours looking serene but letting their attention go everywhere, whilst another person can mindfully engage in an activity like emailing, dancing or watching television[9]. As Pirsig puts it, 'The Buddha ... resides quite as comfortably in the circuits of a digital computer or the gears of a cycle transmission as he does at the top of the mountain, or in the petals of a flower' (1976: 18). Throughout the rest of the book I will try to give examples of both explicit meditations and of how to do everyday activities mindfully.

Summary and conclusions

In the Introduction we began to get an idea of what it means to be mindful and what that experience feels like, as well as exploring key aspects of the concept of mindfulness. In this chapter we've considered the theory behind mindfulness and the common practices it involves. We've also covered how these are rooted in the history of Buddhism and how this has been taken up in the western world.

We've found that the main theory underlying Buddhism proposed that suffering is rooted in craving, and that suffering can be addressed by accepting that it exists and by cultivating ways of letting go of craving.

Meditative practices and bringing mindfulness to daily life are ways of cultivating this practice of noticing our habitual ways of behaving in response to craving, letting go of these and finding other ways (often middle ways between grasping things and hurling them away). A diversity of meditation and everyday practices are possible, many of which we'll experience and explore during the rest of this book.

Now that we understand what mindfulness is, where it comes from, what it is aiming at and how it might be practised, we can go on to explore how therapists and counsellors might engage with it. There are three main ways of doing this: we might encourage clients to practise mindfulness; we might practise mindfulness ourselves; and we might engage mindfully in the therapeutic relationship.

---

[9]The topic of engaging in new technologies mindfully is regularly explored by the Buddhist Geeks: see www.buddhistgeeks.com.

Further reading

I would highly recommend the two books which first engaged me with Buddhist theory and practice as accessible introductions to a secular version of Buddhism and to the range of meditations which you might try, many of which I also include throughout this book. These are Martine and Stephen Batchelor's books:
Batchelor, M. (2001). *Meditation for life*. London: Frances Lincoln.
Batchelor, S. (1997). *Buddhism without beliefs*. London: Bloomsbury.

You can also access the work of the Batchelors on their website: www.stephen batchelor.org.

For a good, clear, concise history of Buddhism from its origins to the present day, see:
Keown, D. (1996). *Buddhism: A very short introduction*. Oxford: Oxford University Press.

This book includes references to longer histories of specific branches of Buddhism if you are eager to follow up any of these.

A more in-depth overview of key teachings in the Buddhist Pali canon, with commentaries and contemporary Dharma teachings, is:
Analayo (2003). *Satipatthana: The direct path to realization*. Birmingham: Windhorse.

There are further resources on Buddhist theory and practice listed at: http://social mindfulness.wordpress.com/references/buddhism and http://socialmindfulness. wordpress.com/references/practice.

TWO Mindful therapy: the client, the counsellor, the relationship

Aims

This chapter aims to:

- introduce the main ways in which counsellors and therapists might engage with mindfulness,
- explore the ways in which mindfulness ideas and practices can be offered to clients,
- consider the value of therapists themselves practising mindfulness,
- suggest ways in which the therapeutic relationship itself might be (more) mindful.

In the previous chapter we began to explore the theory behind mindfulness and the key practices involved. In Chapter 3 we will develop our understanding of how we can integrate these theories and practices with our existing therapeutic approaches. In this chapter, I want to explore more generally how all counsellors and therapists might bring mindfulness into their work.

There are three main ways in which this can be done: we can teach mindfulness to our clients; we can practise mindfulness ourselves; and we can attempt to create an explicitly mindful relationship with our clients (or supervisees if we are supervisors). Of course these areas overlap because many argue that it is necessary to experience mindful practice ourselves in order to teach it effectively, and personal cultivation of mindfulness is probably necessary in order to engage in relationships mindfully.

Therapeutic approaches differ in which of these engagements they embrace or emphasise. On the one hand, the focus of many mindfulness versions of cognitive-behavioural therapy (CBT) has been on teaching mindfulness to clients as an adjunct to therapy, or instead of therapy (often in group-based workshops or via self-help books and audio materials). On the other hand, humanistic and psychodynamic engagements with mindfulness have tended to emphasise mindfulness practice as a means for the therapist to cultivate qualities which aid the therapeutic relationship (such as Roger's (1957) core conditions or Freud's ([1912] 1961) 'evenly hovering attention'). Some practitioners from these modalities are cautious about therapists taking a more educational role or explicitly teaching techniques to clients (e.g. Watson, 2008). In my view there is value in all three ways of engaging with mindfulness, and each is likely to enhance the others. Hopefully, this chapter will help you to determine which modes of engagement you would consider in relation to your own therapeutic work.

Teaching mindfulness to clients

Why might we explicitly teach mindfulness to clients? One reason would be if we fully accepted the Buddhist understanding of suffering presented in the previous chapter and agreed that meditation and mindful engagement with everyday life were the best ways of addressing that suffering (as in the various forms of Buddhist psychotherapy that exist)[1]. However, mindfulness practices also fit well with more conventional western psychotherapeutic understandings of suffering.

When my co-authors and I were putting together our edited textbook on counselling and psychotherapy (Barker, Vossler, & Langdridge, 2010), we were struck by the fact that approaches we had previously imagined to be quite different actually had some clear commonalities. I will try to express the major commonality here, whilst recognising that this is necessarily an oversimplification given the complexity and multiplicity of all of these approaches (something we will tease out further in Chapter 3 when we focus on each modality in turn).

It seems to me that all of the main therapeutic approaches share the idea that patterns are laid down in people's pasts, becoming solidified

---

[1]See, for example, the Karuna institute, www.karuna-institute.co.uk, or the forms of Buddhist therapy/counselling of authors such as Bien (2006), Brazier (1995), Epstein (1995), Kawai (1996), Watson (2008) or Welwood (2000). A full list of books setting out Buddhist psychotherapies can be found on http://socialmindfulness.wordpress.com/references/therapy.

through repetition in ways that impact (adversely) on their present experience and limit future possibilities (see Wetherell, 2012). Suffering can be alleviated by bringing these patterns into awareness (through observing how they unfold in the present and/or understanding how they got laid down in the first place) and shifting them in some way: this is perhaps the key role of therapy.

So, in psychoanalysis we encourage repressed material into consciousness; in person-centred therapy we explore clients' conditions of worth; in CBT we raise awareness of negative automatic thoughts and the beliefs that underlie these; in existential therapy we attempt to loosen sedimented ways of viewing the world; in systemic therapy we address stuck dynamics between people; and in more constructivist and constructionist types of therapy we examine the dominant cultural norms or stories that people take on board, and explore alternatives to these[2]. Different approaches emphasise different elements of such patterns, such as the internal thought process or feelings involved, the personal history of the individual, how patterns operate in relationship with others, or the wider cultural or existential contexts in which they emerge and recur.

The therapeutic encounter is one space in which people can become more aware of such patterns, challenging them, loosening their traction and/or opening up alternatives. However, mindfulness practice has very similar aims and enables the same kind of awareness to develop, as well as creating an explicit space in our lives for shifting patterns.

By slowing down and noticing how events impact us, or by observing the thoughts and feelings that bubble up when we are still, we come to recognise the patterns through which we engage with the world. Instead of our usual response of avoiding this knowledge, or reacting in the habitual ways these patterns set up, we can deliberately do something differently. For example, in meditation we can practise letting go of a tough feeling rather than proliferating it, or we can deliberately cultivate a compassionate, rather than judgemental, response to someone who irritated us. Through mindful everyday practice we can then act differently, shifting the pattern[3].

The comic in Figure 2.1 illustrates patterns of shameful responses that I became aware of through meditation on retreat. These spirals of memory welled up after I'd felt exposed when somebody pointed out my inept washing up!

---

[2]This general theory is potentially compatible with the Buddhist understanding of suffering as rooted in craving because the patterns which are laid down could be regarded, in various ways, as patterns of aversion and attachment.

[3]In Chapter 3 we will briefly consider the neurological processes underlying such processes.

Figure 2.1   No wonder my back hurts

Noticing the connections between these shameful memories revealed a pattern of the kinds of situations that result in shame for me, and a pattern of responding with self-berating and withdrawal from others. In meditation I can deliberately practise other responses to such situations, such as self-compassion, and in everyday mindfulness I can attempt to slow down and try another response (e.g. a single, genuine apology, or an explicit acknowledgement that different groups might find the same behaviour praiseworthy or blameworthy).

Many clients report that therapy is useful to them because it provides a space in which to slow down and reflect upon the patterns they have got into. Some engage with therapy at regular intervals in life explicitly as a way of creating such space. However, there are other ways of doing this besides therapy. Towards the end of our sessions many of us encourage clients to think about how they will open up such spaces in their lives in order to maintain the awareness they have gained and/or changes they have made during therapy. For example, we might consider, with clients, activities like journal writing, talking with supportive people, taking time out for themselves or other forms of self-care (Barker, 2010a). In relationship therapy in particular, many counsellors deliberately spread latter sessions further apart and encourage clients to start having the same conversations (about the dynamics between them and how to shift these) in between sessions, without the therapist mediating (see Chapter 10).

If we are keen to build mindfulness into our one-to-one therapy we might consider similarly encouraging clients into a regular practice whilst they are still coming to see us, providing enough time in therapy to discuss their experiments in finding out what works for them, how to build it into their lives, and what hinders their practice[4]. Then, after therapy has finished, clients will have a regular way of bringing patterns into awareness and shifting them. We could see such cultivation of personal practice as part of ethical therapy (especially in times of economic hardship) as well as potentially empowering as it develops clients' own skills rather than giving the impression that an expert is required. Of course such a view of difficulties (as ongoing aspects of the human condition rather than as problems to fix) and the counselling relationship (as facilitative) fits better with some modalities than others.

We can see here that there is a spectrum of how heavily we might invite clients to engage with mindfulness. At the light end of the spectrum meditation and everyday mindfulness might be two of the many practices which we suggest that clients could engage with post-therapy. At the heavy end we could explicitly teach and encourage mindfulness from the first session onwards with all clients (and Chapter 3 will present some protocols of how we can do this). In the middle we might bring mindfulness in in different ways with different clients and at different stages of the process. This would fit with Cooper and McLeod's (2011) pluralistic approach, which emphasises that different things work for different people at different times, as well as highlighting the importance of working collaboratively with clients to determine what support best fits them and their situation.

It is important to carefully consider how we present mindfulness to clients if we do want to bring it into our therapy in this way. With Buddhist clients there may be ongoing practices already present (although I have found that it is vital to explore the forms of Buddhism that the client subscribes to, and the practices and theories involved, rather than assuming that they will share my own understandings). With clients from other religious and spiritual traditions we might need to consider whether mindfulness or meditation could be integrated with existing practices (such as prayer or religious ritual), whether it might be seen very separately (e.g. as a psychological rather than spiritual activity), or whether it would be problematic to bring in something from a different tradition which could be experienced as disrespectful to their beliefs. We could follow writers such as Kabat-Zinn (1994) in presenting a psychologised version of mindfulness, perhaps not going into its Buddhist roots, but rather emphasising outcome research on its efficacy (see Chapter 4). This might fit better for non-religious or atheist clients. However, given that clients are likely to associate meditation with Buddhism, or 'Eastern'

---

[4]Martine Batchelor's (2010) reflections on the common hindrances can be useful here (see Chapter 4 of her book).

beliefs more generally, it may well be necessary to explore such associations as part of assessing the potential for engagement.

Some of the possible practices, and the pitfalls to engaging with them, which we might explore are covered in the previous chapter, and I will introduce others through the rest of this book. There is also a useful overview of various practices and how they can be taught in therapy in Christopher Germer's (2005b) chapter on teaching mindfulness in therapy.

As well as encouraging clients to engage in mindfulness practices in between therapy sessions and reflecting on this experience, and what it reveals, in sessions, we could also consider building explicit mindfulness practices into counselling sessions as something we practise together. For example, we could bring in the beginning and ending meditations which I outlined in the previous chapter to ground ourselves and the client, we could employ a meditation during the session to reveal automatic thoughts, or we could pause briefly at points during the session to bring our attention to the here-and-now (see Chapter 3). We'll return to some of these ideas again towards the end of this chapter.

Although this book focuses mainly on one-to-one, face-to-face therapy, mindfulness is also something that has frequently been taught to clients via group workshops and self-help materials (including many popular books on the topic, computer programmes, online activities and applications). We will cover the popular group-based programmes in Chapter 3, and you may want to consider suggesting that clients supplement individual therapy with group workshops and/or self-help approaches, or even delivering groups or creating such materials yourself.

Pause for reflection

Having read this section, and experienced mindfulness practices for yourself in previous chapters, do you see it as something that you could usefully teach to your clients? If so, how can you imagine bringing it into your work? How might you introduce it to clients? How might you integrate it into sessions?

Practising mindfulness ourselves

There are two main reasons, from a therapeutic point of view, why we might practise mindfulness ourselves. The first relates to the previous section on teaching mindfulness, and the second to the later section on the therapeutic relationship.

In relation to what we have already covered, many have argued that it is necessary to experience mindfulness ourselves in order to teach it to others. Indeed, it could be seen as rather arrogant to teach something that we have not attempted ourselves. Any notion that 'they' (our clients) require mindfulness in a way that 'we' (the therapists) do not sets up an unhelpful 'us and them' division (Richards, 2010) that is antithetical to the underlying understanding of universal human suffering (see Chapter 1). Purely pragmatically, experiencing mindfulness practices ourselves alerts us to the potentials they offer and also to the difficulties that our clients, like us, will have for example in committing to such practices and in letting go of desires to fix ourselves through mindfulness. Thus therapeutic conversations about mindfulness can be imbued with a shared understanding of how challenging it is.

In relation to the therapeutic relationship, we might engage with mindfulness in order to improve our own therapeutic practice in various ways and to cultivate the skills required for a good therapeutic alliance. There is overwhelming evidence that it is the relationship between therapist and client that is of most importance in determining the outcome of therapy (more important than any specific approaches or techniques used)[5]. Yet most counselling and psychotherapy training courses emphasise teaching their particular approach over developing relational skills. Mindfulness is a practice that develops exactly the abilities which have been found to be key to the therapeutic relationship (see Fulton, 2005; Hick 2008). Here we will briefly consider four of these: attention; empathy and compassion; the ability to sit with difficult emotions; and self-awareness.

Attention

Perhaps most obviously, mindfulness can cultivate attention (Valentine & Sweet, 1999), which is vital for the therapeutic endeavour (Morgan & Morgan, 2005). Remembering back to the samatha and vipassanā forms of meditation introduced in the previous chapter, practising the 'laser beam' of samatha may help us to tune in to our clients rather than becoming distracted or bored. Through mindful practice we become used to noticing when we have drifted off and to bringing our attention back to what is at hand. The 'broad searchlight' of vipassanā can cultivate something more like Freud's 'evenly hovering attention'. This is the kind of spacious attention we need in order to simultaneously hear what our client is saying and relate that back to what we

---

[5]For a review of the recent evidence on this, see Cooper (2008).

have heard from them before, as well as being aware of the relationship between us, the point we are at in the therapeutic process and session, and any thoughts and feelings that we are having ourselves, filtering out what is relevant and considering what we might say next and whether that is in the client's interests. Cultivation of this form of spacious attention can prevent us from becoming attached to particular aspects of what is going on at the expense of others.

At its best, for me, therapy involves a quality of intense attention to the client, within a more open awareness of all that is going on within myself as well as between and around us. This seems rather similar to the combination of focus and spaciousness in breathing meditation.

Hopefully our clients will experience such attention as the therapist being fully present to them and listening closely. Also, just as meditation can reveal our own patterns to us, such attention on the part of the therapist may yield insight into the client's habitual ways of being. Our personal practice in being detached enough to recognise our own patterns, and how they might be otherwise, can translate into the therapy situation.

Empathy and compassion

The therapist qualities that correlate most highly with client outcomes are those relating to empathy, compassion and understanding (Cooper, 2008). Empathy is the capacity to understand others in general, and to communicate this understanding to them, whilst compassion relates specifically to feeling for their suffering.

Research has found that mindfulness training increases empathy. This may well work by improving self-empathy and self-compassion, which has a knock-on effect of improving our empathy and compassion for others (Shapiro & Izett, 2008). As we increase our self-understanding we may have better insight into why other people are the way they are. Also, as we are kinder towards ourselves (e.g. by seeing the reasons why we are suffering rather than blaming ourselves for it), we may extend this understanding to the suffering of others as well. As we judge ourselves less we may find ourselves becoming less judgemental of others, which can aid us in a genuine acceptance of our clients. Such genuine acceptance prevents the common problem of therapists retaining prejudices and judgements of client behaviour under a veneer of unconditional acceptance. Given that we live in a culture that encourages judgement, monitoring and comparison to others, it is likely that we will need to practise a different way of being rather than it just being something that comes easily (Barker, 2012a).

On a basic level, self-caring practices such as meditation also decrease stress (see Chapter 6), and often mean that we tune in to our needs (for sleep, food, rest, exercise, etc.) better. This leaves us with more emotional energy for others and less likely to experience burnout or compassion fatigue (Christopher & Maris, 2010). On a more complex level, mindfulness practice cultivates our ability to detach from our own experience rather than identifying strongly with it, meaning that we may be more able to hear and understand our clients rather than defensively worrying what they think of us, or seeing them through the lens of what they mean to us (Barker, 2010a).

As well as general mindfulness practices cultivating empathy and compassion, we can engage in mindfulness practices that explicitly aim to do this, such as the loving-kindness practice included in the previous chapter. Here is another example which attempts to cut through the ways in which we generally perceive other people in terms of what they are for us. Such perceptions are often based on fixed images we have formed on the basis of limited experiences (e.g. we feel happy and relaxed about a friend, uncomfortable and defensive about an enemy, and neutral and disinterested about a stranger).

Practice: Cultivating empathy and compassion

Sit as you were for the breathing practice in the Introduction. After a few minutes bring to mind a friend. Visualise them at the moment of their birth, crying and covered in blood. Imagine them through their childhood, growing into adolescence and adulthood with all the triumphs and tragedies they experienced along the way. Consider the dreams and fears they developed, and the values and feelings that they now hold dear, just as you do yours. Picture them moving into the future, facing illness and old age. Finally, imagine them at the moment of their death.

Now do the same visualisation for an enemy (or somebody you find difficult), and then for a stranger[6].

Such practices might also be useful explicitly in relation to our clients. We could embark on such meditations to equalise our perceptions of clients who we find easy and challenging to be with.

Many Buddhists find it useful to meditate on the fact that, if you believe in reincarnation, everyone has once been our mother and we

---

[6]This is based on a Tibetan meditation as interpreted by Batchelor (1997). A version of this is also suggested in Morgan and Morgan (2005).

should treat them as such. For those of us who do not hold this belief, we could think about how we feel about a client we have been seeing for months who we have really managed to tune in to and who has trusted us enough to reveal themselves. We understand why they suffer the way they do and we see how courageous they are being in facing that suffering, given the situation that they are in. Perhaps we could learn to see each new client, or each person we come across more widely, as somebody we would reach that point with if only we had the chance.

The ability to 'sit with' difficult material

Another way in which mindfulness can help us as therapists is in the ability to sit with the difficult feelings, memories, fantasies or other material which clients bring up. The way we relate to tough emotions, thoughts and sensations during mindfulness practice is to welcome them with acceptance and curiosity, not trying to eradicate or hide from them, but equally not treating them differently to anything else that emerges (and will inevitably pass away again). We can be a witness to our feelings and how we relate to them, rather than becoming embroiled and tangled up in them or identifying with them strongly.

Paul Fulton (2005) uses the mindfulness therapy metaphor of adding salt to water in his consideration of developing such 'affect tolerance'. If we add a tablespoon of salt to a cup of water then it will taste very salty. If we add it to a jug of water it will be less salty, and added to a bathtub it will be barely noticeable. Through cultivating our ability to bear difficult feelings in an open mind, we become a larger container. The emotions are still there but their power to disturb us is diffused.

Researchers have found that therapists who trained in mindfulness indeed reported being more able to sit with emotions (e.g. rather than rushing to reduce their own anxiety, or that of their client). This can also protect the therapist from the risk of 'vicarious traumatisation' on hearing about intense or distressing client experiences.

A key concept in Buddhism is that of 'equanimity', which relates to this ability to be with whatever comes in a calm and even manner, rather than rushing to make things different or better. Drawing on the work of Joan Halifax, Andrew Bein (2008) likens the combination of equanimity and open empathy to having a 'strong back, soft front'. The grounded postures we use to practise mindfulness are a way of fostering equanimity: some imagine themselves sitting like a mountain, strong and firmly able to withstand even extremes of weather that pass over them. In therapy the 'strong back' of equanimity enables us to sit firm in the face of turmoil, suffering, confusion and despair, as our 'soft front' compassionately welcomes all the experiences of our client.

Of course equanimity does not mean not acting at all, rather that we do not rush to react or to diminish difficult feelings. Instead we attempt to fully consider what will be the most ethical response (in therapy, that which will be in the best interests of the client). We recognise that we will not always know for sure, and also have a willingness to take responsibility if we don't get it 'right' (as we sometimes won't).

Self-awareness

Edel Maex (2011) also relates equanimity to recognising the client's responsibility for their own experiences and behaviours. He says that many therapists, in their aim to be supportive, disempower people by trying to fix their suffering for them or by trying to make things feel better. Obviously this runs counter to the Buddhist view of suffering as inevitable and the importance of seeing it clearly. In equanimity we can stop flailing in the face of difficulties in order to see the full picture. We can acknowledge our client's perspective and feelings without identifying with them.

An important part of this is awareness of our own motivations as a therapist. Mindfulness practice can help us to recognise, for example, our desire for validation that we are a 'good therapist', or our yearning to help people who remind us of ourselves. If we are more aware of our own patterns in life then we are less likely to act them out in therapy. For example, one pattern I learnt when I was younger was to interpret silence between people as a sign that there was something wrong, and I often rush to fill the gap. Observing myself doing that, and opening up to other possible meanings of silence, has been important in enabling me to allow moments of quiet in therapy sessions. In such moments I can check my urge to say something and consider different possible meanings and responses more carefully. Similarly, as therapists, it is useful to mindfully explore our patterned responses to different emotional states (in ourselves and others) to become aware of the ways in which we tend to interpret and respond to these.

Fulton (2005) also suggests that mindfulness practice can help us to treat our therapeutic models more lightly. It is very easy, as therapists, to make generalisations about this kind of patient or that kind of 'disorder' or 'dysfunction'. Mindfulness invites us to experience the person in front of us rather than acting on the basis of expectations, assumptions, or even previous experience of them. The importance of this kind of 'not knowing' attitude is something that has been advocated by therapists such as Wilfred Bion and Ernesto Spinelli, and could be seen as particularly vital when working with groups who are stigmatised against in wider society (Barker, 2010b). This is particularly important given that we know that many therapists unwittingly perpetuate negative stereotypes of minority groups in ways that are detrimental to them (Richards & Barker, 2013). We can be more aware of the ways in which wider social norms operate through us, for example, and work to 'swim against the stream' of these (something we will return to in the concluding chapter to this book).

Research suggests that therapists who practise mindfulness do indeed report becoming less preoccupied with themselves, and that this, in turn, enables them to help their clients to fully experience themselves (Fulton, 2005).

Pause for reflection

Are you convinced of the value of practising mindfulness for your therapeutic practice? Take some time to consider the possibilities raised in this section of the chapter. In what ways do you cultivate these skills already? What mindfulness practices might you build in to cultivate them further? Draw up a plan for how you might incorporate such practices into your therapeutic work (e.g. before and after seeing clients) and your life more broadly.

The mindful counselling relationship

From the previous sections we have seen that it is possible to encourage clients to practise mindfulness, or to practise mindfulness ourselves in order to cultivate the skills that enhance the therapeutic relationship. Beyond this, mindfulness is also a quality that can be present within the relationship *between* client and therapist. As we saw in the Introduction, the aim is to be mindful in our whole life, not just in meditation, so what do we mean by a mindful relationship?

This is a topic that we will return to in more detail in Chapter 10 when we consider relationship therapy and working with clients around relationship issues. A mindful relationship has something in common with concepts like Buber's (1958) 'I–thou' relating, Mearns and Cooper's (2005) 'relational depth', or the idea of therapeutic presence (Gehart & McCollum, 2008). It happens when we relate to other people as full human beings, rather than attempting to fix them as just certain aspects of themselves (e.g. their career, cultural background, diagnostic label or sexual identity). Related to this, the mindful relationship involves seeing the person as they are rather than through the lens of what they mean to us. Even in therapy it is easy to slip into focusing on the person as a client (and assuming that the vulnerability or defensiveness they display with us is indicative of how they are in the rest of their life), or to invest in problems that seem similar to our own, or in their role as somebody we might rescue, or in the fact that we need their ongoing payment. Going beyond the kind of empathy that focuses on ways in which we are similar to another person, mindful relating accepts the other person in all their differences to us.

Clearly this links to the 'strong back, soft front' combination of equanimity and empathy explored above as we demonstrate that we are okay with the client as they are (through sitting with whatever they bring) and that we understand and care about their concerns and suffering.

In the therapeutic relationship we can attempt to relate to our clients in such ways, something which is likely to be aided by practising mindfulness alone. We can also then model this way of relating to our clients and, implicitly or explicitly, encourage them to relate back to us (and to others in their lives) in similar ways.

In Chapter 10 we will also explore some of the mindfulness practices that can be carried out between people in interaction which can be employed in the therapy session as well as in other forms of relationships (Kramer, Meleo-Meyer, & Turner, 2008). For now think yourself about how you might engage mindfully before, during and after therapy with the following client, and I will then suggest a few possibilities that I have found helpful.

With this, and all of the other case studies given in this book, if you find it too hard to imagine yourself in the situation you can always consider how you would advise a colleague or supervisee who brought this case to you.

Case study: Pauline

Pauline is a woman in her fifties who has been attending counselling with you for four weeks. She came because she is feeling rather lost in life after her children recently both left home. She becomes anxious when trying to imagine what she might do next. She tries to have a lot of contact with her kids, and encourages them to visit, but senses them pulling away when she does this.

You are frustrated by your work with Pauline so far because you find yourself asking lots of questions during the sessions and even making suggestions, which is something you rarely do with other clients. You've noticed that you feel

(Continued)

(Continued)

anxious when there is a pause in conversation and tend to fill it. Aware that Pauline is unfamiliar with counselling, you wonder if you're trying to be what you imagine she expects a counsellor to be.

Think about

- How might you cultivate mindfulness in yourself *before* the session with Pauline?
- How could you attempt a mindful relationship with Pauline *during* sessions?
- If Pauline was interested in mindfulness herself, how might you suggest she engages with it *after* the session?

One way forward

One practice that I always make time for is an hour before therapy where I sit in a café and write in my journal about what is going on for me in life at the moment. This is a way of putting down my stuff in order to be available to clients, and also of raising awareness of what issues might seep into my therapy today. I write in a similar way to the way in which I meditate, trying to be aware of everything, noticing the ways in which I'm responding to things, and considering other ways of perceiving the situation (see Goldberg, 1998; Adams, 1990). Such a practice also builds some self-compassion such that I'm not too hard on myself about any struggles in my therapeutic work. Those who work with a heavy client load may consider building such practices into their daily routine (e.g. over breakfast or lunch).

You could also use journaling or meditation practice to reflect specifically on the situation with Pauline. It would be useful to consider the assumptions that you have about her (in relation to her situation and what she wants from you, and on the basis of her gender, race, age and other aspects of her identity). You could engage in some compassion exercises to open up to seeing her as a full person, and to remind yourself of your own patterns which you are likely to fall into in this relationship.

Right before therapy you might do a short breathing meditation. If you work in this way, you could bring mindfulness to reading over her notes from previous settings. As you walk to the door to collect Pauline you could remind yourself of the human being on the other side in all their complexity.

During the session you could try to be aware of the whole of Pauline, noticing her gestures, posture and voice as well as her words. You might encourage her to engage more deeply with her own experiences, describing what it is like when she thinks about the future, or speaks to her kids, for example.

When you notice your desire to leap in with questions or suggestions, you could try to pause and accept the stillness instead of just reacting. Perhaps Pauline will say something more. You could speak to her about it: 'When you stopped talking just now I felt an urge to quickly say something, but I want to give both of us more time rather than rushing in like that. How is it for you if we are quiet for a moment?' Being explicit about the process of therapy in this way can help you to feel calmer as you have explained why you do what you do (so it won't be mystifying for Pauline). It could also lead to explorations of her expectations of therapy and what it can and cannot offer. And it may be helpful in terms of her presenting issue (are the dynamics between you reflective, in some way, of those between her and her kids? Is it that she would like somebody else to fill her time so that she doesn't have to face the emptiness that has opened up in her life?)

If communication with her children and others in her life becomes something to explore, then you could try mindfulness communication practices within your sessions (see Chapter 10) and encourage her to practise those in interactions with other people too. If she is interested in mindfulness, you could also talk her through basic practices that might help her to relate to anxiety differently (see Chapter 6) or treat herself more compassionately and fully as someone who is more than 'just' a mother (see Chapter 5).

Summary and conclusions

In general there are three main ways in which we can engage with mindfulness as practitioners: we can teach mindfulness to clients as practices which might help them with their suffering; we can practise mindfulness ourselves as a way of developing the attention, empathy, equanimity and self-awareness necessary for therapeutic relationships; and we can attempt to cultivate mindful relationships with our clients through practising a mindful form of relating, and potentially drawing on specific mindfulness techniques before, during and after sessions. However, perhaps it is problematic even to separate out these three ways of engaging with mindfulness. As we will see in Chapter 10, Buddhist thought challenges our simple distinctions between ourselves and other people, so perhaps the mindful therapist will inevitably and simultaneously bring mindfulness to themselves, to the relationship and to the client. As one practitioner put it:

> If I'm actually truly allowing myself to be as I am which can include feeling hopeless, helpless, impotent, all of those things which as a therapist it can be so hard to sit with. If I can be sitting with those with compassion and acceptance then I will allow my clients to do the same and that would feel good. (Nugent, Moss, Barnes & Wilkes, 2011: 9)

Having considered how we might bring mindfulness into therapy in general, in the next chapter we will bring mindfulness into dialogue with specific therapeutic approaches. We have seen in this chapter that research strongly supports the value of therapist mindful practice in cultivating the skills needed for a good therapeutic alliance, which we know is probably the most important factor in the effectiveness of therapy. In Chapter 4 we will turn to the research evidence on the value of mindfulness for clients, and for people in general.

Further reading

I found two edited collections to be particularly useful. Both include several chapters expanding upon the ideas presented here about the ways in which therapists can engage with mindfulness in their work, and why this might be useful:

Hick, S. F., & Bien, T. (Eds.). (2008). *Mindfulness and the therapeutic relationship.* New York, NY: Guilford Press.

Germer, C. K., Siegel, R. D., & Fulton, P. R. (Eds.). (2005). *Mindfulness and psychotherapy.* New York, NY: Guilford Press.

This book is a helpful exploration of being a mindful therapist:

Siegel, D. J. (2010). *The mindful therapist.* New York, NY: Norton.

There are also several books available developing different authors' perspectives on how therapists in general might usefully engage with Buddhist and mindfulness theories and practices. A list of these can be found at: http://socialmindfulness. wordpress.com/references/therapy.

Some of these will also be brought into Chapter 3, when we consider different therapeutic approaches.

THREE Integrating mindful therapy with other approaches

Aims

This chapter aims to:

- explore ways in which the mindful theories and practices covered in Chapter 1 may be integrated with specific forms of psychotherapy: cognitive-behavioural therapy (CBT), psychodynamic therapies, and humanistic and existential therapies,
- summarise the theoretical and practical features of three of the main 'third wave' cognitive-behavioural therapies which integrate CBT with mindfulness in various ways,
- describe various historical engagements between psychoanalysis and Buddhism and to introduce some of the recent writings that have integrated psychodynamic and Buddhist understandings,
- explore the resonances between mindful, humanistic and existential approaches,
- highlight some of the challenges and tensions involved in integrating each of the main forms of western therapy with Buddhist theories and practices.

In the previous chapter we explored ways in which all of us as counsellors and therapists might bring mindfulness into our work, focusing on the practices that we might employ to cultivate our therapeutic skills and how we might share these with clients to help them with their issues.

In this chapter we will consider how we can integrate mindfulness into our own current approach towards therapy. Most of us will be largely trained in one of the main western perspectives (cognitive-behavioural therapy, psychoanalysis/psychodynamic therapy, or humanistic/existential therapy), although some of us may already integrate two or more of these (or other) approaches in our work.

There have been many attempts, already, to integrate mindfulness with each of these perspectives. This is most notable in the area of cognitive-behavioural therapy (CBT), where the integration with mindfulness has become known as the 'third wave' of CBT (after the first wave of behavioural therapy, and the second wave bringing in cognitive understandings). CBT is the type of western therapy that has delivered the highest number of new named types of therapy drawing on mindfulness in recent years, as well as being the focus of most research on the efficacy of mindfulness (see Chapter 4). There have been engagements between psychoanalysis and Buddhism from early on (starting with Carl Jung), and many popular books, such as those of Mark Epstein, weave together psychodynamic and Buddhist ideas. Humanistic and existential approaches have tended to engage less with mindfulness, although some of the existential philosophers were influenced by Buddhism early on, and there have been recent attempts towards mindful forms of person-centred and existential therapy.

In each of the following sections I will briefly introduce the key therapies and writings emerging from existing integrations. I will also draw out some of the resonances between each therapeutic approach and mindful understandings, as well as reflecting on some of the tensions which need to be addressed by therapists integrating these perspectives. I'll spend a little more time on CBT than the other approaches because, as mentioned, there are several specific forms of 'third-wave' therapy to cover, all of which have developed new theories and understandings that may be useful to all practitioners. Some of these, like compassion-focused therapy, also draw in elements from psychodynamic or humanistic approaches.

Readers should read this chapter alongside the following chapter (4) on research where I will summarise the key findings in relation to the efficacy and effectiveness of these therapies so far.

Cognitive-Behavioural Therapies (CBT)

Most texts list the 'third-wave' CBT approaches as mindfulness-based cognitive therapy (MBCT), acceptance and commitment therapy (ACT) and dialectic behavioural therapy (DBT). However, here I will only expand on the first two of these because DBT was developed very specifically to address people diagnosed with borderline personality disorder and may be of less use to the more general counsellor or therapist for this reason. Interested readers can find a brief book on DBT in the Further Reading section, and I will touch upon one key aspect of DBT towards the end of this section. Instead of DBT I will include in this section compassion focused therapy (CFT), which is another recent attempt to integrate CBT with Buddhist understandings and practices and also draws upon some psychodynamic theories. For this reason I will detail this approach last; it forms a kind of bridge between this and the next section of the chapter.

Before we start, here is a practice which demonstrates well the resonances between mindfulness and CBT, as well as how mindfulness-based approaches differ from conventional CBT. In CBT people are often encouraged to record their negative automatic thoughts (NATs) in order to begin to notice how these bubble up and are linked to experiences like anxiety and depression. Once people recognise these when they happen, they can endeavour to challenge or replace them. The following meditation does something similar, but you can see that here thoughts are allowed to emerge and fade away again rather than being challenged or replaced. This captures something of the difference between the second and third waves of CBT as the focus shifts from change to acceptance.

Practice: Thoughts meditation (adapted from Batchelor, 2001: 49)

Sit and focus on the breath as in the breathing meditation (see Introduction). For 15 minutes, notice carefully what takes you away from this focus of concentration. Particularly notice the 'stickiness' of thoughts: how you easily get pulled along with them. Each time that happens, just come back to the here-and-now of your experience.

- If you find yourself going obsessively over the past, notice that you are 'mulling over' and return to the breath.
- If you realise that you are day-dreaming, notice the enticing quality of these fantasies and bring yourself back to the present.
- If you start making plans for the future, notice 'planning' and come back to the sensation of the breath.
- If you become aware that you are speculating, judging yourself or others, calculating or making mental lists, again just label those thoughts and let your mind rest back on the breath.
- If you find yourself thinking 'I'm meditating. It's working!' or 'I'm a terrible meditator!', notice it and let that thought go as well.
- Let the thoughts be light as bubbles: gently coming and going.

When you are done, stand up and stretch. Try to notice those thoughts bubbling up in everyday life in the same way, letting them go rather than proliferating them.

Figure 3.1   Letting go of thoughts

Other practices which focus on sounds, sights, feelings or sensations (or simply 'all that arises', see below) adopt a similar strategy of noticing something and letting it go. The cartoon in Figure 3.1 attempts to illustrate the difference between ruminating on thoughts and letting them go.

Mindfulness-Based Cognitive Therapy (MBCT)

MBCT was developed by Mark Williams, Zindel Segal and John Teasdale as an integration of Jon Kabat-Zinn's (1996) mindfulness-based stress reduction (MBSR) and existing cognitive-behavioural therapy for depression (Segal, Williams, & Teasdale, 2002). Like MBSR (see Chapter 6), MBCT takes the form of group sessions over eight weeks with up to twelve participants, although there are also self-help books and CDs available to take individuals through a similar programme (Williams, Teasdale, Segal & Kabat-Zinn, 2007). Mindfulness meditation is the foundation of both MBSR and MBCT. Because MBCT was developed specifically to prevent relapse in people prone to depression, we will consider it specifically in relation to depression in Chapter 5. However, since its inception, MBCT has been adapted more widely than this, with groups tailored to anxiety, pain, chronic fatigue, sexual problems and many other difficulties. Here I will outline the main theoretical understanding behind MBCT and outline the key practices involved in the programme. We will touch upon variations that have been applied to specific problems in future chapters.

MBCT locates suffering in the fact that we spend much of our life 'on automatic pilot' (Crane, 2009). This is evolutionarily useful, enabling us to engage in many complex tasks at once, such as when driving a car. However, the way that we think on automatic pilot is harmful if we approach our emotional experiences in this way. The *doing mode* of automatic pilot is goal-oriented: we try to reduce the gap between how we would like things to be and how they are, as well as widening the gap between unpleasant experiences and how things are (the processes of attachment and aversion; see Chapter 1). We do this through *ruminative thinking* (going over and over, trying to analyse and fix our situation). Although the aim of this is probably to prevent us making the same mistake twice, it often paradoxically increases our sense of how unsatisfactory things are. We also attempt to address these gaps between how things are and how we want them to be through *experiential avoidance* (trying to avoid difficult experiences or feelings). This creates greater suffering because it disconnects us further from our experience. Due to ruminative thinking and experiential avoidance we often become sad about being sad, frightened about being frightened or angry about being angry, for example. It is these extra layers that are added to the original suffering that are involved in the kinds of distress which are often labelled depression, anxiety, anti-social personality and so on.

MBCT therefore attempts to raise awareness of how people are in 'doing mode' (through meditation where we can notice what this is like experientially) and how this is involved in their suffering. It tries to cultivate more of a 'being mode', where experience and feelings are welcomed, accepted, opened up to and tuned in to (rather than being avoided). Attention is brought to the present rather than ruminating on gaps between how things are in the present and how they were in the past or how they might be in the future. Basic breathing meditations are useful for highlighting 'doing mode', whilst bodily meditations (see Chapter 9) are particularly helpful for tuning into experience. Generally the first half of the programme focuses on raising awareness of internal processes, and the second half on cultivating different ways of being and applying these to everyday life.

The shape of the MBCT programme is eight weekly two- to three-hour group sessions (following orientation and assessment), as well as 45 minutes of individual daily mindfulness practice (meditations and bringing mindfulness to daily activities) and additional individual practices and reflections. Below is a brief overview of what is covered each week (adapted from a fuller version in Crane's book listed in Further

Reading below). I have focused on the different ideas and practices that are added each week, whilst many of the previous ones are also continued. Of course this programme can be adapted by different practitioners and for different groups.

MBCT Programme (adapted from Crane, 2009)

Week 1 – Automatic pilot

Introductions and ground rules. Eating a piece of fruit mindfully and body sweep (see Chapter 9).

Home practice: Body sweeps and everyday mindfulness.

Week 2 – Dealing with barriers

Thoughts and feelings exercises. Adding breathing meditations (see Introduction).

Home practice: Adding breathing meditation, recording pleasant events.

Week 3 – Mindfulness of the breath (and body in movement)

Exploration of pleasant experiences. Standing mindful stretches and walking meditation (see Chapter 6). Three-minute breathing space (see Chapter 1).

Home practice: Adding stretching/moving meditation and three-minute breathing space, recording unpleasant events.

Week 4 – Staying present

Exploration of unpleasant experience and specific topic of the group (e.g. depression, stress, sex). Seeing/hearing meditations (see Chapter 8), sitting meditation (noticing all that arises, see Thoughts Meditation practice above).

Home practice: Sitting meditation. Adding in three-minute breathing space at difficult times, as well as regularly (see Chapter 1).

Week 5 – Acceptance and allowing/letting be

Discussion of Rumi's poem *The Guest House*[1] about welcoming all feelings. Explore habitual reactions and cultivate being present through sitting meditation.

Home practice: As above.

---

[1]See www.panhala.net/Archive/The_Guest_House.html.

Week 6 – Thoughts are not facts

CBT ideas about alternative ways of interpreting experiences (such as someone ignoring us). Addressing difficulties with sitting practice.

Home practice: As above, working on building a sustainable practice that works for you and a relapse-prevention action plan.

Week 7 – How can I best take care of myself?

Generating list of nourishing activities to build in, considering links between activity and mood.

Home practice: As above. Developing an early warning system for detecting relapse and an action plan for this.

Week 8 – Using what has been learnt to deal with future moods

Review of early warning system and action plans. Review of course. Focus on how it can help with what is most valued. How to keep up momentum.

Home practice: Settle with sustainable plan (ideally reviewed in a follow-up session).

Acceptance and Commitment Therapy (ACT)

Like MBCT, ACT shifts the focus of CBT away from the content of people's thoughts or cognitions (e.g. trying to change NATs) to the process of how people relate to their experience. We saw in MCBT that this involves moving from 'doing mode' (which is all about trying to change situations for the better or avoid bad experiences) to 'being mode' (where people are in tune with their present experience). ACT similarly aims to cultivate acceptance of the present moment. The idea is not to remove unpleasant thoughts, emotions or sensations, but to live a rewarding life even when these are present (Flaxman, Blackledge, & Bond, 2011). However, ACT has quite different theoretical foundations to MBCT, it often focuses on individual therapy rather than group training[2], and it has developed a number of unique exercises and thought experiments that therapists can employ with clients. Here I will briefly outline the theory underlying ACT before presenting several of these practices.

---

[2]Although it can be used in group-based programmes, and there are also ACT self-help books such as Hayes (2005).

ACT was developed by Steven Hayes (Hayes, Strosahl, & Wilson, 1999). In common with both Buddhist and existential perspectives, it assumes that significant amounts of distress are an inevitable part of the human condition. This is the reason why it focuses on finding ways to be with difficult experiences rather than trying to change them.

ACT is based on relational frame theory (RFT). According to this theory, it is language that enables humans to evaluate their experiences in a negative way (e.g. comparing ourselves unfavourably to others, or creating that gap between how things are and how we would like them to be, which MBCT emphasises). Certain verbal links are reinforced by our culture and during our lives, meaning that they become taken-for-granted 'truths'. For example, imagine the stimulus experience of being publicly criticised. Our response to this depends on how we have learnt to verbally frame such situations. For example, if our verbal framing is that people who are publicly criticised have done something wrong, and that people who have done something wrong are unworthy, then it is understandable if we reach the conclusion 'I am unworthy' and even 'I am bad'. ACT emphasises that such links are constructed, rather than representing any reality of experience, and employs methods of *cognitive defusion* to point out the arbitrary nature of such links and to remove the meaning of problematic words.

Like MBCT, ACT also emphasises *experiential avoidance* and the fact that this can cause harm and compound problems (see Chapter 6). ACT encourages strategies which move people from a sense of self-as-content (we are the content of our thoughts, emotions, memories, sensations, etc.) to self-as-context (we are the person having, or noticing, those experiences, but we are not them)[3]. Mindfulness practices through which we notice our experiences and return to the present are included in ACT to help with this.

Finally, the 'commitment' part of ACT is about people clarifying their values and behaving in a way that is consistent with these. Values are ways of behaving (which people have some control over), rather than outcomes (which they don't). So, for example, if somebody was looking to develop a close relationship their value would be about being a certain way in their relationships which would help with this (e.g. open and compassionate), rather than about gaining a certain type of relationship (see Chapter 10).

---

[3]This can clearly be helpful when people feel that all that they are is their tough feelings, or a certain thought process or identity, but can be more problematic for people who already feel that their self is very diffuse (for example, people who become lost in trying to be what they think others want them to be, or in the case of some 'psychotic' experiences, see Chapter 8).

Figure 3.2 illustrates the six core processes of ACT described above. In combination their aim is psychological flexibility, with three relating more to mindfulness and acceptance, and three to commitment and behaviour change.

In addition to mindfulness meditation and sitting with difficult experiences (see above), ACT therapists have developed several practices relating to each of these core processes. The initial hexaflex functional dimensional experiential interview (HFDEI) includes evaluating on a Likert scale how well the client currently embodies each process. Clients might be encouraged to let an ice-cube melt on the hand in order to experience acceptance of changing sensations, or to try not thinking of an object (e.g. an elephant or a banana) in order to realise how attempting to control things can often have the opposite effect. Gestalt exercises are incorporated, like getting the clients to put their emotion into an 'empty chair' in order to externalise it and fully describe it. Then they imagine welcoming it back into themselves to experience the different way of responding to difficulties (welcoming rather than avoiding).

Language exercises can be used to detach words from their meaning; for example, a client is asked to describe milk and then to say the word

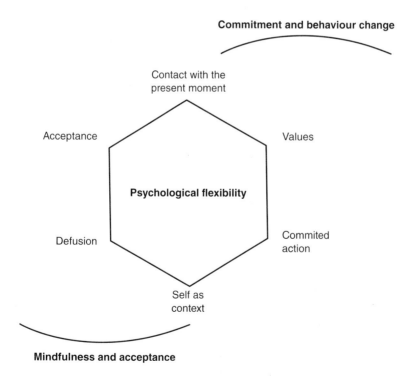

**Figure 3.2 ACT core processes (adapted from Hayes, Follette, & Linehan
2004: 16)**

'milk' over and over again. They find that it loses its meaning. They can do the same with critical words that they use to describe themselves (e.g. coward, lazy, arrogant). A more narrative-based exercise involves them telling their life story, then separating out the key events and telling a story through them which connects them in different (more useful) ways, giving them different meanings.

Several metaphors have also been developed to clarify aspects of ACT, for example:

- *Person in the hole:* A person in a hole keeps digging because a shovel is the tool that they have to hand, but the hole gets deeper. All the ways we've tried to deal with our struggles so far (list these) are like this digging. We need to notice when and how we dig (the things we do which dig us deeper).
- *Polygraph:* Imagine being hooked up to a polygraph which shows any change in your state. You have to stay calm. What happens? The client sees that trying to control ourselves like this makes it more likely that we will get anxious.
- *Two scales:* Ask the client where they are on a 0–10 scale of what they are struggling with (e.g. anxiety/depression), then where they are on a 0–10 scale of how willing they are to feel that feeling. Generally as the willingness scale goes up, the other one goes down.
- *Tug-of-war with a monster:* The monster is whatever the client is struggling with. They are in a tug-of-war with it over a deep pit. The monster is trying to pull them into the pit and vice versa. Another option rather than continuing to pull is to let go of the rope.
- *Clean vs. dirty discomfort:* Clean discomfort is the difficult thought, feeling, memory or sensation; dirty discomfort is what is layered on top of it (e.g. worry about worry, guilt about illness, shame about depression, etc.).
- *Quicksand:* Our difficulties are like quicksand. Struggling more makes us sink deeper. We need to let go of the urge to fight and instead spread out to have maximum contact with the surface (tuning into experience).
- *Passengers on a bus:* The client is the driver of a bus. Some of the passengers (thoughts, sensations, urges, memories, etc.) are unpleasant or scary and want to change the direction of the bus. Trying to placate or remove them is counterproductive. The direction of the bus is the client's values.

Following on from such exercises, more conventional therapeutic approaches are used to help clients to clarify their values (how they want to live their lives) and to set goals and to move towards these.

Compassion Focused Therapy (CFT)

As previously mentioned, I am covering CFT last in this section because it integrates CBT with both Buddhist understandings and psychodynamic approaches (notably Jungian archetypes and attachment theory). I also won't go into as much depth about CFT as the other two approaches because we will return to it, in some detail, in Chapter 5. This is because lack of self-compassion is such a key issue in many experiences of depression.

In recent years several authors have brought Buddhist ideas of compassion (see Chapters 1, 2 and 10) together with western therapeutic approaches such as CBT (see Germer, 2009; Neff, 2011). Paul Gilbert's approach, outlined in his popular book *The Compassionate Mind* (2010a), has been developed into CFT and applied to several difficulties beyond depression, including 'psychosis' (see Chapter 8) and 'overeating' (Goss, 2011; see Chapter 9).

While CFT borrows Buddhist teachings and practices, it is theoretically rooted in an integration of evolutionary psychology, neuroscience, psychodynamic theories, and sociological and social psychological understandings (Gilbert 2010b). CFT presents the sense of belonging and being safe and cared for as an evolutionary need that people have which is highly linked to well-being. From Jung, CFT takes the idea that we have an innate need to seek and form attachments, and from Bowlby the idea that early attachments can be secure (meaning that we are open to love and care), insecure (meaning that we are anxious about such relationships), or avoidant (meaning that we might shun close relationships). Experiences in life, and wider culture, are also viewed as reasons why people learn to evaluate themselves negatively in ways that lead to shame and self-criticism.

CFT suggests that there are three feeling systems in the brain: one for excitement, seeking resources and drive; one for threat and anxiety; and one for soothing, caring and contentment. CFT aims to develop the latter system and to move people from the anxiety and threat system to the caring system. We tend to get stuck in threat/anxiety systems because our safety strategies often fuel further distress (see the discussion of experiential avoidance above and in Chapter 6). The attentional shift from the threat system to a different affective system facilitates a different kind of processing. Gilbert argues that modern society overstimulates the drive system (wanting more and competing with others) (see Chapter 1) and the threat system (with unstable work lives and relationships). CFT is focused on bringing these systems into equilibrium, mainly through stimulating the soothing system, but, like ACT, it balances this with the drive system which is involved in committing to our values. Importantly CFT aims to develop the feelings of warmth associated with compassion, and not just a cognitive or verbal kind of caring. Courage is also emphasised as this is required to sit with difficult feelings or to face unpleasant experiences.

In CFT these understandings are relayed directly to clients in order to help them to understand the neuroscientific and social foundations of their experiences. The aim of this is de-shaming, through making it clear that the tough things they are experiencing are not 'their fault' (as many fear) but rather understandable aspects of the ways that their brains have evolved, what they have learned, and the society they live in (see Chapter 4). Imagery might be used to aid understanding of this. For example, clients may be encouraged to consider the way that the image of a delicious meal or sexual situation stimulates the same physical responses as the actual meal or situation. This helps them to understand that the same brain/body processes that happen when they are bullied and criticised also happen when they treat themselves in these ways with self-critical thoughts and images. Whilst they are not viewed as the cause of their problems, clients are encouraged to take responsibility for ameliorating them through cultivating a different, more compassionate, way of being.

CFT draws upon mindfulness meditation to notice self-critical messages and to cultivate the ability to sit with difficult experiences as well as classic CBT techniques such as Socratic dialogue and gradual exposure (see Salkovskis, 2010). In addition to these, CFT employs many other specific practices to help to bring clients to a more compassionate relationship with themselves. Some of these will be considered in further detail in Chapter 5.

There is an emphasis on imagery in CFT, given that imagining things is viewed as stimulating the same brain/body processes as when they actually happen. So, for example, guided imagery can be used to help clients to build a 'safe place', to imagine a compassionate self (perhaps an older version of themselves), or to remember somebody being compassionate to them. Compassion and loving-kindness meditations may be used (see Chapters 1, 2 and 10). The Gestalt chair technique can be employed to enable conversations between the compassionate and self-critical selves. Memories or dreams involving self- or other-criticism can be reimagined in compassionate ways. The client can write letters to themselves from a compassionate point of view.

Importantly, Gilbert emphasises that the positive feeling states (of compassion and of drive) can both be experienced negatively if they have been linked to negative things in the past, for example if a person was abandoned or treated badly when they opened up to be cared for. Therapy in these cases may well involve grieving for lack of compassion in the past and gradual desensitisation to situations of being cared for.

Pause for reflection

Having read about these three CBT approaches which draw on mindfulness, what do you think the main resonances are between conventional CBT and mindful approaches? What are the key tensions involved in integrating these perspectives?

Mindfulness and CBT are both concerned with internal processes that exacerbate suffering, such as ways of relating to thoughts and feelings. Also mindful practices can complement CBT well in enabling us to slow down and notice the ways in which thoughts can spiral, for example, or the safety-seeking behaviours that we habitually employ and their impact.

However, as recognised by the third-wave approaches above, conventional CBT, which is based on diagnosis, risks fixing people[4] as well as setting up a gap between where they are and where they wish they were, in exactly the ways that mindfulness cautions against (see Chapter 1). Paradoxically, the approach of welcoming or accepting the state that we are in and ourselves as we are (as suggested by MBCT, ACT and CFT) is more likely to relieve suffering than the approach of trying to alter ourselves and our experience. However, as we will see in the concluding thoughts to this book, there are problems if such 'acceptance' is seen as accepting the social status quo. Being with the situation as it is does not mean being politically and socially apathetic.

Marsha Linehan, who developed DBT, acknowledges the tension between CBT (emphasising change) and Buddhism (emphasising acceptance). She points out that if we only urge clients to accept their problems then it can seem that we don't recognise how intolerable their struggles might be. However, if we only focus on trying to change the client they can feel invalidated and reinforced in their beliefs that they can't trust their own responses and interpretations. A balance – or dialectic – may need to be struck, as in ACT, between acceptance and change, but we need to be aware of this tension in our work, and how we are addressing it.

This becomes complicated also when third-wave CBT is linked to the positive psychology movement, as it often is, and is presented as a way of achieving happiness. Striving for happiness is the very thing that

---

[4]There is a similar problem with attachment theory if attachment styles are seen as fixed aspects of personality.

many Buddhist and existential thinkers locate as the reason for much suffering (something that we will touch upon in the next two sections)[5]. The dualistic split in cognitive therapy between emotion and reason – with attempts to control emotions by employing reason – also seems likely from a mindful perspective to exacerbate suffering rather than alleviate it. This is somewhat addressed by the focus on emotion in third-wave CBT, but it often retains a sense of dualism which does not fit well with Buddhist understandings (see Chapters 4, 5, 9 and 10 for more on this).

Psychodynamic Therapies

Unlike CBT there has been a history of engagement between psychoanalysis and Buddhism from the earliest days of the approach. Sigmund Freud regarded meditation as a regressive experience which attempted to regain an infantile or foetal state, echoing the colonialist approach towards eastern cultures of the time (Safran, 2003). However, Carl Jung studied eastern philosophy, along with other religions, and was a key figure in early dialogues between Buddhism and psychoanalysis. He wrote an introduction to D. T. Suzuki's ([1949] 1969) book, *An introduction to Zen Buddhism*, and his goal of a unity of consciousness and unconsciousness, through letting go and allowing Self or God archetypes to guide us, can be seen as analogous to some meditative states. Jung himself was against western cultures copying Buddhist ideas and practices, believing that it was important for each to find their own path (Stanley, 2012b). However, it is perhaps Jungian theory that has been most frequently brought into dialogue with Buddhist understandings in recent decades (see Young-Eisendrath & Muramoto, 2002).

Despite Freud's own perspective on meditative practices, when psychoanalytic thinkers began to engage further with eastern philosophies after the Second World War, many were struck by the similarities between Buddhist meditation and the 'evenly hovering' attention that Freud regarded as vital to free association (see Chapter 2). Psychoanalysts such as Wilfred Bion and Karen Horney stressed the importance of therapists having disciplines of practice in order to refine the attentive process, perhaps because of the great temptation to leap from such evenly hovering attention too early into the

---

[5]See http://northernexistentialgroup.wordpress.com/2012/03/03/happiness-at-the-northern-existential-group.

selection of one particular aspect to interpret (Mace, 2008). Horney and Erich Fromm both engaged in dialogue with D. T. Suzuki, and Horney's concept of 'wholehearted attention' resonates with mindful attention in many ways, as it is described as 'unlimited receptivity' allowing everything to 'come up, emerge, and ... be observed' (Horney, 1987: 20–21).

In relation to classic psychoanalysis, we can see that mindful practice could be a discipline for cultivating the kind of evenly hovering attention that is required by the therapist. Indeed, Nina Coltart explicitly states that her Buddhist practice helps her to concentrate on what is going on in the session, and that her sessions become similar to meditations (Coltart, 1998). There could also be commonalities between the experience of the client in psychoanalysis and the meditator in that things may be brought into awareness rather than remaining unaware through bringing our attention to the flow of thoughts, feelings, memories, sensations and the like. As we notice the connections that we make, or the thoughts, memories and fantasies that evoke painful feelings or tension, it is possible that, from a psychoanalytic perspective, we might reveal what is usually repressed and come to observe our defence mechanisms in action. Psychoanalysis perhaps also shares something in common with some traditional schools of Buddhism in that an expert or senior person is required to facilitate this process. However, it differs from more recent forms of mindfulness meditation which happen alone, or in groups, and emphasise the ability of the individual themselves to become more aware, and in control of, their processes.

Moving to more contemporary forms of psychodynamic therapy, how might mindful engagement be useful for those approaches that emphasise the relationship between analyst and client as the focal point of therapy (Safran & Reading, 2008)? In such approaches there is a shift from regarding the therapist as an expert neutral observer to a more collaborative relationship which understands that the therapist is involved in co-creating the therapeutic encounter and that they contribute consciously and unconsciously to the relationship just as the client does. The relational patterns that emerge in the encounter are the focus of the analysis as these represent the personal histories, internal processes and other interpersonal relationships of both client and therapist. The goal is a collaborative process of helping the client to explore these patterns and their impact. The aim is to bring their unconscious patterns of relating into consciousness by focusing on how interactions are maintained by disowning or dissociating from certain aspects of themselves and their experience.

Interestingly, the adult relationships styles identified by attachment theory map well onto the mindful model that people tend towards

grasping (insecure) or hurling away (avoidant), whilst secure attachment has a lot in common with the idea of holding things, including
relationships, lightly (see Martine Batchelor's metaphor of the precious object in Chapter 1). Like more recent attachment theorists,
mindful approaches would not see these modes of relating as fixed,
but as possibilities that people can move between.

In relationship-focused psychodynamic therapy mindful practice
can, again, be helpful in honing the therapist's attentional skills so
that they can be aware of everything that is going on in the encounter
and within them. This will enable them to be more aware of the trans-
ference and countertransference processes going on with the client.
In addition to this, cultivating mindfulness, and non-attachment, can
help the therapist to be accepting of all the thoughts, feelings and so
on that bubble up for them in the moment. In this way they can be
very aware of their part in the process, and what they bring, and thus
more able to understand what aspects of the encounter express the
client's histories and conflicts. Safran and Reading (2008) state that a
key element of this type of therapy is metacommunication. This is
where the therapist speaks openly with the client about the implicit
communication that is going on between them. They argue that this
is, in itself, a kind of mindfulness in action as it involves noticing all
that is there and bringing it into awareness. There is also a continued
return to the here-and-now of present-moment experience which is
akin to some forms of mindful meditation (see Chapter 1). The work
of Irving Yalom (2001), which highlights the importance of the here-
and-now relationship, could be regarded as particularly mindful in
this way, and forms a bridge between psychodynamic therapy and
the more humanistic/existential approaches that we explore in the
next section.

Returning briefly to the historical engagement between psychoanalysis and Buddhism, Fromm's writings are interesting (see Fromm,
Suzuki & Martino, 1970), as is the subsequent dialogue between
Kornfield, Dass and Miyuki (1979) because, rather than simply bringing
psychoanalysis and Buddhism together, both draw on their engagements with Buddhism to take a critical perspective on western focuses
on 'civilisation' or 'psychological adjustment' and 'personal growth'
(see Chapter 1). This trend of using Buddhist philosophy to critique
some aspects of both psychoanalysis and contemporary western culture has been continued by authors such as Mark Epstein (2001, 2005)
and Barry Magid (2008). Both authors highlight key tensions between
psychodynamic and Buddhist understandings, and this means that the
therapeutic approaches that they propose depart in important ways
from more conventional psychodynamic therapy.

> ## Practice: Where is the self? (adapted from Batchelor, 1997: 23)
>
> Try searching for your self in meditation. What is it that is you? Is it your bodily sensations? Your mood? Your thoughts? A particular trait? Notice how everything that you might fix upon as the self actually ebbs and flows. It is not something that you can pin down.

Mark Epstein's (2001) integrations of Buddhism and psychoanalysis highlight the tension between their understandings of the self. Psychoanalysis, like conventional western understandings, tends to assume that there is a real, core self which we can reach some certainty about through psychoanalytic practice. As we experience when we meditate on the self, whilst the self appears real to us – enduring, fixed and separate – it isn't actually a lasting essential object in its own right. From a Buddhist perspective the self we experience cannot be separated from the matrix of circumstances that formed it or from the relationships in which it is expressed (see Chapter 10). Mark Epstein concludes, therefore, that therapy should be more about breaking open the self as opposed to digging down to reveal it. Following psychoanalyst D. W. Winnicott, his emphasis is not on integration into a cohesive self but on 'unintegration', which emerges in play and creativity where we don't have to create static selves to display to the world. Elsewhere in his work, Epstein (2005) brings Buddhist and psychoanalytic understandings of desire into dialogue and encourages an 'openness to desire' rather than locating it as the root of suffering. Epstein's therapeutic practice emphasises sitting with unexperienced and feared feelings and can include the therapist bringing in Buddhist stories and/ or meditative practices.

In his writing, Magid (2008) questions the idea, common to CBT and many psychodynamic therapies, that there is something wrong with people that needs fixing, and particularly the idea that we should be pursuing happiness. He cautions that such ideas can easily stray into western Buddhist practices too, because they are so omnipresent, such that we meditate with the secret aim of perfecting our self and finding happiness. Magid's integration of psychoanalysis and Zen emphasises ordinary life and leaving our minds alone rather than judging and trying to improve ourselves.

Finally, the psychodynamic understanding of the unconscious differs from mindful understandings which have more in common with the existential approach that we will turn to in the next section. In these, awareness is compared to a torch in a darkened room: everything is available to awareness, but we shine the torch in different places. It is not that there are some things that are unavailable and need to be dug out to be revealed. Meditation practices can facilitate shining the torch in different places, and diffusing the light to enable a spacious awareness of the entirety of experience.

Humanistic and Existential Therapies

Humanistic and existential therapies have engaged with Buddhism and mindfulness much less explicitly than CBT and psychodynamic therapies, arguably because their theories and practices are more similar already, particularly those of existential-phenomenology.

Beginning with person-centred therapy, in Chapter 2 we saw that mindful practice can cultivate the therapist's quality of empathy, which is one of Rogers' main core conditions for a therapeutic relationship (see Moore & Shoemark, 2010). Mindful practices which emphasise non-judgemental acceptance of whatever arises can cultivate the core condition of unconditional positive regard. This involves radically accepting the client as they are, rather than perpetuating conditions of worth which suggest that only certain parts of them are acceptable, or that they are only acceptable as a person if they act in certain ways. Finally, the kind of self-awareness which is cultivated in mindful practice would be beneficial for the core condition of congruence. Rogers describes this as 'openly being the feelings and attitudes that are flowing within [himself] at the moment' and 'a close matching ... between what is being experienced at the gut level, what is present in awareness and what is expressed to the client' (Rogers, 1980: 115), so it is very similar to mindful awareness. In these ways, the way of being of the person-centred therapist with the client mirrors the ways in which we try to be with ourselves when we are mindful. Qualitative research has confirmed that person-centred therapists do indeed report that meditation is useful to their work through fostering the core conditions (Bazzano, 2009).

Pause for reflection

Do you see any differences between the person-centred and mindful understanding of the person, and what helps them when they are suffering, which might result in tensions when integrating these approaches?

Like psychodynamic approaches, person-centred therapy does have an idea of a core, or organismic, self which can be in conflict with the self-concept that is created under conditions of worth. In other words, the kind of self that we really are can be in tension with the kind of self that we think we should be. As we have seen previously, Buddhism regards the belief in oneself as a separate, essential and permanent entity as a delusion which results in suffering (see Fulton, 2008). The Buddhist understanding of the self would be more in tune with existential-phenomenological, systemic and narrative therapy approaches which emphasise the self as plural rather than singular and as fluid rather than fixed (Barker, 2012a). Consider this quote from existential thera-pist Ernesto Spinelli:

> 'The self' that emerges at any given intentional moment is phenomenologically 'real', singular and relatively coherent insofar as it is able to experience or 'story' a temporal narrative incorporating (selective) past experience, current mood and future expectations or goals. But, at the same time, this 'self' is also revealed as an impermanent construct that, at best, is a partial expression of an infinity of potential interpretationally constructed selves. (2005: 83)

There may be related tensions, for example, in humanistic therapy ideas such as 'owning' one's emotions, since who is to do this 'owning' and might this be similar to 'identifying' with emotions, which mindful approaches warn against[6]? Thus, integration of mindful and humanistic perspectives requires rethinking of common western understandings of the self, something we will return to in the Concluding Thoughts to this book.

Perhaps for these reasons, many of those who have written on person-centred therapy and mindfulness have also drawn in existential-phenomenological therapy (e.g. Walsh, 2008). Buddhist theorists Stephen Batchelor (1983) and David Loy (1996) also explicitly bring together Buddhist and existential approaches in their work. It is clear that the existential and Buddhist perspectives share a great deal in common, including:

- the notion of the self as actively created in interaction with the world (Heidegger's being-in-the-world being akin to Thich Nhat Hanh's interbeing, see Chapter 10),
- the inevitability of uncertainty, and
- the impossibility of dualistic splits between mind and body (Nanda, 2006).

---

[6]See http://socialmindfulness.wordpress.com/2012/04/27/owning-emotions-versus-identifying-with-emotions.

Some of the bodily mindful practices, such as attending to sensations and the body sweep (see Chapter 9), are similar to the 'focusing' techniques of humanistic therapist Eugene Gendlin (2003), which have also been popular amongst existential therapists. This involves bringing attention to the body, describing in detail the sensation of feelings in the body, checking descriptions for accuracy, and staying with the experience, noticing what happens over time.

Mindful practice is, in many ways, very similar to Edmund Husserl's phenomenology, which underlies most existential therapy[7]. The non-grasping approach of allowing thoughts, feelings and sensations to ebb and flow shares a lot with the rule of horizontalising, where we avoid placing aspects of the client's experience in a hierarchy. The practice of attending to the world as a whole rather than attempting to fix, label or identify with certain sounds, ideas or memories can be seen as rather like the phenomenological aim of bracketing, where we set aside our preconceptions to be open to the world of the client. In existential-phenomenological therapy we ask 'What does this mean to you?' rather than making assumptions, just as in mindful practice we try to engage with the world openly rather than through habitual reactions. Phenomenology aims at a rich, full understanding of lived experience through an initial stance of unknowing, which is very similar to the Buddhist idea of cultivating 'beginner's mind'. Daniel Stern's writing (2004) brings together psychoanalysis and phenomenology in a way that resonates with these ideas, and emphasises attention to the present moment in psychotherapy.

In Chapter 5 I will explore further how mindful meditations can serve to reconnect the alienated and estranged 'self' with the various dimensions of human existence. Some of the main forms of mindful meditation also explicitly bring the person up against the 'givens' of human existence (Claessens, 2009). Indeed, the story of the first Buddha's journey to enlightenment begins when he is confronted with the existential conditions of sickness, ageing and death (see Chapter 1). One key meditation is to reflect upon the statement 'Since death alone is certain and the time of death uncertain, what should I do?' (Batchelor, 1997: 27). This confronts the meditator with the fact of their death, the impermanence of existence, and the onus on them to create meaning in their life in the knowledge that death could come at any time. Of course the answers that emerge may well be different on different occasions. ACT similarly uses a technique, also used in existential therapy, of having the client write their own epitaph. Jyoti Nanda

---

[7]Although perhaps it is more akin to more recent reflexive styles of phenomenology which acknowledge that we always view situations from somewhere, than the Husserlian idea that we can achieve a god's eye view of phenomena.

(2010) has recently proposed a specifically mindfulness-based form of existential therapy (MBET).

There are relatively few tensions involved in integrating mindful approaches with existential therapy in general, given the common theories and practices involved. However, most existential therapists draw on one of the main existential philosophers more than others (e.g. Heidegger, de Beauvoir, Sartre or Merleau-Ponty) and this is where tensions may occur, given that each of these philosophies differs both from the others, and from Buddhist understandings in places. It is important for existential therapists to explore what flavour of existential therapist they are (Langdridge, 2013) and then, if they do want to integrate this with mindfulness, to pay attention to the commonalities and tensions between the approaches. For example, Sartre's early views of humans as inevitably in conflict (hell is other people) do not fit well with notions of interbeing and interconnectedness (see Chapter 10), and neither do Neitzschian or Heideggarian notions of the 'herd' or the 'they'.

Summary and conclusions

In Chapter 2 we covered the general commonalities between mindful practice and the therapeutic encounter, and how the former could cultivate the qualities needed for the latter. We also saw that the mindful approach was compatible with a general theory shared by most western therapies that suffering results from patterns laid down in the past which can be alleviated by bringing these into awareness and shifting them or letting them go. In this chapter we have explored, in more detail, how mindful practice can be integrated into CBT, psychodynamic therapy and humanistic/existential therapies in order to bring such awareness to the client. We have also covered some of the key tensions between Buddhist and western therapeutic perspectives. Rather than bolting mindful understandings and practices onto our existing modalities, we need to remain aware of these tensions, and consider how we are holding or resolving them when we integrate these approaches.

Further reading

Cognitive-behavioural therapies

If you want to learn more about any of the third-wave of CBT approaches, the Routledge CBT Distinctive Features Series is a great place to start. These small books summarise the main theoretical and practical features of MBCT, ACT, CFT and DBT:

Crane, R. (2009). *Mindfulness-based cognitive therapy.* London: Routledge.

Flaxman, P. E., Blackledge, J. T., & Bond, F. W. (2011). *Acceptance and commitment therapy.* London: Routledge.

Gilbert, P. (2010). *Compassion focused therapy.* London: Routledge.

Swales, M. A., & Heard, H. L. (2009). *Dialectical behaviour therapy.* London: Routledge.

A more detailed list of books bringing mindfulness and CBT together, including the main texts on each of these types of therapy, can be found at: http://social mindfulness.wordpress.com/references/therapy/therapy-cbt.

You can also find links on the Social Mindfulness website to the centres of many of the third-wave approaches covered in this chapter.

Psychodynamic therapies

There are a number of edited collections bringing Buddhist understandings together with psychodynamic approaches. The following one is particularly useful as it includes some of the early dialogues mentioned in the chapter, as well as contemporary perspectives by many key writers:

Molino, A. (Ed.). (1999). *The couch and the tree: Dialogues in psychoanalysis and Buddhism.* London: Constable.

A list of books by the psychodynamic authors touched upon in this chapter, as well as further edited collections, can be found at: http://socialmindfulness.wordpress.com/references/therapy/therapy-psychodynamic.

Humanistic and existential therapies

Two key publications on the engagement between Buddhist mindfulness and humanistic and existential therapies are:

Moore, J. & Shoemark, A. (2010). Mindfulness and the person-centred approach. In J. Leonardi (Ed.). *The human being fully alive.* (pp. 90–111). Ross-on-Wye: PCCS.

Claessens, M. (2009). Mindfulness and existential therapy. *Existential Analysis, 20* (1), 109–119.

A list of further books and papers bringing Buddhist and mindful perspectives together with humanistic and existential approaches can be found here; the work of Manu Bazzano and Jyoti Nanda is particularly helpful as both have engaged in detail with the resonances between mindful and existential/humanistic approaches: http://social mindfulness.wordpress.com/references/therapy/therapy-humanisticexistential.

FOUR Researching mindful therapies

Aims

This chapter aims to:

- overview the research on mindfulness, meditation and mindful therapies,
- propose a non-dualistic, biopsychosocial approach whereby the different strands of research can be woven together,
- draw together what is known about what mindfulness is; whether it 'works' in various ways, how it does so, and what the experience is like.

There has been an explosion of research on mindfulness in recent years such that it would be impossible to summarise even a fraction of the studies that have now been published. It is estimated that there are currently over forty new research publications on mindfulness every month (BBC, 2012). Obviously the fast rate of publication in this area also means that any chapter summarising mindfulness research will quickly become out of date. Here I will attempt to overview some of the key studies, and the ones that have most captured the public imagination in recent years. The Further Reading section at the end of the chapter includes websites that update their material on mindfulness research regularly. For the reader who is interested in a particular aspect of mindfulness I would suggest using an academic search engine to find the most recent reviews and meta-analyses on mindfulness and the topic that they are interested in. These articles tend to bring together everything relevant in the area and are therefore a good place to start.

This chapter will focus on research about the value and impact of mindfulness on clients and people in general, given that we have already considered the impact on therapists and the therapeutic relationship in

Chapters 2 and 3. We will also touch only relatively briefly here on research about the particular issues that are covered in the rest of the book because we will consider relevant research in more depth in the subsequent specific chapters.

The bulk of existing research focuses on the impact of mindfulness interventions on brain, body, experience and behaviour, and on the relationship between people's levels of mindfulness (as quantified on questionnaire measures) and other variables, such as attention, well-being or pain[1]. However, as I mentioned in the Introduction, I will try to include some of the 'shyer' stories in mindfulness research, as well as these more 'boastful' ones! That means also attending to qualitative research on the experience of mindfulness, and the small but burgeoning area of the social psychology and sociology of mindfulness.

Many key mindfulness authors, from various approaches, have argued for better integration of research into mindfulness, rather than separating off, for example, neuroscientific work from outcome research on interventions, from phenomenological studies on the experience. Daniel Siegel attempts a synthesis of these strands in his writings, bringing together personal experiences and neuroscience in particular (Siegel, 2007); Mark Williams and Jon Kabat-Zinn (2011b) argue for an interface between first-person experience of mindfulness and the third-person perspective of scientists; Daniel Goleman (2003) deliberately brought a group of scientists and philosophers together in discussion with the Dalai Lama; and Varela, Thompson and Rosch (1991) set out a detailed model for how cognitive science and human experience might be brought back together by focusing on 'embodied cognition' via Buddhist understandings.

Such integrated approaches are consistent with Buddhism, which has a non-dualistic perspective. This means that it doesn't separate the mind and body in the way that we have become familiar with in western cultures. Rather there is something more like a *biopsychosocial* understanding of human beings (Toates, 2010) that regards us as simultaneously embodied biological beings, psychological experiencers and inextricably located in our social worlds. As Steven Batchelor explains the Buddhist concept of contingency:

> We have been created, moulded, formed by a bewildering matrix of contingencies that have preceded us. From the patterning of the DNA derived from our parents to the firing of the hundred billion neurons in our brains to the cultural and historical conditioning of the twentieth [now twenty-first] century to the education and upbringing given us to all the experience we have ever had and

---

[1]This is clear in the headings of the regular mindfulness research newsletter: www.mindfulexperience.org/newsletter.php.

choices we have ever made. these have conspired to configure the unique trajectory that culminates in this present moment. (Batchelor, 1997: 82)

This 'bewildering matrix' makes a nonsense of simplistic splits like mind/body, nature/nurture and hard-wired/chosen behaviours. It challenges the common scientific goal of delineating simple cause-and-effect relationships, which becomes very difficult with 'open systems' like human beings anyway[2]. Certainly the assumed causal relationship from bio to psycho to social is challenged by recent research demonstrating that social experience determines whether certain genes are expressed or not (Carey, 2012) and influences the structure of the brain (Davidson, 2012), as well as biological vulnerabilities making certain psychological and social possibilities more likely (but not inevitable). Experiences often happen on all levels simultaneously – the flood of neurotransmitters and tensing of muscles; the spike of excitement and fear; and the social messages flowing through us – that the situation we find ourselves in, such as public speaking, should be anxiety-provoking.

We will explore the implication of such a non-dualistic, biopsychosocial understanding for emotional experiences in Chapter 5, and for bodily experiences in Chapter 9. For the purposes of this chapter, we will consider each aspect (bio, psycho and social) separately, but it is important to be mindful throughout that they are not really separable. Indeed, mindfulness research is particularly helpful in evidencing this very point as it demonstrates the impact of mindful practice on all levels.

Bio(psychosocial): Mindfulness and the body/brain

In 2007 Buddhism hit the headlines with the claim that scientists had found the 'happiest man in the world': Matthieu Ricard, a French academic-turned-Buddhist monk who interprets for the Dalai Lama[3]. Ricard took part in one of the recent spate of studies on the impact of meditation on the brain and was found to have huge levels of activity in the left pre-frontal cortex, thought to be related to the experience of positive emotions.

Studies using electroencephalograms (EEGs) and the neuroimaging techniques of functional magnetic resonance imaging (fMRI) and positron emission tomography (PET) have been important in the shift

---

[2] See http://en.wikipedia.org/wiki/Open_system_(systems_theory).

[3] See www.independent.co.uk/news/uk/this-britain/the-happiest-man-in-the-world-433063.html.

to a more biopsychosocial understanding of humans since they reveal the significant *neuroplasticity* of the brain: the fact that experiences, like meditation, can have a marked impact on aspects such as levels of synaptic neurotransmitters, neural activity in certain areas, the strength of links between neurons, and the thickness of the grey and white matter (all of which are interrelated). This challenges previously commonly held assumptions that brains are relatively fixed. Of course every time we learn anything new, have a new experience or lay down a new memory, there is a change at the level of the brain (neurons connecting up differently, etc.). However, somehow meditation research has been particularly powerful in demonstrating this to people who previously thought that brains could impact on behaviour but not vice versa. Such neuroscience seems to reflect metaphors that Buddhist teachers use to explain the impact of mindful practice; for example, the analogy that rainwater wears a groove as it finds its way to the ground, but if we wear a new, deeper channel, it will follow that instead (Batchelor, 1997).

Research in this area began back in the 1960s when Kasamatsu and Hirai (1966) used EEGs to study the neuro-electric response associated with meditation (a measure of the electrical activity of the brain). The study suggested that a different kind of activity occurred to that which happens during sleep or relaxation, and also that experienced meditators responded to each new stimulus they received (a series of clicks) as if it was new, rather than habituating to them. This evidence of 'beginner's mind' has not been replicated, but there are clear EEG differences between relaxation, concentration meditation (e.g. focusing on the breath) and the more spacious kind of meditation when people attend to whatever experience emerges (see Chapter 1 for more on the distinction between vipassanā and samatha forms of meditation) (Dunn, Hartigan, & Mikulas, 1999). Differences between focused attention and wider, more open, awareness may also be related to the specialisations of the left and right hemispheres of the brain[4].

PET and fMRI studies confirm that meditation differs from rest and sleep, and also that different brain regions are involved in different meditative practices (Lazar, 2005). A recent review linked neuroscientific findings on mindfulness and meditation to evidence on the behavioural, cognitive and emotional changes in people who practised mindfulness and their self-reports of this experience (Hölzel, Lazar, Gard, Schuman-Olivier, Vago, & Ott, 2011). Table 4.1 summarises a mechanism that the authors proposed for how the different elements of mindfulness work.

---

[4]See http://socialmindfulness.wordpress.com/2012/04/25/divided-brains-and-mindfulness.

Table 4.1   Potential mechanisms of mindfulness (adapted from Hölzel et al., 2011)

Mechanism	Example types of mindfulness practice	Self-report and experimental behavioural findings	Associated brain areas
Attention regulation	Sustain attention on object (e.g. breath), returning to it when distracted (see Introduction)	Enhanced performance on attention tasks, feeling more alert	Anterior cingulate cortex (ACC)
Body awareness	Focus on sensory experience of breath, emotion or body sensations (see Chapter 9)	Increased scores on body awareness questionnaires, reporting more awareness	Insula, temporo-parietal junction
Emotion regulation: reappraisal	Approach emotional experience with acceptance (being with) (see Chapter 5)	Increasing positive reappraisal of emotions	(Dorsal) prefrontal cortex (PFC)
Emotional regulation: approach/ exposure	Exposure to whatever is present, letting yourself be affected by it, refraining from reacting/avoiding (see Chapter 6)	Decrease in reaction to inner experience	Ventro-medial PFC, hippocampus, amygdala
Changing perspective on the self	Not identifying with static self (see Chapter 3)	Self-reported changes in self-concept on various measures	Medial PFC, posterior cingulate cortex, insula temporo-parietal junction

In each case neural events and mental activities are seen as being related, or 'co-arising', rather than one influencing or causing the other.

Hölzel et al. report that the components in each row of Table 4.1 are highly interrelated with each other, and state that making such distinctions is artificial because each component may mutually facilitate the other. For example, sustained attention to body awareness can lead to emotional exposure, which facilitates reappraisal and changing perspectives on the self. We need to understand the ways in which these aspects integrate across the whole brain, as well as examining each individual component.

Attention regulation, however, is often suggested to be a prerequisite for the other components. This supports the key role we gave attention in our understanding of mindfulness (see Introduction). Hölzel et al. also report that self-compassion has been found to be highly correlated with mindfulness and that this might be a major aspect of the success of mindful interventions (see Chapters 3 and 5), although the mechanisms of this are not as well understood yet as the other components above (see Gilbert, 2010a).

From focusing on the brain we will now turn our attention to the body. However, again it is important to be cautious of separating brain and body because, of course, the brain is part of the body, and all the bodily changes that take place are related to changes in neural activity in complex feedback loops. Mindfulness and meditation have particularly been found to be associated with changes in physical arousal, breathing, heart-rate, immune function, blood pressure and telomerase activity (involved in cellular replication). For example, a few years of mindful meditation practice seems to increase breathing rate, whilst those who have practised for six or more years display a decrease. Mindfulness also seems related to variability in heart-rate (which is associated with better outcome in heart disease), and to improvement in immune function (Davidson et al., 2003).

Pause for reflection

What do you make of the bio(psychosocial) research reported in this section of the chapter? What might its value be to the practitioner and the client? What cautions might you want to have around it?

Given a non-dualistic biopsychosocial approach to human experience, it is certainly important to understand how mindful practices operate on all these different levels and, importantly, how these interrelate. However, there are a couple of notes of caution here. One is the emphasis that is given to neuroscientific studies (in terms of funding and scientific and popular attention) in comparison to other kinds of work. There still seems to be a commonly held perspective that demonstrations of activity in the brain, for example, somehow makes something more 'real'. Of course that can be of use to a practitioner who wants to prove the legitimacy of mindful practices to a client, but in doing so are we also reinforcing the idea that 'bio' equals 'real' in a way that 'psycho' and 'social' (e.g. experiential reports and social theory) does not?

We should be particularly cautious about this given that neuroscientists and biological psychologists themselves emphasise the interrelationship between biopsychosocial aspects of experience and the limitations of neuroimaging studies. For example, they point out that it is difficult, in such research, to know what is being captured: a moment when the meditator is being distracted or focusing, or bringing themselves back from distraction to focusing? Static images can be difficult to interpret in terms of the *process* of mindfulness, and it is also difficult to know the significance of 'active' and 'inactive' areas of the brain:

the latter may be just as important as the former. We still don't have a clear map of what areas in the brain are responsible for what: patterns are not easy to interpret and may well not be entirely generalisable across people anyway. This is one reason to be sceptical, for example, about the broad claims that are frequently made about 'left' and 'right' brains, or 'male' and 'female' brains. Hölzel et al. remind readers that different mechanisms may be involved in mindfulness for different people, and Varela et al. (1991) illustrate this with findings that, for example, during a visualisation task about half of the population show activity in the visual cortex of the brain, and half do not. He uses this as reason to bring together first-, second- and third-person research: attending equally to the person having the experience (first), to the reports of a highly trained interviewer (second), and to objective measurements of brain activity (third).

(bio)Psycho(social): The psychological impact and experience of mindfulness

Turning now to psychological explorations of mindfulness, I will begin with quantitative attempts to measure mindfulness and its relationship to various other psychological factors (such as well-being, concentration, compassion, etc.), and will then turn to more qualitative explorations of the lived experience of mindfulness.

There is an emphasis in psychology on quantifying experiences in order to determine their significance. For example, if we want to measure how mindful different groups are, whether mindfulness is related to happiness or attention, or whether mindful interventions really do increase mindfulness and help people, then we need to be able to quantify mindfulness. In order to quantify something, an 'operational definition' is necessary. In other words, we need to know what we mean by mindfulness in order to study it.

Many questionnaires have been developed in order to measure an individual's degree of mindfulness; for example, the Mindful Attention Awareness Scale (MAAS), the Freiburg Mindfulness Inventory (FMI), the Kentucky Inventory of Mindfulness (KIM), and the Cognitive and Affective Mindfulness Scale (CAMS) (Baer, 2011). Baer, Smith, Hopkins, Krietmeyer, & Toney (2006) compared these existing questionnaires and came up with five factors that seemed to be common across them:

- Observing (noticing internal/external stimuli like thoughts or sounds).
- Describing (labelling these mentally).
- Nonjudging (not evaluating inner experiences).

- Nonreactivity (letting thoughts and feelings come and go without getting caught in them).
- Acting with awareness (attending to current behaviour rather than reacting on automatic pilot).

This research led to a further questionnaire, the Five Factors Mindfulness Questionnaire (FFMQ). Bishop et al. proposed another operational definition of mindfulness, based on a series of meetings with experts in the field, which is frequently employed in the literature:

> A process of regulating attention in order to bring a quality of nonelaborative awareness to current experience and a quality of relating to one's experience within an orientation of curiosity, experiential openness, and acceptance ... gaining insight into the nature of one's mind ... [adopting] a de-centred perspective ... on thoughts and feelings so that they can be experienced in terms of their subjectivity (versus their necessary validity) and transient nature (versus their permanence). (2004: 234)

Measures based on such work have begun to explore the trajectory of mindfulness when people are learning to practise. This research suggests that mindfulness is a capacity that people can learn and which develops over time (Mace, 2008). There have been suggestions that mindfulness can be both a 'state' and a 'trait': that people can be in a state of mindfulness at certain times, but that also some people can be more mindful (as a trait that they possess) than others, and that such a trait can develop with practice.

Table 4.1 displays some of the key findings about the relationship between mindfulness and various cognitive and emotional capacities. Such studies compare experienced and non-experienced meditators, or people before and after a mindfulness course, on various measures and experimental tasks, finding that mindfulness is associated with superior attention, body awareness and emotional regulation, as well as an altered perspective on the self.

It seems likely that the mechanisms suggested in Table 4.1 may explain some of the findings of outcome research on mindfulness interventions: the evidence that rates of various difficulties (stress, anxiety, depression, addiction, sexual difficulties, etc.) decrease following mindful therapy or mindfulness training, when compared to rates in control groups who go through similar therapies and trainings without the mindfulness component. For example, attention regulation is important in attention related problems (sometimes diagnosed as attention-deficit/hyperactivity disorder) and depressions that negatively impact attention and memory. Body awareness is particularly relevant in eating and addiction related issues, and emotion regulation is relevant across a wide range of issues, including phobias, obsessions, anxieties and depressions.

Recent reviews report the results of randomised control trials (the gold standard of outcome research) for mindfulness and depression. Mindfulness-based cognitive therapy (MBCT) has been found to be significantly better than 'treatment-as-usual' in preventing relapse (Chiesa & Serretti, 2010). There are also promising findings for MBCT and mindfulness-based stress reduction (MBSR) on anxiety, and some suggestion that vipassanā meditation may be helpful with alcohol and drug addiction. However, further research is needed in many areas because many of the existing studies have small numbers of participants, who are not randomly allocated to groups (Barkham & Barker, 2010). Research in this area also suffers from many of the problems of outcome research more broadly, including the fact that most research tends to be conducted by those who are invested in mindfulness, who will therefore tend to find more positive results; that significant results tend to be published whilst non-significant ones do not; and that it is very hard to create control groups who go through everything else that the mindfulness groups go through except the mindfulness itself, with the same practitioner (Cooper, 2008). Also, as mentioned in the previous chapters, some mindful therapies (notably MBCT and MBSR) have been researched much more extensively than others, and it is difficult to determine how much people have been practising mindfully between sessions and in what ways. More detail of specific studies will be provided in subsequent chapters on specific psychological issues, and we will also consider more physical conditions in Chapter 9.

Whilst researchers within quantitative psychology have urged better operational definitions of mindfulness, and more randomised control studies of mindful interventions and treatments, another set of challenges have come from more qualitative researchers and Buddhist scholars who feel that the rush to capture and apply mindfulness has caused it to drift too far from its origins (Grossman & Van Dam, 2011). As we saw in the Introduction and Chapter 1, Buddhism presents being mindful as a practice or process, not as an object, and mindfulness also cannot easily be extracted and isolated from related concepts such as compassion, courage and commitment to ethical action. In addition, many have highlighted a seeming tension between the focus on treating psychological 'disorders' and enhancing well-being and the central Buddhist teachings that question the desire to fix and label ourselves, and regard the entitled pursuit of happiness as the root of the problem (see Chapters 1 and 3, and Concluding Thoughts; Cohen, 2010).

It is here where some authors call for a return to the self-experiential foundations of mindful practice, which are arguably too quickly short-cut by some of the biological and psychological science approaches

(Depraz, Varela, & Vermersch, 2003; Stanley, 2012c). This is important because mindfulness is a slippery concept and there is a lack of consensus around what it includes, and paradoxes inherent in trying to make it more tangible (Moss & Barnes, 2008).

Practice: Phenomenological enquiry into being mindful

Commit to a daily mindful practice for a week, deciding in advance what this will involve. For example, you might decide to meditate for 20 minutes each morning and evening, employing the breathing meditation from the Introduction, or a more spacious meditation where you just attend to whatever (thoughts, sensations, feelings, etc.) emerge, noticing them, and neither grasping them nor trying to avoid them. Alternatively, you might incorporate different practices such as mindful washing of dishes (see Chapter 1), walking (see Chapter 6) or eating (see Chapter 9).

Over this time keep a daily written or audio diary of the experience (either writing in a journal or speaking into a recorder). Describe the experiences of mindful practice themselves as well as how you experience your daily life, and professional practice, during this time.

At the end of the week consider the key themes that come up in your diary. If a friend or colleague does a similar enquiry, you can compare your accounts.

Mace (2008) suggests that qualitative research, such as diary studies, interviews, focus-group discussions and autho-ethnography (where the researcher reflects on their own experience, as you did above) (Etherington, 2004) can help to illuminate the range of experiences that are possible, as well as contextualising the variation in experience in the diversity of people's lives. It can also yield much richer descriptions of what mindfulness means to people, and what they understand and experience when being mindful.

Mace's discussions with active mindfulness meditators echo the diary studies of Nugent et al. (2011) with new mindful practitioners, which we touched upon in the Introduction. Both groups spoke of the discomfort that mindfulness could bring. Mace's participants talked about failing to live up to their own expectations, realising how intolerant they could be of other people, and facing up to aspects of themselves that they found difficult (see Chapter 10). Nugent et al.'s participants also spoke of the challenge of sitting with uncertainty and said things like:

> There's just such a huge instinctive drive to push it [pain] away. So not only have you got the discomfort, but also over and above that are the thoughts that

como in whioh arc likc 'I don't like', 'why have I gul', um 'huw can I gel rld of it', 'I'm feeling fed up about it'. (2011: 7)

There is a also the striking similarity that both sets of participants felt that there was a value to facing these challenges and discomforts as they helped them to learn to be with difficult experiences and to cultivate equanimity.

Participants in Mace's study made comparisons between mindfulness and other, similar, practices such as yoga and playing musical instruments, which perhaps demonstrates value in considering overlaps between mindfulness and other, more familiar, practices rather than isolating mindful meditation specifically. Nugent et al.'s participants emphasised everyday mindfulness beyond formal practice and both groups noticed mindfulness permeating their daily lives over time, particularly in their sensitivity towards other people (see Chapter 2).

In terms of what they felt was specific to mindfulness compared to other practices, Mace's participants highlighted inclusive awareness (to the internal and external world, including the body), a single-minded attention to what is with equanimity, suspending attempts to control experience, and letting go of thoughts. Nugent et al.'s participants emphasised that mindfulness could both encourage acceptance and open up space for change:

> The first thing that you might notice is feeling physically very tense um ... down, stressed, fed up. Perhaps not having been aware ... why or how you've got to that point. And I guess being mindful of it gives you an opportunity either to just be aware, just be mindful and think 'oh my mind's very busy or fretting about work'. Or maybe it's about, it gives an opportunity to take some practical action over it. (p. 8)

Nanda's (2005) in-depth interviews with practitioners who also engaged in mindfulness practice found a similar both/and approach to acceptance and change. The two key themes emerging from her research were of 'being with what is' and 'transformational relational change'. For example, participants said both that 'Instead of manipulating events, and trying to control events, there is much more an experience of being with the event as it is arising from moment to moment' and that in a meditative state 'I go into the small, clear state of quiet awareness. I just come from a much stiller place; less influenced by my personal agendas. So I tend to be much calmer, much more understanding, much less reactive' (p. 330). There was a sense of enhanced intimacy with others, and, rather than enforcing change, a sense of the inevitable change and impermanence involved in life.

For therapists who want to research their engagements with mindfulness, an alternative to outcome research is process research. This focuses on how therapy unfolds over time and more frequently uses qualitative methods, although combined questionnaire measures and qualitative approaches can be valuable here. For example, if you were building mindfulness into your practice, you might want to encourage clients to keep diaries of their experiences, or to record some of their sessions to examine the mindful relationship between you, or to reflect over time on your own mindfulness practice in relation to your therapy (McLeod, 2010).

(biopsycho)Social: The social psychology and sociology of mindfulness

There has been far less research into the social aspects of the biopsycho-social experience of mindfulness than on the biological and psychological aspects. Here we will consider the related research of social psychologist Ellen Langer, before exploring further what more (biopsycho)social explorations of mindfulness might look like.

Langer's (1989) work is still psychological, in that it is mostly based on experimental research on the impact of mindful, or mindless, cognitive processes. However, it is also social in that it is mostly applied to social situations such as workplaces, situations of prejudice, education, healthcare and ageing.

Importantly, Langer's conceptualisation of 'mindfulness' is not equivalent to the understandings we have considered so far in this book. She did not come to her research through Buddhism but rather through observing how people commonly think and behave 'mindlessly' and researching whether the opposite might be beneficial. Whilst she is clear that her mindfulness construct is not the same as the Buddhist or mindful therapy ones – and she doesn't explore meditative practices at all – there are clearly some overlaps which make it worthwhile to consider her work alongside other types of mindfulness research.

What Langer means by 'mindless' is our common habitual way of thinking and behaving where we act on automatic pilot, take things for granted, and follow rules and routines. Mindfulness, under her definition, is the capacity to see things in different ways: being open to new information, considering alternative perspectives, being aware of the impact of context, and creating new categories. The distinctions here resonate with current thinking in psychology and economics, which highlights the biases and errors that are inherent in automatic, intuitive responses compared to more conscious, engaged or attentive ways of thinking (Kahneman, 2012).

Case study: Vineet

Vineet, an Asian man in his mid-sixties, has been 'bullied' into coming to counselling by his family. They say that since he retired from his successful medical practice he has become an 'old man' over night, napping in the daytime and showing little interest in the things he used to be passionate about. His wife, who is in her fifties, is particularly frustrated as she had been looking forward to all the things they would do now that they had more time. She finds herself having to do everything for Vineet because he can't do it himself.

Think about

- Under Langer's definition, how might you respond to Vineet mindlessly?
- How might a mindful response – again using Langer's definition – differ to this?
- How might Langer's concepts of mindlessness and mindfulness be useful in working with Vineet?

One way forward

Short vignettes, such as the case studies presented in this book, in a way encourage us to think mindlessly as we draw conclusions about people based on limited information. However, this is often the first kind of information that we have to go on with a client. Notice how reading the description of Vineet (and the others in this book) conjures certain images and assumptions. In this case perhaps you already have a sinking feeling about the difficulty of working with clients who don't choose therapy for themselves, or doctors who are likely to prefer medical to psychological interventions. Maybe you have an image of an 'Asian family', and your own assumptions about when 'old age' kicks in, and what is appropriate at that time. The danger is that we are primed to view Vineet in certain ways, and this may well become a self-fulfilling prophecy both in terms of the ways in which we treat him and the ways in which he may act.

To be mindful with Vineet we would want to be open to new information, ready to explore what each aspect of the situation (coming to counselling, family, retirement, old age, passion, etc.) mean to Vineet himself. We would consider alternative perspectives: sleep and lack of passion could be signs of depression, or an underlying medical condition, of feeling the need for a well-deserved rest, or of changing interests, for example. We would want to be aware of context; for example, what were/are the commonly held beliefs in Vineet's family growing up? In his religion (if he has one)? Amongst his colleagues and friends, and in his family now? And we would want to be open to creating new categories rather than sticking Vineet in a problematic broad category of 'old', 'Asian' or 'depressed', for example. This might involve considering the intersections of race, culture, class, religion, gender, sexuality, geography, generation, age, etc. (das Nair & Butler, 2012) and being mindful of the wide variety of experiences under 'depression' (see Chapter 5).

(Continued)

(Continued)

Langer's work on mindfulness might be particularly helpful with somebody like Vineet as she has found that people often get stuck in mindsets about being old. If this is part of the issue with Vineet, we might work with him to open up different understandings of age which are available, even drawing on some of Langer's (2009) experiments, such as increasing choice and responsibilities, having people act as if they were 20 years younger, encouraging people to do things differently rather than believing that they can't do them, or shifting language from absolutes to conditionals (e.g. people in their sixties 'may', 'might be' or 'sometimes are' rather than 'are' ...).

We can see that Langer's mindfulness resonates with the version we are more familiar with in that it is about freeing ourselves from habitual patterns, unlearning previous connections, and being present to what is (see Siegel, 2007). Langer also emphasises the importance of a non-dualistic approach to mind and body (given her findings about the health benefits of mindful thinking and behaviour) and the value of embracing uncertainty rather than expecting certainty, both of which are ideas key to Buddhist philosophy.

Interestingly Langer's research differs from much quantitative research in focusing more on what is possible rather than on averages. She argues that only one participant is necessary to show that something is possible (such as ageing without memory loss), and that such people can provide a model that others may learn from. However, Langer has also demonstrated some compelling impacts of mindfulness with more conventional research. For example, after a week of acting as if they were 20 years younger, including having more control over their schedule and plans, older people had better hearing, memory, flexibility and intelligence, they were judged to look younger by others, and their life expectancy increased. In a learning context, people became more creative when using conditional rather than absolute language, and emphasising the perspective that information was coming from led to better learning (e.g. 'three reasons for the war, from the perspective of ...' rather than 'the three reasons').

Langer's work emphasises the ways in which *social constructs* limit us. For example, the words, environments and habits surrounding old age, disability or mental health often subtly suggest to people that they are dependent and require care and that they should therefore accept their treatment mindlessly rather than engaging mindfully with it. This perspective links Langer's writing with more critical social psychological and sociological work, which tends to be social constructionist in flavour, often using qualitative research to demonstrate how 'dominant discourses' in society position people in certain ways. For example, the dominant discourse of masculinity, which a client like Vineet will likely draw on, emphasises rationality and being a strong protector and breadwinner. There might be other discourses available to him, like being more of a Homer Simpson 'regular bloke' or even a 'new man', but social constructions of gender will likely make it difficult for him to suddenly embrace a very emotional or nurturing way of being, for example. The kind of lethargy Vineet is feeling might once have been regarded as sinful or related to the impact of supernatural forces; it may then have been assumed to be a purely physical condition; these days it is more likely to be regarded as psychological in nature.

Steven Stanley and myself have recently begun to explore how mindfulness might be useful in the work of social constructionist social scientists like ourselves. One interesting possibility is the use of mindful practices as a form of research themselves, in order to gain a rich understanding of experience as it is lived (Stanley, Barker, & Edwards, forthcoming). I am particularly interested in whether the slowing-down and noticing practices of mindful meditation, and their open curiosity to all that is, can help us to understand the processes by which social messages, or dominant discourses, operate through us. For example, we might notice how our responses to people are based on judgements of attractiveness, which involve comparison against a mental image of the ideal body drawn from cultural images. Or we might slow down mid-argument and become aware of how our 'instinct' to blame and defend is related to social constructions of conflicts as being one side's 'fault' and the shame attached to being wrong (see Chapter 10). Being mindful we can notice how we take up, reproduce or resist such social messages.

Theorists have suggested that our internal conversations intervene between the social pressures that surround us and our own individual behaviour, opening up the possibility for choice and agency (Archer, 2003). So, as well as being a research practice itself, we could explore mindfulness as a way of enabling people to act differently: what Buddhists refer to as 'swimming against the stream'. This has important implications for social arenas such as conflict, discrimination and sustainability, and relates back to Langer's work that links mindfulness to the ability to make choices.

Beyond this work, there is scope for more sociological research into the cultural contexts in which mindfulness becomes so appealing (perhaps the self-monitoring, consumerist context that we mentioned in Chapter 1), and also the elements of mindfulness that do and do not take hold, and the ways in which they are integrated (see Loy, 2008). This brings us back to the 'boastful' and 'shy' stories of mindfulness that started this chapter. From a sociological perspective we can ask some interesting questions about the popularity of neuroscience studies, the quest for positive outcome research, or the enthusiasm for meditation practices as opposed to other ones. We will return to these issues in the Concluding Thoughts to this book (see Schipper, 2012).

Summary and conclusions

In this chapter we have explored the diversity of research that is possible on mindfulness, and the ways in which the studies that have been conducted so far illuminate different aspects of mindfulness as a biopsychosocial experience. So far it seems that we can conclude that mindful practices can be of therapeutic value, and that they probably operate through various mechanisms which can be tentatively linked to particular brain/body processes. Qualitative and quantitative research point to some similarities across experiences of mindfulness (around attention and openness), but also warn that different aspects of mindfulness may be emphasised for different people, and at different times, and that these may have different mechanisms and impacts, which may also vary across individuals and groups.

Hopefully the continued commitment that we have seen in many authors to integrate first-, second- and third-person research will continue to illuminate all aspects of mindfulness, improving our understanding of the ways in which bio, psycho and social aspects are interwoven, and emphasising both diversities *and* similarities in experience.

Further reading

An accessible overview of the biological and psychological elements of mindfulness can be found in:
Siegel, D. J. (2007). *The mindful brain: Reflection and attunement in the cultivation of well-being.* New York, NY: Norton.

An argument for an increased emphasis on the social aspects of mindfulness, and critique of the emphases of current research, can be found in:
Stanley, S. (2012). Mindfulness: Towards a critical relational perspective. *Social and Personality Psychology Compass,* 6 (9), 631–706.

You can also read more about Steven Stanley and my visions for social mindfulness at: http://socialmindfulness.wordpress.com/about.

A more detailed list of books and articles on mindfulness research can be found at: http://socialmindfulness.wordpress.com/references/psychological-research.

There are also links to the major centres of mindfulness research on the Social Mindfulness website.

The *Mindfulness Research Guide* website publishes a monthly newsletter containing the new scientific publications on mindfulness: www.mindfulexperience.org.

PART TWO

Practising mindfully across issues

FIVE   Depression

Aims

This chapter aims to:

- mindfully explore the experience of depression,
- present a non-dualistic, mindful understanding of depression,
- consider common elements of depression and how they might be addressed mindfully,
- summarise existing work on mindful therapies for depression.

Since this is the first of the chapters in the book to focus on specific issues, we will begin with a general consideration of mindful approaches to diagnosis and to understanding such issues biopsychosocially. Much of what is considered here will also apply to the subsequent chapters so will not be covered in such depth there.

We will then go on to consider specifically how we might work with depression in a mindful way, touching upon awareness, being present, tuning in to experience and turning out towards the world, and developing self-compassion.

A mindful approach to diagnosis

Much of the existing mindfulness literature on depression works from the starting point that there is one coherent thing called 'depression' that we can point to and treat. This concurs with the view of depression that prevails in popular culture, and within most western psychiatry and psychology: depression is a disorder that people can be diagnosed with; some people have depression and some people don't.

If we take a mindful approach to the whole concept of depression, however, we might want to approach it again with a 'beginner's mind':

attending curiously to the experience of depression and being cautious about fixing it or identifying with it (see Chapter 1).

Such an approach is taken by Ellen Langer (2009), who we met at the end of the previous chapter. She points out that the mindset of being depressed often involves believing that depression is a constant factor in our lives: it is all that we are and all that we will ever be. This may well be reinforced by receiving a diagnosis of depression and by popular views that divide people into mentally ill and mentally healthy. Drawing on her version of mindfulness, which emphasises openness to novelty, Langer suggests encouraging ourselves to notice the *differences* between bouts of depression: checking in with ourselves about how we are actually feeling right now rather than gathering evidence to support the fact that we are 'depressed' again in exactly the same way as we were yesterday, last week or last year. Langer argues for replacing a retreat into the familiar and mindless meaning of 'depression' with a mindfulness about our changing mental states. Paradoxically this mindful focus, in itself, may well reduce depression.

What might this mean for the practitioner working with somebody who is depressed? Langer gives the thought experiment of what it would be like if, rather than believing in one thing called 'depression', we suggested that there were several types and encouraged the client to figure out which one they had right now: this might tune them in to difference and novelty rather than sameness and familiarity. Other ideas here would be to work with the client to build up a full and rich description of their individual experience of depression, including the ways in which it shifts over time. We might ask clients to remember, or record, times during the week where they noted subtle shifts in their experience where they felt less depressed, for example, or we could encourage them to notice the ways their experience shifts in a five-minute meditation (see Morgan, 2005). Of course the mindful meditation practices we've covered so far can cultivate the ability to do this, and also provide frameworks for slowing down and being with the experience as it is in the moment.

Pause for reflection

Take some time now to reflect on your own experience of being depressed. You might like to start with some breathing meditation (see Introduction) before focusing on a specific memory of the last time you felt this way. Try to approach the recollection with openness and curiosity to the whole experience, attending to feelings, thoughts, bodily sensations and all of the senses. It might help to consider what images and thoughts come to mind and the colour and texture of the experience. When you are done, allow yourself some time returning to the breath and to your current surroundings to ground you back in the present.

When I reflected on the different experiences that cluster under the label 'depression', I thought about the colour terms that are popularly associated with it. In the film *Breakfast at Tiffany's* Audrey Hepburn distinguishes between the 'blues' and the 'mean reds': whilst the blues are a kind of rainy-day sadness, the mean reds are a horrible feeling where 'suddenly you're afraid and you don't know what you're afraid of'[1]. Depression is also associated with night and darkness: being in a black pit or followed by Winston Churchill's black dog. It can be experienced as greyness like living in a black and white film, or as the bleak white of a life leached of all colour. The story *The Yellow Wallpaper* (Perkins Gilman, [1892] 1998) uses yellow as a metaphor for a stifling sickly claustrophobic depression. Some describe a kind of muddy brown of all the colours of the emotional palette being mixed together rather than being able to experience them separately[2]. It is clear from this that there are many related experiences that can be grouped together under the term 'depression'[3].

In relation to diagnosis, it may well be counterproductive to dismiss labels that other professionals have applied to the client and/or that they have embraced themselves, but we might usefully explore with clients the gains and losses that come with a label like 'depression'. For example, embracing such a diagnosis might give them a sense of legitimacy, a recognition of shared suffering with others, and a practical way of obtaining paid leave from work. However, they may also feel stigmatised by the label, aware that their experience of depression is not identical to that of others, and a sense that they can't now escape being a person with depression (see Pilgrim, 2010). Such a reflective approach to diagnosis could enable them to hold a label like 'depressed' (or

---

[1]See www.youtube.com/watch?v = 4jsUIgchHXU.

[2]See http://northernexistentialgroup.wordpress.com/2012/03/03/happiness-at-the-northern-existential-group.

[3]As well as helping us see the variety of experiences that can be termed depression, an exercise like this can help to break down the 'us and them' thinking which can occur between therapist and client in detrimental ways, see http://rewritingtherules.wordpress.com/2011/10/16/mental-health-beyond-the-1-in-4.

'anxious', 'addict' or 'disordered') more gently, rather than clinging to it or hurling it away (see Chapter 1).

A cautious approach to diagnosis and labels also fits rather better with the Buddhist understandings of suffering that we explored in Chapter 1 (whether we are operating on the basis of this or from the more western psychotherapeutic understandings covered in Chapter 2). As we saw, Buddhist thought does not really separate out different forms of suffering. It sees suffering as a universal aspect of human experience (rather than distinguishing those who are, and are not, mentally ill), and it understands all human distress as having the same roots in craving patterns of attachment and aversion: trying to get more of what we want and less of what we don't want. It also offers the same approach to addressing all forms of suffering: attending to experience, being with the situation as it is, and developing compassion and equanimity.

Such an approach fits well with evidence that the separation of different disorders is a problematic endeavour. For example, the two most common mental health problems, depression and anxiety (see Chapter 6), almost always occur together (Bentall, 2009). Also two seemingly different sets of feelings and behaviours (such as angry aggression with others, and depressed self-criticism) could well be expressions of the same suffering on different occasions, or on the same occasion, depending on whether our pain is being turned outwards or inwards, and similar understandings and approaches may be valuable for working with them (Barker, 2012b).

For these reasons it will be useful to read this chapter and the subsequent chapters together, particularly Chapter 6. Whilst I have separated out the 'issues' chapters in this book in ways that will be familiar to the western practitioner, it is worth being mindful throughout that they may well not be so easily separable, and that there is a risk that by labelling and addressing something as 'anxiety', 'addiction', 'psychosis' or 'eating disorder', for example, we are reinforcing the idea that it is a static, permanent feature of identity, rather than an experience that might be there sometimes and not others, and which will vary over time in terms of the experience and its meaning for the client.

A useful example of this, which highlights the importance of attending to meaning, is 'self-harm'. A person who sometimes cuts or hits themselves may be labelled a 'self-harmer': a label that comes attached to stereotypes of suicidality and/or attention seeking. However, the same behaviour may well mean very different things to different people. It may also have different meanings to the same person at different times, or at the same time when multiple meanings may be present. Meanings could include being a form of stress-relief; control over the body when everything else feels uncontrollable; self-punishment that enables self-nurturing to follow; marking a particularly profound experience so that it isn't lost; or jolting oneself out of a particular emotional state (amongst many other potential meanings). There are also significant overlaps with more socially acceptable behaviours (such as dangerous driving, heavy drinking and strenuous exercise), which can be erased by the division of people into 'self-harmers' and 'non-self-harmers' (Favazzo, 1996).

Mindful understandings of depression

As well as understanding depression as just one form of suffering in its wider sense, and as being a cluster of different experiences with a variety of potential meanings for the sufferer, a mindful approach would also involve a non-dualistic, or biopsychosocial, understanding of the experience (see Chapter 4).

This is particularly vital in relation to depression because the common view of the experience, in both the mainstream media and amongst clients and people in general, is that it is an entirely biological or psychological condition. The popular perception is that it is internally, rather than externally, caused in one of two ways. If you are depressed:

Either
you are ill, you need help, but at least
this means that it is not your fault;
or
you are not ill, and therefore don't need help,
but this means that you are to blame for your
own suffering (the 'pull your socks up' attitude).

Such understandings catch us in a double-bind whereby we have to accept that there is something wrong with us or that we are blameworthy. Both of these can be problematic because the one suggests that we have no power to address the situation and that we have something wrong with us, and the other suggests that we are personally deficient and mustn't ask for help. Many people oscillate between the two positions as neither side really captures the complexity of depression.

The fact that neither position really 'fits' means that each possibility remains haunted by the other. Those who do not identify as depressed are haunted by the fear that perhaps there *is* something terribly wrong with them that needs fixing. They attempt to hide this fear, and any signs that they might be struggling, and this puts them under additional pressure. Those who do embrace the label 'depression' are often haunted by a huge sense of guilt that maybe they are not really ill and that they will be 'found out', and so they must prove that they really are depressed. This exacerbates any suffering they were already experiencing. It may particularly be the case, for example, for a person who does not fit diagnostic criteria perfectly, or who is not depressed all the time or in the way that other people expect (e.g. being unable to get out of bed, having poor appetite, feeling suicidal).

As we have seen, a more mindful approach views suffering as something that all people will experience in life, moving us away from separating out those who are, and aren't, *really* depressed. It also recognises that distress, in its various forms, happens for a complex multiplicity of reasons, and that we can have a personal role in exacerbating and ameliorating it, but acknowledging that such a role does not mean that we are totally 'to blame'. It also opens up the possibility of support being something that anybody can access at the points in life when they need it, rather than it being something only for a certain few who are 'properly' depressed.

A final, and vital, point about the entirely internal understandings that most people have of depression is that they deny any social role in the experience. Suffering is exacerbated when something that has such a strong social component is regarded as being something which is internal to the individual themselves.

Depression is social in two key ways: specific social situations can have a major role in somebody becoming depressed; and the current societal expectations of us are intrinsically related to our suffering.

In terms of specific social situations, of course much has been written about the potential role of poverty, abuse and neglect in childhood in depression, but we should also attend to experiences outside the family and in later life. This is particularly important, for example, when we consider the huge role of the taken-for-granted abuse of 'school bullying' in many people's lives, and the crushing impact that loss, pain and violence can have in adult life. Marked differences in rates of 'mental health problems' depending on the gender, race and sexuality of a person alert us particularly to the role of discrimination, stigmatisation, alienation and oppression in mental health (Barker, 2010b). The ways in which such social experiences might write themselves on our psychology and biology is particularly emphasised in compassion focused therapy (CFT) (see Chapter 3). So, just as we are aware of the ways in which certain biological vulnerabilities impact on our social lives (e.g. having a particular body shape or a form of neurodiversity that impacts on our ability to understand other people or social conventions[4]), we should also be aware of the impact of social experience on the expression of genes and the ways in which neurons link up, as well as being

---

[4]See http://en.wikipedia.org/wiki/Neurodiversity.

mindful of the complex interweaving and feedback loops present in such biopsychosocial processes (see Chapter 4).

In relation to the role of wider societal expectations and depression (and other forms of distress), we have already touched in Chapter 1 upon the role of 'craving culture' in current forms of suffering. Consumer culture and the makeover/reality television idea that we can become beautiful, successful and celebrated overnight exacerbates the sense of the gap between how we are and how we want to be. Mindfulness-based cognitive therapy (MBCT) and acceptance and commitment therapy (ACT) emphasise this in relation to depression. Related to this is what we might call 'self-monitoring culture'. Philosophers have suggested that we are encouraged to scrutinise and judge ourselves at all times in comparison to others we see around ourselves, with advocations to self-improve, to work on ourselves and to present a positive and successful self to the world. Advertising, and many other forms of media, create fears (e.g. we might look bad, be out of date, be a failure) and then offer products to allay those fears (e.g. beauty products, the latest fashion, recipes for success in various arenas). Self-scrutiny and critical comparison against others has a key role in depression and many other problems: that common idea that 'everybody else' had their lives sorted out, so there must be something wrong with us that we can't manage it (Barker, 2012a). This societal role in depression is also supported by the fact it has increased to the point that it will be the second greatest burden of ill health after heart disease globally by 2020 (Murray & Lopez, 1996). We will return to the implications of self-monitoring culture for mindful therapies in the concluding chapter of the book.

In terms of our therapeutic practice with clients, one implication of this biopsychosocial approach to depression (and to the other issues we are covering in this book) is to be alert to purely internal understandings on the part of the client, and to open these out: perhaps by increasing awareness of social aspects and/or helping the client to see the problematic positions that internal understandings put them in. Emphasis on the ways in which our experiences write themselves on body and brain, and on the role of societal forces on our negative views of ourselves, may be helpful for those who tend to self-blame and self-criticism. Emphasis on neuroplasticity and the possibilities of thinking in different ways and relating differently to the world may be helpful to those who feel stuck in depression. We might work with clients to reconnect the biopsychosocial when they have split the different elements off. For example, if they are wholly focused on troubling internal thoughts we might encourage them to relate those to both the wider social messages they receive and to their bodily experience of the feelings that accompany these thoughts.

Mindful therapy with depression

Mindfulness-based cognitive therapy (MBCT) is the form of mindful therapy that was specifically designed for people with depression, particularly in relation to preventing them from relapsing into depression again once they had recovered. As we saw in Chapter 3, MBCT takes people through most of the key mindful practices, weaving these with teachings and experiential work about how we tend to approach difficult thoughts and feelings and how we might do this differently. Evidence so far has been very positive about the outcome of MBCT with depression, suggesting that it can indeed help and prevent relapse (Hofmann, Sawyer, Witt, & Oh, 2010), and readers are referred to detailed books about the approach in the Further Reading section of this chapter.

So it seems that learning about, and practising, mindfulness in general is helpful with depression. In the rest of this chapter I will draw out some specific mindful practices, and illustrate how these may be helpful for clients struggling with depression. Due to the variety in experiences of depression, and in the meanings that it has for clients, it may well be that different ideas and practices are useful to different people and at different stages. For example, for the client who has been going far too hard for far too long in their work and has eventually collapsed into a depression (see Lewis, 2002), key aspects might be tuning them in to their body and emotions so that they are more aware of where they are at. We might also explore how they relate to their work identity and whether this might be held more gently. For the client whose depression is linked to a sense of meaninglessness and not feeling that anything is worth bothering with, the ACT practices around commitment to one's values may be particularly helpful, as might tuning in more to the world around them and recognising their ability to influence it. 'Depression manifests in myriad ways and has multiple causes' (Morgan, 2005: 133): what helps one person might trap another.

Case study: Beverley

Beverley is a woman in her late forties who approaches you because she says that she has suffered from periods of depression throughout her adult life and desperately wants it to stop. Much of the time she enjoys her work and is happy with her partner Janice and their two kids. However, every few years she slides into a depression and withdraws from everybody. At such times she finds it hard to get out of bed and feels as if she is walking through treacle, unable to touch what it is about life that is worth living. She is in such a period at the moment and is also scared that this time it won't end.

Think about

- How would you currently work with a client like Beverley?
- How might you understand Beverley's issues from a mindful perspective?
- What mindful ideas and practices from the book so far might you consider applying or suggesting in this case?

One way forward

In the next section of the chapter on awareness, we will stay specifically with Beverley in exploring how we might work with one aspect of her depression: the struggle to get out of bed in the mornings. Then we will consider other aspects of mindfulness for depression more broadly: being present, turning out and tuning in, and self-compassion. For each of these sections you might find it useful to come back to this case study and to consider how these aspects might be helpfully applied in Beverley's case.

Awareness

A good starting point for mindful therapy with depression, and indeed any of the issues covered in this book, is to encourage the client to cultivate awareness of their experience. Whilst it is important to be understanding about the desperate desire that many clients will have to escape the state that they are in, which may feel utterly unbearable, it is useful to talk with them early on about the need to first have a good knowledge and understanding of things before we can alter them, perhaps using the ACT quicksand analogy (see Chapter 3) of the way in which struggling in distress can easily sink us deeper into it.

For example, we saw above that Beverley struggles to get out of bed in the mornings. If we explored that further with her we might find that every evening she resolves to get up early the next day, but every morning she fails to do so, lying in bed and becoming increasingly angry and critical with herself for this failure. Instead of implicitly joining this criticism by attempting to shift her behaviour, we might encourage Beverley, over the next week, to stop trying to change the situation but rather to openly and curiously notice what it is like as it is. What does her body feel like? What thoughts run through her mind? What feelings does she have? What happens then? And then? And then? Of course basic meditation practices (such as the one in the Introduction) may also be helpful here because if Beverley cultivates this kind of awareness at other, perhaps less demanding times, then it will be easier to bring the same quality of attention to her 'staying in bed' experience.

Such awareness has multiple benefits. It can prevent both therapist and client from making assumptions about the experience and its meaning for the client. For example, Beverley's own assumption that she is being lazy may be challenged if she realises that she lies there thinking furiously about things. The therapist's assumption that Beverley stays in bed because she doesn't feel any sense of purpose might be challenged if she reports back that she lies there feeling a strong desire to get on with important tasks, but a powerful sense that she will inevitably mess them up keeps her paralysed. Understanding what the 'depressed behaviour' means to a particular client can guide where we go next with therapy.

In addition to this, as we have seen before, awareness in itself can demonstrate the kinds of patterns that we get trapped in. For example, Beverley might well notice the kind of thinking that happens when she remains in bed, and the way in which this makes it harder, rather than easier, to move. Rumination is a feature of depression for many people: a stream of repetitive, self-critical thoughts driven by the desire to 'solve' the problem. In Beverley's case it might go something like this:

> Oh it's morning already. I should get up. I'm probably going to struggle like I always do. What's wrong with me that I can't get up like everyone else does? I should just bound out of bed. I've got so much to live for compared to some people. And yet they manage it and I don't. There's so much to do. I ought to get on with it rather than lying here like a lump. But here I still lie. I'm useless. It's probably a good job I'm here: I'd only mess things up anyway.

Finally, just becoming more aware of depressed experience can, in itself, lead to shifts because people tend to notice impermanence (see Chapter 1): the fact that there are subtle changes in experience over time, which can mean that we feel less stuck in depression because we recognise that it is not a static state that defines us.

Of course becoming aware of the experience does not preclude then going on to make changes and experimenting with different ways of relating to times when depression occurs (see comments on acceptance and change in Chapter 3). For example, Beverley might then go on to experiment with what it is like remaining in bed but practising thoughts- or feelings-based meditations (see Chapters 3 and 6), or having a self-compassionate morning ritual instead of remaining in bed, or putting an alarm clock out of reach in order to leave the bed. In each case she might try these alternatives, bringing the same quality of awareness to them and noticing what possibilities are opened up and closed down by the change. A similar approach of noticing and under-standing, followed by curious experimentation, could also be helpful for other behaviours that are linked to depression, such as forms of 'self-harm' (see above), drinking, smoking or watching television a lot (see Chapter 7), insomnia, sexual and eating difficulties (see Chapter 9), indecisiveness, or irritability with others (see Chapter 6).

Being present

Another element of depression that the MBCT and ACT literatures highlight, along with rumination, is 'experiential avoidance'. As in the example above, people generally try hard to escape the situation they are in. The kind of awareness that we are encouraging involves being with the experience as it is rather than continuing to attempt to get away from it. Again, simply moving from avoidance to a welcoming and curious approach can, in itself, shift things. We will consider this in greater depth in relation to fear and anxiety in the next chapter.

Practice: Shikano (adapted from Koshikawa, Kuboki, & Ishii, 2006)

After a short while of breathing meditation, call to mind an unpleasant situation which upset or bothered you and the feelings that it evoked in you. Once you have a situation in mind, allow it to play itself out whilst suspending judgement on it. Try not to weigh up your role in it, or make evaluations about how embarrassing or frightening or bad the situation was.

After you have imagined it through in this way, try to play it through again from different angles of vision: closer up, further away, above the situation, below the situation. You might try altering the angle every couple of seconds as you play it through again. Pause regularly during the replays to return to the breath, and then run through it again. When you have done this a few times, come back to breathing meditation for a while before ending.

The idea is that this playing through of the experience will detach the memory from the emotional significance that we add to it. How does it feel now that you have run it through so many times without evaluating it?

Both the meditation where we allow thoughts to bubble up and drift away without becoming attached to them (see Chapter 3) and shikano practice (above) involve what Pema Chödrön (2002) calls 'letting go of the story'. Rather than stringing together thoughts into a story, we let them bubble up and disappear again. Instead of making a story out of our memory and what it means, we see it as simply what happened.

In the Introduction I emphasised that 'being present' does not always have to mean being in the 'present moment', and we can see this again in shikano practice, which involves being present to a memory. However, the present-moment focus of some mindfulness teachings, such as Jon Kabat-Zinn's, can be particularly valuable with depression because another common feature of depression is focusing upon the past and the future.

Pause for reflection

Try setting a random alarm to go off during the day. Each time it rings, ask yourself where you were when it went off. What were you aware of in terms of thoughts, feelings, sensations and images?

On an everyday basis you may well find that you spend much of the time going over things that happened in the recent or more distant past (e.g. passing judgement on somebody's behaviour yesterday, or rehearsing your story of how you came to be the person you are today), and also in planning and predicting the future (considering what you might say to prove your point to someone who is bugging you, or fantasising about what you would do if you had more money or a different job or relationship)[5]. When you are depressed you might notice this past and future focus is exacerbated: every difficult feeling brings a tidal wave of memories of times of rejection, exclusion or anguish, and the extent of your misery suggests that only a massive future change could make things better, which seems overwhelming and makes you feel worse.

Mindful practices where we ground ourselves in the present can be a huge relief at such times. Focusing on the breath (Introduction) or an everyday task (Chapter 1), bodily sensations (Chapter 9) or the sounds around us (Chapter 8) can all bring us back from rehearsing painful memories, anxiously imagining the future, or yearning for things to be different. This in itself can provide us with a glimmer of what it is like not to be so depressed, which reminds us that the state is impermanent and begins to release our grip upon it.

---

[5]For specific examples of everyday mindlessness and mindfulness see http://socialmindfulness.wordpress.com/2011/04/03/mindfulness-it-aint-what-you-do-its-the-way-that-you-do-it.

Working with alienation and self-criticism:
Turning out and tuning in

When I reflect on being depressed, the experience is one of being simultaneously *tuned* out, but turned in. By *tuned* out I mean the kind of self-
monitoring that I mentioned earlier: being terribly concerned with other
people and the outside world. In depression we often become anxious
about what others will see in us, and judge ourselves harshly, frightened
that we will get things wrong somehow and be exposed in all our use-
lessness. Decisions become very difficult because we are so *tuned* out –
trying to be okay for everyone else – that it is almost impossible to *tune*
in to what we want and need ourselves. We might find ourselves busily
rushing around trying to please everyone and not letting on how much
we are struggling, or we might withdraw from contact as much as possible for fear of what others might see if we let them in close.

At the same time as being *tuned* out, we are also turned in. By this I
mean that when we are hugely concerned with what other people think
of us or how we are being seen out in the world, we don't really see or
hear the people around us because we are so focused on our own struggles. We often spend a great deal of time in internal conversations with
ourselves about whether something is wrong with us, what it is, and how
we might fix it. We view other people in terms of their danger to us ('they
might see me as I really am!'), or the possibility that they might be able
to help ('maybe they have the answer'), but it is hard for us to make the
shift that is necessary to understand how *they* are feeling and what is
going on for them. Often we assume that we are the only person who is
this bad and full of problems, and we are so fixated on not showing other
people that this is the case, or apologising to them for our perceived
wrong-doing, that there is no space available to turn towards *their* experience and let go of all of our own stuff for a moment. Thus we reach the
state of alienation, which is very common in depression: feeling isolated
from other people, and not really noticing the world around us.

One thing that mindfulness can offer to clients with this kind of
depressed experience of *tuning* out and turning inwards is a shift from
turning in to turning out, and a related shift from *tuning* out to *tuning*
in. This involves becoming more mindful of the world around us (turning out) and of our own experience (*tuning* in).

My own experiences of turning out happen when somebody else's pain
pierces my bubble, or in professional mode when I have to put my stuff
down and turn towards another person to hear about their struggles, or I
remember how this works and deliberately reach out to somebody else
and ask how they are doing. Sometimes the relief takes the form of sitting
on a train or walking down the street and suddenly opening up to the fact

that all the people that I see have their own fears and desires, tragedies and triumphs, which are just as precious and concerning to them as mine are to me. So we might encourage clients to engage in imaginative activities where they consider what might be going on in other people's lives, or to deliberately make time to listen to somebody else, or even to watch a film that involves empathising with somebody else's pain. Alternatively, if other people are very difficult to be around, we could encourage a turning out towards the world: noticing the breeze through the trees or the architecture around them. Reconnecting with surroundings on any level can be a step towards reconnecting with others too.

Turning out works in several ways, which we might usefully explain to clients. On a very basic level listening to somebody else, or imagining their world, means that our mind is occupied with something else for a moment and we have a brief relief from the clatter of noisy and critical thoughts that has been exhausting us. Then there is the way that helping somebody else (anything from flashing a kindly smile through to giving them a supportive shoulder to lean on) can leave us feeling better about ourselves: we do have something to offer after all. Perhaps most fundamentally, though, is the sense of connection to others which is an antidote to the sense of isolation and alienation that is a major element of depression for many people. If others let us in by opening up to us, or just reveal their pain on their faces, we might realise that they struggle too, often in similar ways to ourselves. We realise that they also scrutinise themselves constantly with a stream of critical comments running through their heads. We are no longer alone. In fact, that pain is the very thing that links us to everybody else.

Related to this it is often the case that in finding compassion for another person we become able to find a little of the compassion that we need for ourselves (see Chapter 10). This is an important part of *tuning* in. Instead of only being attuned to what other people think of us (whether we are normal or abnormal in society's view, whether or not this person approves of us, etc.) we can *tune* in to our own feelings and thoughts, often being more aware of the full experience of them, including how we are in our bodies (see Chapter 9). Of course many of the mindful practices that we have considered in this book involve some form of *tuning* in to our own experience (see Concluding Thoughts for a complete list of these).

We might explain the importance of turning out and *tuning* in to clients by pointing out that in turning out and really seeing and hearing the other people around us we can realise that they aren't really that concerned with us because they are so busy worrying about themselves. Or, if they are judging us and disapproving of us, we might realise that they are doing this out of their own pain and anxieties rather than because they are seeing any true flaw in us. For example, it might be that putting us down gives them a brief reassurance that they are okay, when they secretly fear that they are not. Even if there is an element of truth in any criticisms they are making of us, we can manage to hear it and bear it because we are no longer trying to present an unreal perfect image to the world. We are turned out enough to be able to appreciate our impact on other people, and *tuned* in enough to own up to such things without thinking that it means that we are a terrible person in our entirety.

When people are depressed, or otherwise suffering, it doesn't really matter whether they start by turning out or *tuning* in. Either one begins to make the other easier. So it might be that we encourage clients to deliberately try to empathise with other people or imagine what they are going through, and that gives them the space to find a bit more compassion for themselves. Or we might start by encouraging them to *tune* in to themselves – sitting with however they are feeling without judging it or criticising it – and that might enable them to open up and see the other people around them.

Self-compassion

This latter kind of *tuning* in is close to Paul Gilbert's (2010a) notion of self-compassion (see Chapter 3), which he locates as the vital antidote to depression. Certainly I often find that the most useful thing early on in therapy with a client who is very depressed is simply to encourage them to open up the tiniest space in their life for kindness to themselves. I often describe depression as a spiral which they have been travelling down for a while and are still spiralling downwards on. Trying to immediately haul themselves right out of this spiral is unlikely to work (although quite likely what they have been attempting to do). However, what they can do is to gradually slow the progress down the spiral and start to change the direction such that they are gradually spiralling up. The way we do this is through starting to develop self-compassion.

One practical way of doing this is to attempt at least one kind act towards oneself each day. The client can list what these might be, aiming for small, inexpensive things which fit well into their current routine and require little of them at first. It might be a hot bath, taking a 10-minute coffee break in a café rather than remaining at the desk all day, walking past a florist and enjoying the flowers, or stroking a pet.

As we saw in Chapter 3, Gilbert proposes that any compassionate activity will make a compassionate, rather than critical, way of being more available to us. Thus we might practise loving-kindness or compassion meditations (see Chapters 1 and 2), or engage in fantasies where we, or others, are nurtured or treated with kindness. One powerful technique is to deliberately engage with memories in a compassionate

way, particularly those memories that are part of our self-critical litany (see Figure 5.1 for an example of how this might work)[6].

If we engage with the Buddhist questioning of the self, which we covered in Chapter 3, self-compassion might also involve practices which loosen our grip on the self (Fulton, 2008), reminding ourselves that we are always changing rather than being fixed, and that we have multiple sides to ourselves which emerge in different relationships and situations rather than being one single thing[7]. This can provide a feeling of intense relief when we are depressed as it often feels, at those times, as though depressed is all that we are and all that we will ever be.

The Buddhist-influenced social constructionist Kenneth Gergen (2009) argues that the self-monitoring, craving way of being that our culture encourages is also linked to an individualistic sense of ourselves as very separate from others. His alternative, 'relational being', reminds us how intertwined with others we are, and encourages us to experience such interconnections. We will return to this idea in Chapter 10.

---

[6]This is similar in some ways to Tibetan Buddhist practices with dreams (see Chapter 9). We might also try re-entering nightmares where we are treated badly and ensuring that we are treated more compassionately.

[7]I provide details of two specific practices to help with this understanding in my book *Rewriting the Rules*. These are also provided, along with other activities, on http://rewritingtherules.wordpress.com/resources-2/1-self.

Figure 5.1   Self-compassion

Summary and conclusions

In this chapter we have seen some of the ways in which mindful therapy might be helpful for those who are struggling with depression, in terms of understanding the experience and working with common features such as self-criticism, rumination, and past and future focus. It will also be useful to think back to what we covered in Chapter 2 about the mindful therapist here. As Stephanie Morgan points out, the cultivation of the 'hard back, soft front' combination of empathy and equanimity can be extremely valuable for demonstrating to clients that we can sit with their distress, whether it is presented as suicidal despair, hostility or grey boredom, without disengaging (Morgan, 2005).

There are some notes of caution about practising mindfully with depression, however. First, as always, we must be careful about how we explain mindful ideas to clients. The ideas of being with depression, rather than trying to escape it, may seem counter-intuitive, and even cruel. Also, questioning diagnostic labels or internal explanations may be difficult for all the reasons we explored above, particularly if the idea of depression as a physical illness is viewed as a protection from the notion that the person is blameworthy and bad. Additionally we need to be mindful in our own relation to labels and explanations. If we are critical of mainstream approaches, as I am, we should ask ourselves whether there are situations where the label 'depression', or an understanding which is heavily weighted towards the 'bio' in biopsychosocial, is helpful and appropriate (e.g. in the case of brain injury or depression following a long illness).

As we will explore in more depth in the Concluding Thoughts to this book, the mindful emphasis on acceptance and being with what is can risk de-emphasising the real, material and social aspects of depression in the same way that more biological and psychological explanations do. For example, when working with Beverley (the woman in our case study), if we found that her depressions were always sparked by periods of unemployment, experiences of domestic abuse, or being the victim of hate-crime, then there would be a vital need to address those experiences directly as well as exploring how she might relate to her response to them. If we are not careful, the emphasis of mindfulness forms of CBT on thoughts and emotions as not being 'objective facts' may inadvertently be taken as a questioning of clients' very real experience of oppression, loss, poverty or violence.

Finally, as previously mentioned, what works well for one person can be problematic for another, or for the same person on other occasions. This was brought home to me when I compared two experiences I had of going on a silent retreat. The first time I found a great relief in being quiet and tuning in to myself and turning outwards to my environment: a powerful sense of my own 'okayness' and resilience during a very difficult time. The second time, despite being in a much happier state at the start, noticing my self-critical thoughts and being with difficult memories was intensely challenging and I felt a real lack of conversation with others and compassionate care. Any mindful practice, or therapy, could be experienced in such diverse ways, and there are potentials in some meditation practices that people will feel more removed from the world and from their own experiences, rather than reconnecting with them (see Chapter 8).

Returning to Beverley, our example case study, encouraging her to become more aware of her experience of depression, and approaching it with curiosity, might well shed some light on what it is she is withdrawing *from* when she retreats into depression. Given how very painful the experience of depression is for most people, we need to address how it became the sensible response rather than just trying to shift them out of depression without awareness of how the depression might be serving a purpose. Drawing on our understanding of this, we might work on both developing self-compassion and turning back outwards to reconnect her to others and to the world around her. However, it is important to do this in a way that is mindful of the reasons for the withdrawal in the first place.

For example, depression might follow a bereavement[8] or other situation which makes the world appear a very frightening place.

In this way, depression and anxiety are often intrinsically related. Depression often involves turning away from experience to avoid what is fearful or causes pain. The mindful turning towards the experience often means having to face fear and anxiety head on. That is what we will focus on in the next chapter.

Further reading

The MBCT approach to depression is described for practitioners and psychologists in:
Segal, Z. V., Williams, J. M. G., & Teasdale, J. D. (2002). *Mindfulness-based cognitive therapy for depression: A new approach to preventing relapse.* New York, NY: Guilford Press.

A more accessible overview for the general reader is:
Williams, M., Teasdale, J., Segal, Z., & Kabat-Zinn, J. (2007). *The mindful way through depression.* New York, NY: Guilford Press.

The specific experiences of loss and bereavement are explored in:
Halifax, J. (2009). *Being with dying: Cultivating compassion and fearlessness in the presence of death.* London: Shambhala.

There is more about cultivating self-compassion in Paul Gilbert's writing (see Chapter 3) and in my chapter on our relationships with ourselves in:
Barker, M. (2012). *Rewriting the rules: An integrative guide to love, sex and relationships.* London: Routledge.

I frequently write about depression from a more social mindfulness perspective on the following blogs: http://socialmindfulness.wordpress.com and www.rewriting-the-rules.com.

---

[8]For more on this specific situation, see Joan Halifax's work, mentioned in the further reading.

SIX   Stress and anxiety

Aims

This chapter aims to:

- explore how the mindful approach of turning towards, rather than away from, difficult experience is particularly useful when working with anxiety, fear, panic and trauma,
- consider how mindful therapies might work with more everyday experiences of stress and worry,
- touch upon mindful approaches to other experiences linked to fear and anxiety, such as those related to control and anger,
- summarise existing work on mindful therapies for stress, anxiety and related difficulties.

People who are unfamiliar with mindfulness might see it as an appropriate approach when people are worried or frightened because they imagine that meditative practices are relaxing. They might assume that meditating creates a kind of calmness that is the opposite of being anxious and stressed out. This is not a complete misconception, because the experience of watching the breath (see Introduction) or listening meditation (see Chapter 8), for example, can ground us and calm us when our mind and body are racing. Continually returning to the present can be a relief from frightening imaginings of the future, as we saw in the previous chapter. A body sweep meditation (see Chapter 9) can alert us to points of tension in a way that enables us to relax them. However, relaxation is not the aim of mindfulness, and neither is it the most important thing that it has to offer for experiences related to fear. Most authors in this area agree that the vital element of mindfulness for anxiety-related difficulties is that it involves turning towards these experiences, rather than away from them, which is our common habitual response to things that frighten us.

As we saw in the previous chapter, depression often involves a turning away from experience in the hope that this will enable us to avoid or escape from emotional pain. Mindfulness proposes the opposite: a turning towards suffering so that we engage with it in an open and welcoming way (see Chapter 1). But this requires a new approach to anxiety because we are often confronted with fear when we turn towards experience. Living in an engaged, rather than avoidant, way involves facing our fears of the uncertainties and inevitable sufferings of life, as well as the possibility that we may be hurt and/or hurt others. It is therefore worth reading this chapter together with Chapter 5, as depression and anxiety often co-occur and indeed may be two sides of the same coin.

It is also worth considering briefly the mindful approach towards diagnosis that we explored at the beginning of Chapter 5, in relation to stress, fear and anxiety. When we can't escape from, or avoid, a frightening experience it is often tempting to identify with it, believing that we must therefore be an anxious person, neurotic or 'a worrier'. Such labels can easily become self-fulfilling prophecies, and even more reason to try to avoid potentially fearful experiences. Here I am reminded of the character in the book *Cold Comfort Farm* who retreats to her room because she once 'saw something nasty in the woodshed', requiring her whole family to operate in certain ways to keep her safe even though she can no longer remember what the 'something' was (Gibbons, [1932] 2006).

Mindful ideas run counter to the conventional western approach of seeing somebody as anxious or phobic, or identifying them as having a 'disorder' such as post-traumatic stress or obsessive compulsion. As we've seen, Buddhist teachings do not distinguish different forms of suffering, and the Buddhist perspective of the self is that it is in a constant state of process and becoming (see Chapter 3) rather than being fixed. So whilst we will touch upon some such categories in this chapter, it is useful to refer back to Chapter 5 to consider how we, and clients, might hold them lightly rather than becoming stuck in a fixed story and solidifying 'anxiety' as if it was one thing with one cause (Watson, 2008). It can be useful, as with depression, to remind ourselves of the different experiences that can be described as anxiety, and the multiple different meanings we can attach to it: from the excited, giggly fear of the camp-fire ghost story to the paralysing terror of the thought of harm befalling a loved one, for example.

Despite the very bodily experience of many anxious experiences (e.g. increased heart-rate, shortness of breath, sweating, palpitations and nausea), as with depression a biopsychosocial approach is more in keeping with mindfulness than one that separates out the physical or psychological features (see Chapter 9). Again, social experiences are often key in triggering anxiety (e.g. being out in public or experiencing a violent attack). The ways in which we socially make sense of things influence what situations are regarded, and experienced, as particularly traumatic or as an appropriate object of fear or worry. Consider, for

Figure 6.1 Walking meditation

example, the way we can become hyper-vigilant to certain symptoms if we read a news report about a health scare. In addition, the societal encouragement to self-monitor, which we touched upon in the previous chapter, may well be involved in attempts to avoid revealing our fear to others, or in attempts to control situations which we find frightening and uncertain. Again, it will be useful to refer back to Chapter 5 to consider how the bio, psycho and social aspects of the various forms of stress and anxiety that we touch upon are intrinsically linked. This can be usefully explored with clients.

Due to the very physical experience of fear- and anxiety-related problems, some find that mindful practices which involve movement can be particularly helpful. Yoga, qigong and tai chi all involve focusing on slow movements, but the most basic meditation – for those who are unfamiliar with such practices – is slow walking.

Practice: Walking meditation

In walking meditation we simply walk very slowly backwards and forwards across a room or garden attending to the full experience of gradually lifting, moving and placing our feet, and the sensations in our body as we move.

> Where breathing meditation (see Introduction) uses the breath as the object to return to when we drift off, walking meditation uses the sense of movement. Each time we find that we were not fully in the experience (e.g. when we start thinking about something else) we bring our attention back to walking.

I will now go on to a detailed consideration of the process of turning towards difficult experiences, something that we began exploring in Chapter 5 when we considered being present to depression and cultivating awareness of the experience. After considering the implications of this for working with experiences such as phobia, panic, anxiety and trauma, I will move on to explore more everyday experiences of stress and worry, and how we might work with control and anger (two experiences that can be related to anxiety).

Facing the fear

Pause for reflection

Think about something in life that scares you. It may be a particular phobia, a kind of situation that you find anxiety-provoking, something in the past that was scary to live through or something that you always worry about happening. How do you usually relate to this thing? What happens if it comes to mind, or if you are confronted with the actual situation?

The notion that facing fears might be a better approach than attempting to avoid them is one that has been popularised far beyond Buddhist teachings. For example, in the sixteenth century, French writer Michel de Montaigne famously said 'he who fears he shall suffer, already suffers what he fears'[1], capturing well the problem with avoidance strategies. One of the best-selling self-help books of the late twentieth century was Susan Jeffers's ([1987] 2007) classic *Feel the Fear and Do It Anyway*. Gradual exposure has been the CBT treatment for phobias for many decades: the process of engaging more and more directly with the object of our fear.

---

[1]http://en.wikiquote.org/wiki/Michel_de_Montaigne.

However despite this, as you probably observed if you considered the Pause for Reflection, we generally find ourselves attempting to escape fearful situations and avoiding the things that we find anxiety-provoking. Both acceptance and commitment therapy (ACT) and mindfulness-based cognitive therapy (MBCT) talk about 'experiential avoidance' as triggering and maintaining anxiety and depression (see Chapter 3). MBCT locates this in the fight-or-flight response whereby we habitually respond to perceived threat with physical avoidance or defensive attack (Crane, 2009). ACT emphasises the ways in which experiential avoidance can cause harm and actually compound the thing that precipitated our anxiety (Flaxman, Blackledge, & Bond, 2011). For example, avoiding the situation through drinking, smoking, 'overeating' or undereating, or never going outside may harm our health long term (see Chapter 7). Procrastination or avoiding conflict can mean the thing that we are scared of becomes even more fearful; for example, now we only have one day left to revise for that exam, or our friend is even more angry with us for not answering their calls. Additionally, like existential therapy (see Chapter 3), ACT emphasises the ways in which experiential avoidance can move us away from a meaningful life; for example, if we can't face the fear of the potential failures involved in pursuing a challenging career, or the exposure of vulnerabilities inevitable in intimate relationships (see Chapter 10).

Both ACT and MBCT advocate shifting ourselves from avoidant mode into approach mode, where we move towards experience in a welcoming and open way. This is very much what I described in the previous chapter when considering slowing down and noticing the experience of depression while aiming to be present to how it is in the moment.

One key mindful practice here is called 'vedana' or 'feeling tones'. Each time we receive any kind of stimulation (a sensation, somebody saying something to us, or a memory being triggered), we immediately assign it a feeling tone of pleasant, unpleasant or neither-pleasant-nor-unpleasant (neutral). This is the very first micro-emotional response, which generally occurs beyond conscious awareness, and which will build into a full proliferating emotional experience and a reaction of either attachment (if it is registered as pleasant) or aversion (if it is registered as unpleasant) (see Chapter 1).

In vedana practice we begin to tune in to the first tiniest movements towards avoidance or approach. We can just notice how the micro-emotion spirals into something more. Additionally we can begin to experiment with what happens if we play with that first feeling tone, for example by leaning into a 'negative' tone rather than instinctually pulling away from it. We could do vedana in various kinds of meditation (e.g. when noticing thoughts, see Chapter 3; or sounds, see Chapter 8). However, it is most frequently done in more bodily forms of meditation (see Chapter 9).

Practice: Vedana (adapted from Stanley, 2012c)

After spending some time on breathing meditation (see Introduction), broaden out your awareness to include bodily sensations: feel the contact between your skin and your clothing, your body against the chair or the floor, the way that the sensations of breathing in and out ripple across your body.

Notice when any distinct 'feeling tones' co-arise with the sensation of contact. Do you have a sense of a pleasant, unpleasant or neutral feeling accompanying a particular sensation? Does this also co-arise with a reaction of aversion or attachment, such as a desire to scratch an itch or to try to maintain a comfortable position? Can you separate out the sensation, from the feeling tone, from the response? Each time it happens, notice it and return to a focus on sensation.

After some time you might play with what happens when you attempt to engage with 'unpleasant' sensations in more of an open and curious 'approach' mode.

My sister, Jess, gave me a great example of how such an approach might be usefully applied in the world. She was on a train where a fellow passenger had his music turned up so loudly that it was bothering her and other passengers. This was exactly the kind of potential conflict situation which she – like many of us – usually finds anxiety-provoking, so she decided to engage with it in a different manner to usual: with approach rather than avoidance. There is no conventional happy ending to the story. The guy responded abusively and didn't turn down his music. But my sister determined to remain sitting directly across from him as long as the music remained loud, and used it as an opportunity to notice what happened in herself and in the carriage around her. She was aware of her physical responses, and the stories she wanted to tell herself about what might happen or what other people were thinking of her. She was also able to notice the man's discomfort and the way her actions drew others in the carriage into a sense of solidarity with her.

In addition to meditative practices such as vedana, it may well be very helpful to deliberately engage in anxiety-provoking situations in real life. Most people have been strongly discouraged from engaging with things that they find frightening and even rewarded for disengaging, for example by other people protecting them. For this reason, deliberate engagement can be powerful and can gradually inculcate a different response to fear where leaning in becomes as possible as pulling away. Personally engaging with my fear of heights by rock-climbing has taught me at least as much about being mindful as sitting on a cushion. It can be useful to explore with clients what their fears are and to consider ways in which they might experiment with them in a gradual and risk-aware way.

Although there are similarities between this and the classic cognitive-behavioural therapy (CBT) 'gradual exposure' technique, there are some differences. Our focus here is on welcoming our experience of fear and noticing what it involves rather than on calming it down. With phobias this might begin with the memory of the feared object and build to engaging with the object itself.

Similarly, in relation to the experience of panic attacks, conventional CBT focuses on challenging anxious thoughts whilst mindful therapies focus on increasing people's willingness to experience emotions. One of the key books on mindful approaches to anxiety gives the following helpful example of the difference between CBT and mindfulness approaches to panic:

> *CBT approach:* Identify catastrophic thinking ('I will die of a heart attack') and challenge it ('Will you? What are the chances? What else could a heart palpitation mean?')

> *Mindful approach:* Explore the experience of heart racing and related thoughts in detail as they arise ('Heart beating ... thinking I will die ... always seems to beat faster when I think that ... thinking about heartbeat ... could be the pizza I just ate'). (Germer, 2005c: 154–5)

From a mindful perspective, attempting to control thoughts risks perpetuating the problem, as that can be another way of avoiding the experience. Mindfulness CBT approaches to panic include the exposure, psychoeducation and relaxation elements of CBT, but they add mindful meditations and cultivating an approach, rather than avoidance, response (see Levitt & Karekla, 2005).

Social anxiety is a similar case: therapeutic approaches that try to control the experience (e.g. suppressing anxious thoughts) tend to fail long-term. An ACT approach of identifying values and working towards them in a way that accepts inevitable anxiety may well be more effective (Herbert & Cardaciotto, 2005).

There are similar issues in the treatment of post-traumatic stress disorder (PTSD). Attempts to avoid trauma-related thoughts and feelings are key criteria for diagnosis, and there is evidence that people with a delayed or dissociated emotional response to trauma develop more severe symptoms (Batten, Orsillo & Walser, 2005). Again, mindful therapists suggest that traditional exposure therapy (to memories of the trauma and associated thoughts and feelings) could be complemented by enhancing willingness to engage with the full range of experiences involved in PTSD. Importantly, exposure techniques such as writing and reading over an account of the trauma aren't put forward as a way of increasing control over experience, but rather as a way of changing how the client relates to them.

One useful book in this area puts forward a mindful alternative approach to crises, which involves considering the process before, during and after a crisis hits, rather than just working 'post' trauma. Perhaps cultivating mindful attention can make us more aware of impending crises, or the conditions under which they hit hard (e.g. when we are overloaded and tired). It can also aid our ability to be with the experience as it happens, to find moments of stillness in 'the eye of the storm', and to know when we need to retreat and just take care of ourselves while it passes ('weathering the storm'). Finally, it can help us to address how we relate to the memory once it is over (see Owen, 2011).

Overall it seems that mindful approaches to anxiety and fear involve reconceptualising the issue in a very similar manner to that quote by Michel de Montaigne. Experiencing anxiety isn't regarded as a problem (or a setback in therapy), rather *fighting* anxiety is the problem.

Working with everyday stress and worry

Mindfulness was first popularised in the west by Jon Kabat-Zinn's (1996) work applying it to stress, culminating in his Mindfulness-Based Stress Reduction (MBSR) programmes (see Chapter 3) which have been found to be effective at reducing stress and anxiety, as well as increasing self-compassion (Chieasa & Serretti, 2009). Kabat-Zinn proposes shifting from 'reacting' to stress into 'responding'. By that he means cultivating moment-to-moment awareness such that we can slow or halt the usual plunge into hyperarousal and desperate casting around for solutions. Like vedana practice, the idea is to be fully present to the event as it unfolds. This awareness includes opening up to the full context, rather than approaching it in the blinkered way in which we generally perceive things when we are overwhelmed. There are many occasions, for example, when I have found myself in crisis mode after receiving an email, only to realise that I had misread it when I go back to it and that it isn't the emergency that I assumed. Personally I find the Taoist phrase 'There is so much to do, there is so little time, we must go slowly' extremely helpful at such stressful times. If I remember it early, I find that I can now respond by slowing down instead of following the desire to speed up and get everything done.

Kabat-Zinn emphasises the need for regular mindfulness training to be able to bring this quality of awareness, equanimity and openness to a stressful situation. He also suggests that we can learn to notice feelings of anger, fear or hurt rising in our bodies and to specifically use these as a signal that a mindful approach is required. Of course Kabat-Zinn also emphasises that we will not respond to every situation in this way and we shouldn't beat ourselves up for struggling to change the habits of a lifetime. When we do manage it, such an approach can help, for example, in enabling us to see the full situation, in recognising how our previous experiences might be colouring our interpretation, in acknowledging that the stressful thing has now happened rather than wishing it away, or in realising that we have more than one option in terms of what we do next.

Case study: Namiko

Namiko is a woman in her thirties who approaches you for therapy because she says that she can't stop worrying. Exploring something of her past you find that Namiko left her family in Japan to come and study engineering when she was 18 and she has remained here ever since. Her experience at university was very isolating as there were few international or female students on her course and she was generally ignored by her peers. She determined to be courageous and to study hard and 'show them', and she did indeed excel and now works for a successful engineering firm where she is a highly valued member of the team. However, Namiko spends a lot of time worrying, for example about the possibility that she will make a mistake on a project, or about whether her boss will 'find out' that she is not as good as he thinks she is, or that she neglects her partner and family.

Think about

- How would you generally work with a client like Namiko?
- How might you understand Namiko's issues from a mindful perspective?
- What mindful ideas and practices from the book so far might you consider applying or suggesting in this case?

One way forward

Research suggests that worrying can decrease subjective distress in the short term; for example, by enhancing the perceived sense that you are monitoring everything and therefore in control, or by distracting you from even more distressing possibilities. Hence, despite the unpleasantness of worrying it can be viewed as another way of avoiding experience.

Worry is also very future-focused (see Chapter 5) and therefore takes people away from present-moment awareness. It might be worth exploring with Namiko the potential that worrying will make it more, rather than less, likely that she will make mistakes, and become distant from loved ones because she is less aware of what is going on around her.

Mindful therapy with Namiko might involve first cultivating mindfulness in situations when she is not worrying, and then bringing that quality of open curiosity to her worrying so that she can understand how the process of worrying plays out. Deliberately putting a certain amount of time aside for worrying, and observing the process, can be a good way of bracketing it off from the rest of life. Thought meditations (see Chapter 3) might help Namiko to try letting go of thoughts rather than following them. She might also experiment with developing an approach (rather than avoidant) relationship to things she finds anxiety-provoking. For example, could she have a conversation with her partner about the impact of her long working hours, or try admitting a mistake to a colleague and see what happens?

A similar approach may be appropriate for what is labelled 'obsessive compulsive disorder' (OCD), which involves ruminating thoughts and behaviours that temporarily reduce distress, such as checking that doors are locked several times over. It may well be useful here to approach the things that are feared rather than attempting to control them, experimenting with leaning into the anxiety rather than trying to avoid it. Hannan and Tolin (2005) suggest engaging clients in discussion about the short- and long-term success of avoidance strategies, and also draw in an ACT approach to examine the ways in which behaviours may interfere with committing to their values. The metaphor that all the OCD behaviours are a form of continuing to 'dig oneself into a deep pit' (see Chapter 3) can help clients towards the alternative of putting the shovel (behaviours) down and facing the situation as it is. We might also consider with them whether the energy that they use trying to control their internal experience could be freed up to address any situations that do arise (Orsillo & Roemer 2011) and help them to mindfully attend to the beliefs underlying their behaviours (see also Chapter 7 on addictive habits).

Intrinsic to many of the forms of fear and anxiety that we have considered is an attempt to control what is uncertain. The recognition of the inevitable uncertainty of life, and the move to embrace this rather than attempting to avoid or control it, is central to both Buddhist and existential approaches (see Chapter 3). Pema Chödrön (2002) emphasises this in her work, which draws on mindful and other meditation practices to present a path towards a kind of 'fearless' or 'warrior' way of being. This concept of training as a warrior might particularly appeal to clients who value physical and/or psychological strength, like Namiko whom we met above.

Chödrön (1994) describes embracing uncertainty as an alternative approach to our usual habits of trying to control our lives and searching for security, predictability, comfort and safety. Her warrior path (2001) involves directly confronting difficult feelings (see Tonglen practice, in Chapter 10), looking at our baggage and buttons, taking responsibility, and using difficult experiences as an opportunity to rest in uncertainty: to find the tenderness and vulnerability behind a nameless fear, righteous indignation, or desire to lash out, for example.

Mindful approaches to anger

This latter point brings us to anger. Although, like all broad terms, anger covers a multitude of experiences and has different meanings to different people at different times, there is often an element of covering-over fear, attempting to control what is uncertain, and protecting ourselves from our own vulnerabilities. Anger is also a particularly important topic from a mindful point of view because there is often an assumption that being mindful is about being calm and peaceful: the very opposite of being angry.

> ### Pause for reflection
>
> How would you imagine a mindful approach to anger? Can we even be angry if we are being mindful? Could we have attentive anger or mindful rage? Consider the last time that you were very angry. How might you have engaged with that mindfully?

It is striking that whilst there is much focus on anger from Buddhist teachers such as the Dalai Lama and Thich Nhat Hanh, there has been much less written about it from a western mindful perspective (Mace, 2008). Possibly this is partly because obvious expressions of anger often tend to be criminalised rather than pathologised in a western context. Anger turned inwards on ourselves is classed as depression (see Chapter 5), but externalised anger tends to be regarded as 'bad' rather than 'mad' even when it might equally be a sign of distress. There are, of course, important gender implications of this in cultures where men, but not women, are generally encouraged to express anger outwards (Barker, 2010b) and women, but not men, are generally encouraged to display fear and to require protection.

As with fear, a mindful relationship to anger involves a willingness to approach it rather than trying to avoid it. Nhat Hanh (2001) speaks of anger like a friend who you need to take good care of and treat with tenderness, recognising that it is a form of suffering. He draws a clear distinction in his writing between the experience of anger and the act of aggression. His metaphor of the house on fire may be a useful one:

> If your house is on fire, the most urgent thing to do is to go back and try to put out the fire, not to run after the person you believe to be the arsonist. If you run after the person you suspect has burned your house, your house will burn down while you are chasing him or her. That is not wise. You must go back and put out the fire. So when you are angry, if you continue to interact with or argue with the other person, if you try to punish her, you are acting exactly like someone who runs after the arsonist while everything goes up in flames. (p.24)

Nhat Hanh's approach brings together mindful breathing and walking practice, which enable us to embrace our anger and look deeply into the experience, with compassion practices, which enable us to see the suffering of the other person or people who are involved (see Chapter 10). These are all helpful practices which we might explore with clients who are struggling particularly with anger.

Nhat Hanh also suggests looking at ourselves in the mirror when we are angry and noticing changes in our face when we return to the breath. In this way we are not trying to stop ourselves from feeling angry; rather we are finding ways to avoid escalating it, instead drawing on its power in helpful ways. I find this an important point from a social mindfulness perspective where we might regard anger at social injustice, for example, as vital and something that we wouldn't want to damp down. But we might want to think carefully about the most pragmatic and potentially transformative ways to draw on that energy (see Barker & Heckert, 2011). For example, when we find ourselves angered by somebody who is ignorantly repeating common prejudices, we might turn our anger against the culture in which these prejudices are prevalent (and think about ways of challenging such cultures) rather than against this one individual who is a product of this culture and, like all of us, finds it difficult to step outside of it. Again, these are useful ideas to explore with clients whose anger at other people in their life is distancing them from people, or hurting others (see also Chapter 10).

Summary and conclusions

In summary we have seen that the key element of mindful therapy with anxiety is the shift from experiential avoidance to approaching fear in a welcoming and open way as well as the embracing of uncertainty. Through cultivating a mindful way of being we may be able to move from reacting to our instant appraisals of situations of stress (e.g. with panic or anger) to responding in a way that sees the full situation and all of our options within it. Existing evidence certainly suggests that mindful approaches are effective at reducing anxiety, and that improvements last over time (Hofmann, Sawyer, Witt & Oh, 2010).

Many of the potential limitations of mindfulness that we covered at the end of Chapter 5 apply here also. We need to work from where the client is, and we need to be aware that different things work for different people at different times in terms of understandings and practices. It is also important to attend to, and engage with, real material situations that are involved in anxiety rather than implicitly suggesting that mindful engagement is to be done *instead* of addressing these in any real way. Facing the fear may well involve recognising just how unjust the situation is that we, and others, find ourselves in, and committing to doing something about it.

Specifically, there is a risk that the turn towards, rather than away from, anxiety can be done in a hard and self-berating kind of a way. This is why some authors emphasise the vital importance of integrating mindfulness and compassion in relation to anxiety (e.g. Brantley, 2007). We see this in the words like 'befriending', 'welcoming' and 'gentle acceptance', which are used throughout the literature. Whether we are approaching fear, anger, sadness or any other difficult feeling, we need to do so in a way that is kind and recognises underlying pain and vulnerability. This may involve cultivating compassion and loving-kindness (see Chapters 1 and 10), and trying to rest in the present moment in a gentle rather than a forced way. As we saw earlier, it may be about finding which practices work for us and our clients, rather than feeling that we, and they, must meditate in the way we've been taught. Walking meditation may be a gentler way of being with anxiety for some, rather than sitting, for example. 'Mindfulness without kindness is not mindfulness' (Brantley, 2007: 153).

Further reading

Mindfulness and acceptance-based CBT approaches to anxiety are described for practitioners and psychologists in the following book, which includes specific chapters on panic, social anxiety, general anxiety, post-traumatic stress disorder, obsessive compulsive disorder, and stress:

Orsillo, S. M., & Roemer, L. (Eds.). (2005). *Acceptance and mindfulness-based approaches to anxiety.* Boston, MA: Springer.

More accessible overviews for general readers are:

Brantley, J. (2007). *Calming your anxious mind.* Oakland, CA: New Harbinger.

Orsillo, S. M., & Roemer, L. (2011). *The mindful way through anxiety.* New York, NY: Guilford Press.

Focusing specifically on stress, Jon Kabat-Zinn is a very accessible author:

Kabat-Zinn, J. (1996). *Full catastrophe living: How to cope with stress, pain and illness using mindfulness meditation.* London: Piatkus.

For those who would like an accessible approach to fear and anxiety which is rooted more in Buddhist teachings than in CBT mindfulness perspectives, the work of Pema Chödrön is excellent. Two books which focus on fear are:

Chödrön, P. (1994). *The places that scare you: A guide to fearlessness.* London: HarperCollins.

Chödrön, P. (2002). *Comfortable with uncertainty.* London: Shambala.

SEVEN Addiction

Aims

This chapter aims to:

- present a mindful understanding of addiction as involving intense habits of attachment and aversion,
- consider addiction from a non-dualistic perspective as a biopsychosocial phenomenon,
- describe how mindful approaches like mindfulness-based relapse prevention (MBRP) differ from the conventional moral model, disease model and cognitive-behavioural approaches to addiction,
- explore key ideas from Buddhist and mindful practitioners that are particularly useful in working with addiction and habits.

Commentators often criticise the growing list of things that are viewed as addictions. In recent years we have seen sex, work, shopping, gambling and social networking added to the list, with self-help books and groups springing up around them. Many people are sceptical of putting such behaviours in the same category as drug and alcohol addiction (often called 'substance abuse' or 'misuse'). They regard them as different in kind.

From a mindful perspective, however, it makes sense to consider all of these things together for two reasons. First, Buddhist philosophy, and many of the mindfulness approaches that draw on it, regard patterns of aversion and attachment as universal and as the root of suffering (see Chapter 1). This means that everyone – except possibly those few who have reached some state of total enlightenment – could be regarded as addicted: craving more of what they want and trying to avoid and get rid of what they don't want. Second, as we saw in Chapters 4 and 5, mindful approaches are non-dualistic and tend to see all human behaviour as complexly biopsychosocial. This means that they would not make clear distinctions between 'biological' addictions (e.g. those involving substances which directly affect our physiology) and 'psychological' or 'social' ones (see also Chapters 4, 5 and 9).

Therefore mindful approaches would be critical of the ways in which the idea of addiction gets applied, though not because it is dangerous to put additional behaviours into the same category as 'real' addictions, but rather because everyone demonstrates some form of addiction. Like more social-oriented critics, from a mindful standpoint we might well question why some behaviours become labelled 'addictions' whilst others (often more socially acceptable ones) do not.

This chapter begins by considering these ideas of addiction as a universal biopsychosocial phenomenon in more depth. It then highlights the ways in which mindful therapies for addiction differ from the conventional moral model, disease model and cognitive-behavioural treatments, and summarises some specifically mindful practices and ideas that might be particularly helpful when working with addiction.

Because addiction is often a way of trying to avoid unpleasant experiences, as well as trying to create pleasant ones, it is worth reading this chapter alongside the previous two chapters on depression and anxiety. Perhaps the key mindful practice for addiction involves cultivating the ability to be with difficult feelings rather than escaping into something else (the addiction), and there is more detail about this turn towards, rather than away from, experience in those chapters (5 and 6).

I have used the word 'addiction' throughout this chapter (rather than 'compulsion', 'dependence' or another word) because it is probably the most familiar term. I am defining it as any repeated behaviour that people feel compelled to persist in, despite a potential problematic impact on their lives and/or the lives of others (adapted from Maté, 2008: 128). However, as already mentioned, I am using addiction in quite a different way to the way it is generally used by people who distinguish those who are addicted from those who are not. Whilst we'll consider degrees of intensity of addiction as a continuum, it is important to keep in mind throughout that everyone manifests habitual patterns of craving which could be labelled 'addiction'. Either we need to apply the term to all of us, or avoid using it in favour of a more universal term[1].

Addiction continuum

In his book on addiction, Gabor Maté (2008) evocatively likens the state to the Buddhist hell realm of the hungry ghosts. The inhabitants of this

---

[1]This is probably why Martine Batchelor uses the word 'habit' rather than 'addiction' in her book on the topic (see further reading).

realm are depicted as 'creatures with scrawny necks, small mouths, emaciated limbs and large, bloated, empty bellies'. Maté suggests that we all go into this domain of addiction when 'we seek something outside ourselves to curb an insatiable yearning for relief or fulfilment' (2008: 1). This is true whether our addiction is to drugs or gossip, wealth or television.

Perhaps the common tendency to distinguish 'real' addicts from everybody else is down to an 'us and them' impulse to distance ourselves from others who reflect disturbing tendencies in ourselves. This is reflected in dichotomies of health and illness, normal and pathological, which are such common themes in writing about addiction (Keane, 2002), as well as the often classed and raced nature of which similar substances are regarded as addictive (e.g. cheap beer but not expensive wine) and how those who are addicted are perceived (e.g. crack vs. cocaine; gambling in different contexts). Maté says that 'those whom we dismiss as "junkies" are not creatures from a different world, only men and women mired at the extreme end of a continuum which, here or there, all of us might well locate ourselves' (2008: 2). If the craving patterns of attachment and aversion that Buddhist philosophy highlights is something which we are all engaged in, inadvertently exacerbating our own suffering and that of those around us, then it makes sense that we would want to avoid that knowledge and scapegoat those people who are obvious addicts rather than facing up to the same inclinations in ourselves. Indeed, this very tendency to 'us and them' thinking is itself a form of addiction as it involves the avoidance of a painful, humbling truth by becoming lost in a soothing fantasy of oneself as a healthy, normal, non-addicted person.

There is an element of this 'us and them' distinction in families where one person is viewed as the 'addict' and the others engage in 'enabling' behaviours in their attempt to help and support them. For example this might take the form of down-playing the problem to others, assuming the person is incapable of everyday tasks without help, and providing them with money on the basis that their need is greater than others in the family. It may well be more helpful to explore how we are all implicated in addiction, and how such systems risk perpetuating the very thing that they attempt to ameliorate as people become fixed in 'addict' and 'non-addict' positions (Vossler, 2010).

A common theme in mindful writing in this area, from (auto)biographical explorations like Maté's to more manualised therapeutic approaches like mindfulness-based relapse prevention (MBRP) (Marlatt & Donovan, 2008) is this avoidance of the addict/non-addict dichotomy. Maté weaves together the stories of the drug addicts who he worked with as a medic with his own personal story, and MBRP authors stress that the therapists who run MBRP sessions are seen as participants in a common human experience, alongside the other group members (Marlatt, Bowen, Chawla, & Witkiewitz, 2008). Martine Batchelor's (2007) suggestion that all human behaviours can be light, habitual or intense is a useful way of conceptualising the continuum of addiction, and opens up the possibility of moving up and down it. I may enjoy a glass of wine on occasion for the pleasant taste and the sensations it invokes (light), in times of stress I may long for a glass or two every evening (habitual), and it is possible that I could start to become dependent on alcohol to get through the day (intense).

Pause for reflection

Take a few minutes now to jot down all of the regular cravings and habitual behaviours that you engage in which might be regarded as being on a continuum of addiction. You might find it helpful to consider things that you do in the hope of having, or maintaining, a pleasurable experience, as well as those you do to avoid difficult or troubling feelings. Which of these behaviours would you regard as light, habitual or intense?

Considering my own life at the moment it is easy to notice a regular temptation to check my social networking site as a way of avoiding the harder, and more exposing, work of laying words down on the page. Similarly, poor television, comfort food, sleep and fantasies can all be soothing and comfortable retreats from everyday stress or more existential anxieties[2]. Alongside this, email-checking easily becomes a way of chasing the dragon of 'having the decks cleared', and work itself feeds a compulsion to be successful in ways that everyone would acknowledge and approve of. Occasionally the craving for a wilder thrill away from the mundane realities and difficult complexities of everyday life bubbles up and momentarily compels me to attend absolutely. In such moments it is clear to me why people risk hurting themselves and others for such a hit of pure confidence, freedom and exhilaration (whether that is found in a drug or a poker game, in someone else's body or the applause of an audience, or in a general pattern of constantly moving on to the next new thing).

It may be useful, with clients and with ourselves, to explore broadly which type of addiction they are engaged in, drawing on those Buddhist

---

[2]Not that these behaviours are always necessarily done in addictive ways, see http://socialmindfulness.wordpress.com/2011/04/03/mindfulness-it-aint-what-you-do-its-the-way-that-you-do-it.

notions of aversion and attachment. We are in a pattern of craving, but is it more about seeking to avoid pain or about seeking to gain (and maintain) pleasure? We saw in the previous chapters that depression can be a way of withdrawing from the world and attempting to avoid suffering (Chapter 5), whilst anxiety can be more about the fear that comes with engaging with the world and trying to get what we crave and avoid what we dread (Chapter 6). Related to this, addiction can be more about avoidance/withdrawal or about engagement/attachment. For example, aversion addictions might include retreating into a novel or smoking a joint whenever life is hard or when faced with time alone, whilst attachment addictions might include seeking the confident self who emerges after snorting cocaine or the buff, toned body that spending all our leisure time in the gym seems to promise.

For these reasons the first step in any mindful therapy with addiction is to understand the meaning of the addiction for the individual. This is one thing that sets it apart from treatments which emphasise cessation first and foremost. From a mindful perspective the first step is to observe the behaviour in an open and curious way rather than either trying to eradicate it or letting ourselves be mindlessly pulled along with it. We might encourage a client to notice the times when they feel urges. What is going on at that time? How does it feel in their body? What thoughts and emotions arise? How does it feel if they do follow the compulsion and/or if they hold back for a while? It is important that they don't beat themselves up if they do continue to give into their urges because, prior to such observation and understanding, it makes sense that this would still happen.

Such observations can help a more thorough exploration of what these specific cravings and habitual behaviours mean to the person[3]. We can find out whether it is broadly about avoiding pain or about trying to create pleasure, and also what specific pains and/or pleasures are involved. Of course it is important here to be very aware that different behaviours mean different things to different people, and to the same person at different times. For one person running miles represents an escape from a difficult home situation, for another it is motivated by craving for the endorphin rush. Shopping may be a buzz on some occasions, soothing on others. Also, most behaviours are not simple but will have multiple meanings at the same time, all of which are worth being aware of; for example, smoking might simultaneously involve the

---

[3]The same kind of observation and exploration of meaning is also useful for other behaviours which aren't always placed in the same category as addictions, but which share much in common, such as 'obsessive compulsive' behaviours and 'self-harming' behaviours.

pleasure of the nicotine rush, the sense of connection to the others in the smoker's huddle, a break from the monotony of work, and a feeling of rebellion and freedom.

The work of mindfulness researcher Ellen Langer (1989), whom we met in Chapter 4, supports such an exploration of multiple meanings. She found that people who are able to look at a situation from more than one perspective are more able to quit smoking. This is because they are aware of both the positives and the negatives of smoking for them, whereas most people focus only on the negatives in their attempt to force themselves to stop. It is very hard to give something up if we don't understand its meaning and how it is serving us.

Biopsychosocial addiction

As described in more detail in Chapters 4 and 9, Buddhist philosophy is non-dualistic: it doesn't distinguish between mind and body, or inner and outer worlds, in the ways that are common in western cultures. This means that a mindful perspective towards addiction would see it as a biopsychosocial phenomenon where all of those elements (bio, psycho and social) are complexly interwoven and impossible to tease apart. Indeed, both Marlatt and colleagues (who developed MBRP) and Maté explicitly use the word 'biopsychosocial' in their work on addiction.

This is another way in which mindful perspectives differ from conventional approaches to addiction that tend to emphasise either the biological components (e.g. disease models like the 12-step programmes) or psychological aspects (e.g. moral approaches like the 'war on drugs' which hold people personally responsible; or cognitive-behavioural treatments which emphasise the mental processes, triggers and cognitive biases involved).

Such a biopsychosocial approach is consistent with current research in the field of addiction, which also takes a more holistic approach. For example, most addictive drugs affect neurotransmission, often increasing synaptic dopamine (e.g. cocaine, nicotine, cannabis, ecstasy and heroin), targeting serotonin (e.g. LSD, cannabis and ecstasy) and/or interacting with endogenous opioids (e.g. heroin and alcohol) (Toates, 2011). However, there are also major psychological and social aspects to all drug taking that are vital in developing and maintaining addiction. These may even override more obvious biological components, as in the classic research on soldiers who had begun drug taking in the Vietnam war: they found it much easier to give up their drug use on returning home than those who had remained in the United States because their external justification for drug use was removed (Robbins, David, and Nurco, 1974).

Drug addictions are likely to be influenced by external as well as internal rewards and/or punishments (e.g. peer approval). They are also likely maintained by attentional biases, which make addicted people much more tuned in to the things that they crave than other people are, as well as by routines and rituals which become familiar and rewarding in themselves (e.g. a cigarette first thing in the morning, a line of coke before a party). Additionally, drug taking is clearly contextual if we think about social situations in which drugs are simply unavailable compared to those in which getting involved in drug distribution is the norm, or if we compare levels of alcohol addiction in cultures which have very different norms around alcohol (e.g. comparing Iran, France and England). You might like to reflect on how difficult or easy it is for you, or people you know, to refuse an alcoholic drink in different contexts.

Similarly, more seemingly psychosocial addictions such as shopping, sex or internet addiction will inevitably involve biological processes. This includes the kinds of neural connections that happen with any kind of learning or habit (see Chapter 4), as well as an impact on the same kinds of neurotransmitters that are involved in drug addiction (e.g. dopamine levels in gambling) (Open University, 2010). Again it is impossible to disentangle, for example, the high social desirability of 'falling in love', from the psychological rewards of seeing adoration in the eyes of another, from the neural connections and levels of neurochemicals that are involved (see Chapter 10).

As with other aspects of mental health, the 'social' in the biopsychosocial understanding of addictions requires particular attention because it tends to be de-emphasised by conventional biomedical and psychological approaches which generally take an internal, individual perspective on human behaviour (see Chapter 4 and Concluding Thoughts). Such approaches sometimes consider social 'factors' (e.g. the environment or peer pressure), but they rarely consider more societal contexts such as the popular representation of a certain behaviour or the way in which it fits into wider culture.

Two social elements worth exploring with addiction are the ways in which the wider culture encourages patterns of attachment and aversion, and the dominant understandings around the particular behaviour the person is engaging in. In Chapter 2 I mentioned how current western consumer culture encourages people to seek more of what they desire and to avoid what is unpleasant or fearful. Advertising and mass media present a fairly consistent message that people are lacking in some way, that they should feel bad or anxious because of this, and that that lack should be quickly fixed (generally by their product). From fast food to overnight-success television shows, to the proliferation of medications for various forms of emotional distress, the message is that pain should quickly be eradicated and pleasure should be easily attained.

When addressing addiction with our clients it is important to contextualise it in this wider culture and to normalise the struggles they are having, given the wider structural forces which are pushing them in that direction (see Alexander, 2010).

Similarly it is worth being mindful of wider-circulating understandings of specific addictions and the place of the client's experience within these. In the case of some drugs and 'self-harming' behaviours, it is worth thinking about equally damaging behaviours which are socially acceptable in order to decrease the stigma (e.g. comparing the impact of illegal drugs to cigarettes, or self-cutting to extreme sports). In other cases it might be useful to consider how addictions are used to pathologise certain groups when they may be accepted in others (e.g. comparing working-class teenage girls smoking cigarettes to upper-class middle-aged men smoking cigars, or the way in which gay men may be more likely than heterosexual men to be labelled as sex addicts because of the *kind* of sex they are having as much as whether it is causing any problems for them). Finally, it is helpful to consider social contexts where forms of addiction are normalised and not seen as problematic when they very well might be damaging (e.g. work cultures of long hours and no breaks, or sport, dancing or modelling cultures where troubling levels of exercise, food intake and/or drug taking may be regarded as normal or aspirational) (Keane, 2002).

Mindful approaches to addiction

Probably the three most common existing approaches to addiction are moral models (whereby addicts are punished and held responsible for their actions), disease models (which see addiction as a physiological disorder that is largely out of the control of the individual) and cognitive-behavioural approaches (which focus on identifying and avoiding triggers to the behaviour, substituting more 'positive' activities and improving interpersonal skills and control). We have already seen how mindful therapies differ from these models in their initial emphasis on noticing rather than eradicating behaviours, and in their explicitly biopsychosocial understanding.

Marlatt and colleagues (2008), who developed MBRP, report that moral models which involve imprisoning drug users (with no assistance treatment programmes) are abject failures in relation to both recidivism and relapse. Whilst approaches rooted in Buddhist philosophy would share a sense of ethical responsibility with such moral models, the focus would be more on cultivating compassion for oneself and others (see Chapter 5) rather than punitive treatment that is neither compassionate nor effective.

The disease model of addiction is perhaps the most prevalent given the massive popularity of the 'anonymous' programmes for various addictions which employ the 12-step process towards recovery. Such programmes see addiction as a disease beyond the individual's control, and this is why the goal is total abstinence and there is emphasis on fellowship and putting one's trust in a higher power. Mindful approaches could be seen as sharing with such programmes a spiritual element, which some therapies do not include, although secular western versions of mindfulness do not require any belief in higher powers or afterlife (see Chapter 2) (Marlatt et al., 2004). Also, many mindful therapies, like MBRP, take the form of weekly groups (building, as they do, on mindfulness-based stress reduction; see Chapter 7), and so include mutual support and collaboration. Some have even suggested that mindfulness can be woven into 12-step addiction programmes (Jacobs-Stewart, 2010).

However, there are tensions between 12-step and mindful approaches which need to be taken into account. Mindful therapies would not insist on abstinence as it would be impossible to abstain from all addictions given that they are a pretty intrinsic part of being human. They would advocate gentle observation and engagement rather than suppression. Also they would question the notion that addiction is purely biological and out of an individual's control. By slowing down and noticing our cravings it is possible to respond to them differently, and this experience could be seen as empowering rather than as giving up power. Finally, 12-step approaches often insist that people recognise their identity as 'an addict' whilst mindful approaches would be extremely cautious about fixing identity in this way (see the consideration of the self towards the end of Chapter 3).

Whilst mindful therapies can certainly be integrated with cognitive-behavioural therapy (CBT), as MBRP is, as we've seen in Chapters 3 and 6 there is a difference in the way that mindfulness advocates 'leaning in' to experience with compassionate curiosity rather than trying to avoid it or fix it. The purpose of meditation practices in mindful therapy for addiction would be to enhance awareness of our standard patterns of attachment and aversion and how these are implicated in addiction behaviours, and to creatively engage in experimenting with alternative approaches.

Practice: Urge surfing

One key strategy taught in MBRP is 'urge surfing'. Impulses to engage in the things we are addicted to are conceptualised as a wave of urges which we

may surf rather than being dragged under by. This involves cultivating a welcoming and curious stance towards the urge rather than trying to avoid it or
giving into it.

Next time you experience an urge, try to sit with it for a while rather than giving into it or trying to distract yourself and ignore it. What is the urge like? Try
to describe it in detail: its colour, texture, sensation, feeling. Experience what
it is like to engage with the urge openly and curiously: how does it feel to surf
the wave?

Such slowing-down and noticing can help us to see what temporary
relief or instant gratification we get from our habits, as well as recognising that these may well be short lived. Mindful groups for addiction,
such as MBRP, include other exercises and meditations which encourage clients to be present with painful and uncomfortable experiences
(see Chapters 5 and 6); for example, meditating on bodily sensations
(observing how pains and itches arise and fall, shifting over time; see
Chapter 9). Such activities are followed by discussion of these experiences, and there may be opportunities in the group when cravings or
uncomfortable situations arise, to sit with these experiences rather than
avoiding them or trying to fix them. Here the therapist can usefully
model a more mindful way of being. Of course, such exercises and
approaches could also be adapted for a one-to-one therapy setting (see
Chapter 2).

In her book on habits, the Buddhist scholar Martine Batchelor (2007)
presents a sort of mindful alternative to the 12 steps. The ox-herding
pictures (Figure 7.1) are a useful metaphor for addressing habits and
addictions. At first we are caught in habits and don't even realise it,
although we may have a nagging sense of something not right (1), then
we begin to notice our habits (2) and glimpse that there might be some
way of addressing them (3) because they are sometimes more or less
intense. When we first grasp what is going on it is a struggle because
we are still embedded in patterns of trying to get what we want and
eradicate what we don't want (4), but if we cultivate a different
approach of compassionate curiosity we start to hold these patterns
more lightly and see them more clearly, diminishing their power (5).
Once we are able to break free of our habits of thinking and behaving
we may experience glimpses of joy and freedom from stuckness (6) and
appreciate the ordinariness of life rather than being caught up in cycles
of attraction and aversion (7). We realise that we are not fixed and limited by our stories about ourselves (8) and can return to our worlds in
a less grasping and more appreciative way (9), which also makes us
more open and available to others (10).

Figure 7.1 Ox-herding pictures

A sense of process like this can help when addressing addictions, although Batchelor emphasises that these stages are not linear: we may jump straight to a later one, or back to a previous one, or go through them all in the same day.

Summary and conclusions

The case study below applies some of the ideas that we have covered in this chapter to a specific client to illustrate how they might work in practice.

Case study: Mike

Mike is a wealthy man in his late forties. He set up a charitable organisation 20 years ago, which became a huge success and is now well known nationally for providing support to young people. He also regularly runs marathons to raise funds and awareness of their work. Mike lives in a large apartment in the heart of the city with his partner Brian, but their relationship is in a bad way. Brian complains that Mike is never there because he is either working, running or attending events, and when he does come home most of his attention is on his phone and email. Mike acknowledges that he is never off-duty and that it is taking a toll on him too, but he doesn't know how to change.

Think about

- How would you generally work with a client like Mike?
- How might you understand Mike's issues from a mindful perspective?
- What mindful ideas and practices from this chapter, and from the rest of the book, might you consider applying or suggesting in this case?

One way forward

The starting point with Mike would be to encourage him to notice when he has a craving to check his phone, to take on another task or to go running, and try to surf the urge, leaning into the experience, and curiously exploring it. Mindful meditation may be a useful practice for Mike here if he is willing to consider that (see Chapter 2).

Meanings might emerge, for example, around Mike wanting to be a success, to help others, and/or to be constantly moving. It would be useful to normalise these in relation to social pressures and the common human desire to get more of what we want and less of what we don't want. It would also be worth exploring what Mike fears will happen if he does stop or focuses his energies differently. Rather than pathologising Mike's work and exercise as addictions, or embracing them as good, productive behaviours, it is important to recognise that they can be both positive and problematic and to start him thinking about *how* he engages with them rather than trying to stop them completely, or carry on as he is. If he decides he does want to shift his habits then something like the ox-herding pictures might be a useful way of explaining this as an ongoing biopsychosocial process.

See Chapter 9 for a case study relating to sex addiction, which is more about avoiding experience.

There has been relatively little research on mindful therapy for addiction so far, but initial research on MBRP is positive, suggesting that it can result in a decrease in both substance use and the cravings related to this (see Bowen, Chawla, & Marlatt, 2010).

One potential limitation of mindful approaches in this area would be if they were taken to mean that we should *never* give into cravings. It is highly unlikely that we could engage in everything we do (work, relationships, eating, physical activity, play) without any elements of attachment/aversion being present. As we saw with Mike, mindful therapy is about noticing when we are engaging with such things in light ways, and when they have become more habitual and/or intense, and addressing the latter. Buddhist philosophy does not regard desire as problematic per se, but only when it has become excessive or problematically directed (Keown, 1996). As usual, it is worth being cautious if mindful practice in itself becomes about trying to perfect oneself or eradicate all suffering, and thus being – in itself – a kind of addiction.

Mindful approaches challenge our usual pattern of moving towards the pleasant and away from the painful and emphasise the value of learning to lean into pain, and/or being cautious about what seems pleasant. This is important for addiction since, as we have seen, this often involves attempting to grasp hold of what is pleasurable, or to eradicate or avoid what is painful. The following Buddhist story can be helpful in understanding why it can be useful to treat pleasant/unpleasant and good/bad distinctions lightly:

> The situation ... is like that of the wise Chinese farmer whose horse ran off. When his neighbour came to console him the farmer said, 'Who knows what's good or bad?'.
>
> When his horse returned the next day with a herd of horses following her, the foolish neighbour came to congratulate him on his good fortune.
>
> 'Who knows what's good or bad?' said the farmer.
>
> Then, when the farmer's son broke his leg trying to ride one of the new horses, the foolish neighbour came to console him again.
>
> 'Who knows what's good or bad?' said the farmer.
>
> When the army passed through, conscripting men for the war, they passed over the farmer's son because of his broken leg. When the foolish man came to congratulate the farmer that his son would be spared, again the farmer said, 'Who knows what's good or bad?'.
>
> When do we expect the story to end? (Hagen, 1997: 42)

Further reading

The most helpful practical book on these issues I have found is Martine Batchelor's exploration of habits from a Buddhist perspective:
Batchelor, M. (2007). *Let go: A Buddhist guide to breaking free of habits.* Somerville, MA: Wisdom.

Also helpful is Gabor Maté's book, which draws on his medical experience working with drug addicts, as well as his personal experiences, to present a biopsychosocial understanding of addiction and a compassionate approach to dealing with it.
Maté, G. (2008). *In the realm of hungry ghosts: Close encounters with addiction.* Toronto: Random House.

Details of mindfulness-based relapse prevention (MBPR) can be found in:
Bowen, S., Chawla, N., & Marlatt, G. A. (2010). *Mindfulness-based relapse prevention: A clinician's guide.* New York, NY: Guilford Press.

Thomas and Beverly Bien have written a self-help style book including many Buddhist-inspired practices towards recovery from addiction:

Bien, T., & Bien, B. (2002). *Mindful recovery: A spiritual path to healing from addiction*. New York, NY: Wiley.

Teresa Jacobs-Stewart's book specifically considers how mindfulness could be brought into the 12-step programme for addiction:

Jacobs-Stewart, T. (2010). *Mindfulness and the 12 steps: Living recovery in the present moment*. Center City, MN: Hazelden.

EIGHT 'Psychotic' experiences

Aims

This chapter aims to:

- introduce mindful approaches to understanding, and working with, 'psychotic' experiences such as having 'delusions' and hearing voices,
- locate mindful approaches in relation to more conventional treatments of such experiences, explaining what mindful understandings and practices might have to offer,
- suggest a three-phase model of mindful therapy with people who are struggling with such experiences (forming a therapeutic alliance, developing self-compassion, and engaging mindfully with the experience),
- consider some of the ways in which mindful therapies need to be adapted when applying them in this context, and issues to be aware of in their application.

The chapter focuses on 'psychotic' experiences because such experiences are common to a number of different diagnosed 'conditions'. There is much evidence of overlap between, for example, categories such as 'schizophrenia', 'bipolar affective disorder' and 'schizoaffective disorder', so it is more useful to focus our understandings and therapies relating to particular experiences, or symptoms, rather than on seeking explanations and treatments for separate conditions (Bentall, 2009). Such overlaps are a good reason for holding diagnostic terms lightly, both as a practitioner and as a client. The mindful approach of not fixing people in terms of identity, but considering when certain ways of defining ourselves might be more or less useful (see Chapter 5), relates well to current thinking about 'psychotic' experiences. For example, there is a wide variation in the course that schizophrenia takes, with at least two-thirds of people recovering or having times when they do not have 'psychotic' experiences (World Health Organization, 1973).

Common assumptions that 'disorders' involving 'psychosis' are incurable and inevitably lifelong require challenging (in both clients and professionals) lest they become self-fulfilling prophecies.

'Psychosis' generally refers to some form of loss of contact with reality, such as when we believe in things that there is little evidence for and others don't also believe (sometimes called 'delusions' or 'paranoia') or see or hear things that are not readily apparent to others (sometimes called visual or auditory 'hallucinations').

I have placed the term 'psychotic' itself in scare quotes because, as with addictions (see Chapter 7), very similar experiences may or may not be labelled 'psychotic' by ourselves and/or by others. This depends, for example, on who we are, as people of certain gender, cultural and age groups are more likely to be so labelled (Johnstone, 2000). It also depends on the context of our experience. For example, beliefs such as astrology or popular conspiracy theories may not be pathologised because they are so common. Similarly, there may be an acceptance of experiences that fit into recognised religious or other community contexts, such as hearing the voice of god or of a departed loved one. Of course all of the issues in this book could really be put in scare quotes ('depression', 'anxiety', etc.) within the mindful approach that regards them all as simply forms of suffering, and also due to the wide variability in how such labels are applied to people. However, as we will see, 'psychosis' is worthy of particular caution because of the stigma surrounding it.

Pause for reflection

Take a moment to consider times when you have experienced these kinds of beliefs or experiences. Have you felt paranoid or believed something that you have later come to question? Have you seen or heard things that might not have been there? What were those experiences like? How did you, and those around you, respond to them?

Then imagine yourself immediately in the wake of a very traumatic event (e.g. the loss of a loved one, a serious accident, convicted of a crime, or seeing a negative public report about yourself). What might your experience be under those circumstances? Can you imagine yourself being more fearful, over-estimating danger and threat, or being hyper-vigilant to sights and sounds and misperceiving them (e.g. seeing people who look like the person you've lost, or hearing sounds similar to those you heard in the accident)?

Most writing about working with people who have 'psychotic' experiences, from a mindful perspective, emphasises the importance of a continuity model of these experiences. This is distinguished from a normal/abnormal model, whereby 'normal' people never experience things like that and 'abnormal' 'psychotic' people do. The above Pause for Reflection hopefully illuminates the ways in which these experiences are very much on a continuum with more everyday experiences. When teaching on this topic, if one can de-stigmatise the experiences sufficiently, often around half of the people in the room will admit to having heard voices on occasion, for example. Certainly most of us have experiences akin to this when we are struggling. The kinds of critical voices that many people hear when having 'psychotic' experiences are on a continuum with the self-critical thoughts that are common in depression (see Chapter 5). 'Delusions' and paranoias may be usefully conceptualised as extreme versions of common beliefs that one is really a bad person, or is under threat from things that are not really that dangerous (see Chapter 6). Often the difference is akin to that between simile and metaphor; for example, compare saying that it feels *like* there are worms under my skin, or *like* my mother is telling me off, to saying that there *are* worms under my skin or my mother *is* telling me off.

I personally remember a time when I was having problems at work after having been quite publicly exposed in relation to my personal life. I became convinced that certain people were ganging up against me and was shocked and disturbed when friends suggested that I might be imagining it. Also I often heard my name being spoken in the corridor outside my office, probably mishearing words that sounded similar because I was so hyper-alert to the fear that people were talking about me. This situation made me aware of the ways in which such experiences can both exacerbate existing distress (as we start questioning ourselves) and distance us from our usual support systems (who may begin to distrust our reports, creating a barrier between us). It would be very easy to withdraw from others, and them from us, and this could quickly become a vicious cycle, exacerbating feelings of paranoia and hallucinatory experiences, for example.

However, there is a note of caution to such continuum models which suggests that, like difference models, they should be held lightly. Certainly continuum models are a very useful corrective to the kind of 'us and them' thinking which is prevalent in this area whereby people, many professionals included, regard 'psychotic people' as a different, and alien, category and struggle to treat them as fellow human beings (Richards, 2010). However, in some ways 'psychotic' experiences *can be* different to the kinds of issues that we've covered in the previous three chapters in terms of just how distressing they may be. This is highly linked to the degree of stigmatisation that we face from others if our experiences are viewed as out of touch with reality. We are often labelled as 'psycho' or 'crazy', in a way that those struggling with anxiety, depression or addiction seldom are. Also people around us may feel that they can't cope with us, meaning that hospitalisation and isolation are more common outcomes. In addition to this, our thoughts and feelings are generally dismissed as 'mad', whereas the thoughts and feelings of someone who is depressed or anxious would be treated with more respect. So whilst it is vital to recognise that clients we work with who are having 'psychotic' experiences are as human as we are, and are experiencing something that we ourselves would be likely to experience under similar circumstances, it is also important to respect just how distressing and alienating such experiences can be.

This idea of simultaneously holding the continuum of experience as well as the ways in which 'psychotic' experiences are different to other experiences, relates to the question of whether mindful approaches are appropriate for people who are suffering in these ways. There is a widely held perception, for example, that meditation practices are harmful for people with 'psychosis' (Chadwick, Hughes, Russel, Russel, & Dagnan, 2009). This is problematic as it treats people who experience this as a different category of person, potentially denying them access to a very useful set of practices. At the same time, however, there is a need to apply mindful practices particularly thoughtfully in this context due to the potential for some forms of meditation to render experiences more, rather than less, frightening and distressing (something we will return to in the Summary and Conclusions at the end of this chapter).

The outcome research on mindful one-to-one and group therapies so far, although suffering from all the usual limitations of outcome research on forms of therapy (see Chapter 4), consistently finds that such therapies are helpful in reducing both distress and troubling experiences, so long as they are adapted appropriately (Davis & Kurzban, 2012). The remainder of this chapter will outline what such adaptations might look like, and why they are important.

Distinctions between mindful, and other, approaches to 'psychotic' experiences

Probably the most vital thing that mindful therapies have to offer for people having 'psychotic' experiences is a radically different way of approaching their experience to that which they have likely previously been confronted with in mental health services. The following list highlights three main ways in which mindful approaches differ:

- Rather than treating the person as different and abnormal, the mindful practitioner attempts to engage with them, as with all clients, as a fellow human being who is embroiled in suffering (see Chapter 2).

- Rather than viewing their experiences as nonsensical and meaning-less (as many conventional approaches to 'psychosis' do), the notion that suffering is a constant of the human condition opens up the possibility of speaking about the experiences and attending to the ways in which they are explicable and understandable responses to the circumstances we find ourselves in.
- Rather than working to eradicate the whole experience (as approaches including some drug[1] and psychological treatments do), the focus is upon how we *respond* to the experience, attempting to be with it without either avoiding it or exaggerating it (see Chapter 6).

The literature in this area is in broad agreement that there is a major problem with many conventional approaches to 'psychotic' experi-ences. Treating such experiences as if they are nonsensical, with no basis in reality, makes it more and more unbearable for the client to speak about them because telling people will reaffirm that they are 'crazy'. Additionally, they may have well-founded fears that sharing their experience will mean that they will be hospitalised, taken away from home and support, and given drugs which they may not wish to take. Therefore they are highly likely to withdraw more under such treatment and to feel worse rather than better.

In addition, the experiences themselves may well increase because they are often the way in which the person tries to make sense of threat-ening situations in which they find themselves. For example, imagine a client who is convinced that a secret organisation is trying to harm them because they find themselves highly anxious a lot of the time and bad things seem to keep happening to them. If a professional disbelieves them and tries to get them to challenge this belief, they are put in a terrifying situation of having to accept that they have been wrong all this time and that there is no reason for the things that they are going through. Alternatively they could make sense of the professional's response by assuming that they are in on the conspiracy against them.

For these reasons, practitioners who use mindful approaches gener-ally do not work directly with 'psychotic' experiences at all in the early stages of therapy. When they do engage with them later on their focus is on how we engage with our experiences, rather than whether they are valid or accurate representations of reality.

---

[1]This is not to say that drug treatments would never be used alongside mindful therapies, for example to help calm a person who is in severe distress, but rather that practitioners would use caution, mindful of the ways in which such drugs have historically been over-used and can function to increase stigma (Bentall, 2009). Bach et al. (2006), for example, present a case study in which issues of whether to take medication are addressed mindfully with a client.

The rest of the chapter will act out a three-stage process for working with people who are having 'psychotic' experiences, drawing particularly on the protocol suggested by one of the key authors in this field, Antonio Pinto (2009), and also bringing in some elements from acceptance and commitment therapy (ACT) (Bach, Gaudiano, Pankey, Herbert, & Hayes, 2006), compassion focused therapy (CFT) (Gumley, Brachler, Laithwaite, MacBeth, & Gilbert, 2010) and person-based cognitive therapy (PBCT) (Chadwick, 2006), which incorporates CBT and mindfulness specifically for people with 'psychotic' experiences. The key stages are:

- Foundation: the therapeutic alliance and exploring values.
- Developing self-compassion.
- Engaging with experiences mindfully.

Foundation: The therapeutic alliance and exploring values

Whilst, of course, the therapeutic alliance is extremely important in all counselling and psychotherapy (see Chapter 2), it can be regarded as particularly vital in this context. This is because it is a situation in which many professionals struggle to develop such an alliance, or move away from their usual way of being with clients because they themselves are troubled and scared. Also, clients having 'psychotic' experiences are likely to have been previously marginalised and stigmatised, treated as alien and different by others, including professionals, and therefore work will likely need to be done to overcome their suspicion and distrust and to create a safer space for them to engage with their issues. They may be extremely isolated and require time to close the existential gap that has opened up between them and the rest of humanity. Additionally, as we have seen, they are likely to expect the professional to focus on challenging and changing their experiences, and it will be important to make it clear to them that that will not be the approach taken here, and to build trust so that clients feel able to talk about their experiences without fearing a reaction which will adversely affect their lives.

It is important from the start that mindful professionals demonstrate that they are willing to work in the person's reality, clarifying that the experiences themselves are not the problem but rather the distress that they are causing and the problems people face navigating the rest of the social world with them (May, 2007). There needs to be a commitment to being alongside a fellow human being, no matter how strange or foreign their experience or behaviour may seem. It is important to remember that the contents of experiences which are 'indecipherable to most people ... [may] represent [their] only bridge between a shareable reality and what appears to be total chaos' (Pinto, 2009: 348).

Of course here mindful practice may be very useful for therapists themselves (see Chapter 2) in terms of cultivating openness to all experience and the 'strong back, soft front' combination of equanimity and empathy, such that we are able to model being with difficult experiences and treating people with compassion. In this way we can avoid the temptation to objectify or dismiss 'psychotic' experiences. We can demonstrate our own willingness to attend to, and understand, them, showing that we are interested in the client, that we believe that they are worth listening to and taking seriously, and that we value their thoughts, feelings and understandings as we would those of any other human being. This also involves being attentive to their life history, and the meanings of their experiences in the context of this, as we would be, for example, with somebody who was struggling with depression or anxiety.

One excellent way of building a therapeutic alliance early on comes from ACT (Bach et al., 2006). As we saw in Chapter 3, ACT emphasises identifying and working towards one's life-goals alongside developing a mindful accepting approach to suffering. It can be powerful for clients who have had 'psychotic' experiences to encounter a professional who is more interested in what their goals are, and what they value, rather than the experiences per se. ACT practitioners suggest spending most of the early sessions identifying the client's goals *and* their underlying values (e.g. getting a full-time job *and* being self-sufficient; developing a friendship *and* connecting with others). Thus the professional comes to be seen as an ally in the pursuit of valued goals. Further sessions may involve, for example, considering steps on the way to these goals, or the ways in which it is important to keep moving towards our values even when we don't feel like it (seeing them as like a compass pointing the direction in which we need to move).

There is a note of caution here as those who have had long experiences of stigmatisation and isolation may find it very difficult to make contact with their values and may assume that they can't do things, having been told many times that they cannot. In such cases there may need to be more of an emphasis on finding goals and values, rather than easily identifying them. Also, of course, it is vital to avoid pushing goals and values onto clients; for example, in assuming that somebody who has held a powerful and responsible position in the past ought to work in a very small-scale role due to having had 'psychotic' experience, or setting goals without providing the skills training necessary to meet them. It is important to remember that different people will be in different places, and to do values and goals work with compassion (Spandler & Stickley, in press).

Once such an alliance is in place, the way that the client and others respond to their 'psychotic' experiences may be identified as one of the potential barriers to their goals – and can then be explored in this context – but the starting point is a respect for the client and a collaborative approach towards helping them to move towards and/or find what they value.

Developing self-compassion

This emphasis on the therapeutic alliance links to, and overlaps, with the next part of the therapeutic process, which is to focus on developing self-compassion before, and then alongside, any engagement with the 'psychotic' experiences themselves. As we have seen, mental health services may well not have been experienced as compassionate places by clients. Therefore many authors and researchers in the field of mental health – beyond those taking an explicitly mindful approach – emphasise the vital importance of kindness and compassion[2].

We covered mindful approaches to developing self-compassion, notably CFT, in some depth in Chapter 5 (see also Chapter 3 for an overview of the approach). Many of the same issues are present with 'psychotic' experiences as they are with depression, including the commonality of self-criticism and shame and underlying assumptions that one is bad or deserving of harm. There may also be additional levels of shame due to being diagnosed as mentally ill, hospitalised and/or stigmatised by others.

The CFT approach to 'psychotic' experiences emphasises that when we have such experiences we understandably feel under threat, and the ways in which our experiences function to regulate the emotional distress we are feeling as a result of this. This is explored in the context of life histories and learned responses to threat, with an awareness of the unintended consequences that some coping responses may be having (such as actually increasing their distress or distancing them from others). The focus is on cultivating a 'soothing system' to shift from 'threat' into 'soothing', for example through meditative practices which cultivate compassion or loving-kindness (see Chapters 1 and 2;

---

[2]For example, Bentall (2009) covers this in some depth and Spandler and Stickley (in press) argue for the importance of including compassion in recent recovery approaches to mental health.

and Johnson, Penn, Frederickson, Meyer, Kring, & Brantley, 2009). This ability to treat oneself with more compassion then links to a more compassionate, understanding and open stance to our experiences (see below), as well as being more able to tolerate distress.

CFT often emphasises educating clients about the brain process underlying their experiences (e.g. being stuck in the threat system) and the developmental trajectories and cognitive processes that explain why they respond in the ways they do. Such education can relieve feelings of shame and engender a curious and understanding approach to experiences. In addition to this, from a mindful biopsychosocial perspective (see Chapters 4, 5 and 9), it is also useful to explore with clients the social elements that are a vital aspect of their experience[3]. For example, experiences of bullying, marginalisation and stigma are part of the experience for many suffering from 'psychotic' experiences. A cause-and-effect model may be more usefully replaced by one of co-arising (see Chapter 4), as it is often unclear whether experiences led to being labelled as 'mad' and excluded, or whether such labelling and exclusion led to the experiences: most likely they co-arose, each mutually reinforcing the other. Such understandings can offer the client relief from the impossible process of trying to determine whether they were 'to blame' for what happened to them, or whether external forces were at fault.

It may well also be useful to contextualise experiences of self-scrutiny and judgement, and lack of compassion, in the wider context of current consumerist and individualist culture (see Chapter 1 and Concluding Thoughts). Just as it is understandable in such a context that people struggling with depression think highly negatively about themselves and try to turn themselves into better people, it is also understandable that many 'psychotic' experiences involve the externalising of critical judgements and monitoring (e.g. hearing cruel voices, or feeling that one is being watched).

Engaging mindfully with experiences

Once a therapeutic alliance has been developed, and the client has been introduced to the notion of cultivating self-compassion more broadly, the professional and client can begin to have conversations

---

[3]Biopsychosocial models of paranoia and hearing voices, which may well be useful here, can be found in Bentall (2009) in the chapter on 'brains, minds and psychosis'.

about the 'psychotic' experiences more directly if this is necessary and helpful. In some situations, of course, clients may not respond to the experiences in ways that are problematic for them, and the focus may be more on other aspects of life as with any other client (e.g. relationships, goals, loss, etc.).

When experiences are the focus, the emphasis is on shifting from the view that the experience *itself* is problematic (which clients themselves and other professionals may well have reinforced[4]) to the view that it is the way we have *related* to the experience that is the issue. ACT employs the phrase 'creative hopelessness' for the stage at which we recognise that our prior ways of coping have actually exacerbated our suffering (hopelessness), but at which we are therefore open to engaging with other strategies (creative). For example, we might explore how ruminating on troubling experiences makes us feel worse, or how trying to shut out voices makes them louder, before going on to explore alternative, more mindful, approaches.

In terms of past ways of responding it is likely that the client, and others around them, will have focused on trying to ignore, avoid or eradicate the experience, or on ruminating about it and trying to confront and challenge it. As with other experiences such as depression and anxiety (see Chapters 5 and 6), the mindful response involves leaning into the experience (rather than avoiding it), and gently and openly being with it as it is (rather than evaluating it, challenging it and layering shame, worry, guilt and other feelings on top of it).

Figure 8.1 from the PBCT approach clearly summarises the different approach that we are advocating in mindful therapy with 'psychotic' experiences.

As with compassion, above, the kinds of mindful practices that we have covered throughout this book can be useful for cultivating experiential engagement (rather than avoidance) with 'psychotic' experiences, and for cultivating an open and curious approach to noticing such experiences and how we respond to them, allowing them to ebb and flow rather than trying to stop them or being carried away with them. As with addiction urges in the previous chapter, we are attempting to be with the experience spaciously rather than grasping hold of it or trying to avoid/eradicate it.

---

[4]Many professionals do not see the experiences themselves as problematic, but rather whether or not they get in the way of 'normal' life. Of course it is useful here to interrogate any taken-for-granted assumptions that we have about what 'normal' life should be and to focus on whether the experience is problematic for the person having it.

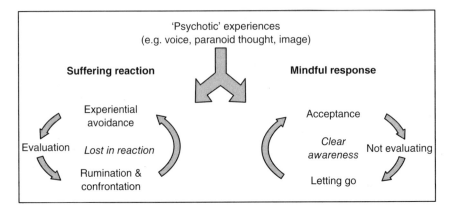

Figure 8.1 **Different responses to 'psychotic' experiences (adapted from Chadwick, Newman Taylor, & Abba, 2005: 352)**

Such an approach importantly differs from conventional treatments, which dismiss 'psychotic' experiences as meaningless and warn professionals against engaging with them at all. Thus it links well to other work around hearing voices, for example, which advocates finding ways of communicating with the voices in order to better understand the meaning behind them (Corstens, Longden, & May, 2012) (see case study below for an example of this).

Summary and conclusions

The case study below gives an illustration of how the three stages above might be applied in a specific situation, as well as a way in which direct engagement with voices might be brought in.

Case study: Bill

Bill is a man in his early twenties who has recently dropped out of college and moved back in with his parents because he struggled to keep up with his studies. He became very withdrawn and spent a lot of time sleeping. His parents were concerned because they heard him talking to himself in his room and asked mental health services to assess him. It emerged that Bill was hearing a voice which told him that he was useless and weak.

Think about

- How would you generally work with a client like Bill?
- How might you understand Bill's issues from a mindful perspective?
- What mindful ideas and practices from this chapter, and from the rest of the book, might you consider applying or suggesting in this case?

One way forward

As suggested above, it is important to first build a therapeutic alliance, showing that we are interested in Bill as a person, and perhaps focusing on what his goals are and what he values in life. We might explore whether Bill shares the critical view of himself suggested by the voices he is hearing, and encourage him to try practices that cultivate a more compassionate approach to himself and others (e.g. building in daily kindnesses, remembering people being compassionate to him, writing compassionate letters to himself).

Then we might bring in the idea of mindfully responding to voices rather than trying to avoid them, or becoming caught up in them, perhaps employing breathing (Introduction) or body (Chapter 9) meditation practices to cultivate that way of being. The focus is on learning to cope with voices and accept their presence, rather than fighting them. As usual it is worth emphasising that this is no easy task, lest any difficulties with meditative practices be perceived as further failure by the client.

Drawing on the Gestalt empty-chair technique employed in CFT (see Chapter 3), we might engage with Bill's negative voice more directly. Voice dialogue methods have been found to be an effective way of cultivating acceptance of voices in many cases, and can also reveal useful information that the voices are harbouring. These techniques involve the client shifting chairs in order to access the voice if they feel safe to do so. The facilitator then asks questions in a tone appropriate to the nature of the voice (e.g. gentle or firm) and the client repeats the voice's responses word for word. Questions are asked directly to the voice and might include, for example, 'Who are you?', 'How do you feel?', 'When did you come into Bill's life?', 'What is your role?', 'What would you advise Bill to do?' and so on. Once the voice or voice-hearer has had enough, the facilitator checks that they are ready to stop, says goodbye to the voice, and the person returns to their chair. The facilitator summarises what they heard. They may discuss new information that emerged and the client may well continue to work, in their own time, on a new relationship with the voice.

We can see then, that generally the mindful approach to 'psychotic' experiences is the same as for all the other issues considered in this section of the book: building self-compassion, leaning into experience instead of avoiding it, and gently noticing what is there rather than layering extra suffering on top of it.

However, there are some cautions with the application of mindful practices to 'psychotic' experiences which are important to be aware of. As with any issue, it is necessary to adapt the therapy or group practice to the specific issue, and this is particularly important here for the reasons we have considered. We have pulled out some of the main adaptations throughout the chapter, including: not rushing to challenge experiences or encouraging clients to do so; ensuring a good therapeutic alliance and working on self-compassion before moving to engage more directly with the experiences when relevant; and treating the client as a fellow human being, with a sense of your own capacity for such experiences under similarly challenging circumstances.

Pause for reflection

Consider what the experience of meditation might be like if you were having hallucinations or feeling paranoid. Do you think that conventional mindful practices might need to be adapted in such situations? Might some work better than others?

In addition to the general points above, there are some more specific kinds of adaptations that are important to consider when employing meditative and mindfulness practices with people who are having 'psychotic' experiences. Whilst, as we have seen, the research so far suggests that mindfulness one-to-one therapy and groups can be very helpful in this context, qualitative research in particular draws our attention to some of the ways in which mindful and compassion practices can be difficult when we are suffering in these ways. For example, some people report difficulty concentrating during meditations, or find that silence is difficult at first because of becoming more aware of negative voices.

Particular challenges might occur around trying to practice for long periods, being silent, having one's eyes shut, and practising at home (e.g. where meditation might be viewed by others as another form of strange behaviour). Flexibility is helpful here, as with all clients, to determine what works best, and generally it would be advisable not to try meditating for extended periods to start with, to avoid prolonged silence (perhaps with guided meditation), and to consider focusing on a visual stimulus (e.g. a candle-flame, the breeze through leaves, raindrops on a puddle), as well as the best place to practice. Consideration of already existing practices is also important. For example, many silent retreats advise against reading or writing whilst attending. For some people who are used to externalising their thought processes as part of making sense of their experience, or as a form of self-care, removal of that form of distributed cognition may be problematic[5].

The spacious awareness of vipassanā meditation may be particularly helpful for those having 'psychotic' experiences as there can be a tendency towards misvaluing things during such experiences[6]. For example, people may see patterns where others would not, such as in something left on the table or in a particular number or phrase that they see or hear. Cultivating the capacity to attend to our full experience, rather than focusing in on such things, could be extremely useful, as it is with depression when we often only focus on what is difficult or troubling (Chapter 5), or anxiety when we focus on what we fear (Chapter 6), or addiction when we focus on the object of craving (Chapter 7). Rather than feeling pulled into overvaluing certain aspects of our surroundings, we can be more spaciously aware and feel more of a sense of control over what we then decide to bring our attention to.

One particular issue with many who have 'psychotic' experiences is that a sense of fragmentation and disintegration is a common, and distressing, element of experience. Therefore meditative practices that encourage an awareness of the fragmented self or a questioning of reality (see Chapter 3) should be employed with extreme caution. Instead, a focus on very grounding and centring practices that anchor the attention, such as those involving the body in motion (see Chapters 6 and 9) or everyday activities (see Chapter 1), is particularly helpful, as is recognition that those who engage in lots of meditation (such as Buddhist monks) also have the slogan 'chop wood, carry water' to emphasise the need to ground themselves, in an embodied way, in everyday material existence. As one author on Buddhist approaches to 'psychosis' puts it, being more centred means that we feel safer in our world and can notice things without being blown away by them:

> Just as we may watch the clouds pass across the sky, so too we can watch the vagaries of our inner world pass. However, we can only do that if we have our feet planted firmly on the ground, or we will let ourselves think we are floating away on the clouds too. (Mills, 2010: 218)

A final practice, which can be useful particularly for those who struggle with becoming stuck on the content of voices is meditating on sounds (see Figure 8.2), described below.

---

[5]See http://en.wikipedia.org/wiki/Distributed_cognition.

[6]My thanks to Christina Richards for this suggestion which I had not come across in any of the writing on mindful approaches towards 'psychotic' experience.

Practice: Listening meditation

Sit comfortably and quietly, shut your eyes, relax any tension in your body.

Start by paying attention particularly to the sounds within your body. Don't imagine them but hear what is there.

Expand your attention out to be aware of all the sounds around you in the room. Don't grasp or reject them, just listen.

Expand your awareness again to include all the sounds that are present. Don't name them or make up stories about them, just open your ears to the sounds of the world. If you find yourself distracted, gently come back to listening.

Notice how the sounds come and go, and how the sounds and your hearing of them is seamless.

Stretch and get up, trying to maintain this quality of attention as you leave.

Figure 8.2   Listening meditation

Further reading

A very comprehensive and practical chapter on applying mindfulness to psychosis in general is:

Pinto, A. (2009). Mindfulness and psychosis. In F. Didonna (Ed.). *Clinical handbook of mindfulness.* (pp. 339–368). Berlin: Springer. Available from: www.springerlink. com/content/u130w2531n755x63.

The PBCT approach is outlined in:

Chadwick, P. (2006). *Person-based cognitive therapy for distressing psychosis.* Hoboken, NJ: Wiley Blackwell.

For more of a focus on the ACT approach, including useful case material, see:

Bach, P. A., Gaudiano, B., Pankey, J., Herbert, J. D., & Hayes, S. C. (2006). Acceptance, mindfulness, values, and psychosis: Applying acceptance and commitment therapy (ACT) to the chronically mentally ill. In R. A. Baer (Ed.). *Mindfulness-based treatment approaches: Clinician's guide to evidence base and applications.* (pp. 93–116). San Diego, CA: Elsevier Academic.

A useful chapter applying Buddhist and Taoist ideas to hearing voices specifically, and focusing on the importance of grounding, is:

Mills, N. (2010). Learning to become centred and grounded and let the voices come and go. In I. Clarke (Ed.). *Psychosis and spirituality: Consolidating the new paradigm.* Hoboken, NJ: Wiley Blackwell.

Isabel Clarke's book on psychosis and spirituality (above) is generally a useful resource, and you can read more about this, and related projects, at: www.isabelclarke.org/psychosis_spirituality.

NINE   The body: pain, sleep, eating, sex

Aims

This chapter aims to:

- introduce a non-dualistic, mindful way of approaching the body,
- explore the ways in which mindful ideas and practices can be helpful for clients with issues relating to bodily experience,
- consider the value of mindful practices particularly for pain, sleep difficulties, eating problems and sexual issues,
- provide a more in-depth consideration of what a mindful sex therapy could be like.

Just as it doesn't really make sense, from a Buddhist perspective, to tease out different forms of suffering as we do in western psychotherapy (see Chapters 5 and 6), it also doesn't make sense to separate the body from other aspects of our experience (as I am doing in this chapter) or to separate out our relationships (as we will do in the next chapter). This is because, as we covered in Chapter 4, Buddhism is non-dualistic: it doesn't distinguish between mind and body, or self and others, in the ways we are used to doing in the western world. As we will see, mindful approaches to the body, and to relationships, are grounded in recognising the impossibility of such separations and attempting to reconnect self and body, self and other.

In this way Buddhist mindfulness is actually consistent with more recent thinking in western theory about the body. The purely biomedical approach to health and illness, which has dominated in the medical professions and in popular understanding, is gradually being replaced by biopsychosocial approaches that emphasise the importance of understanding human experience on all of these levels, and the impossibility of teasing them apart (Fox, 2012).

As we have already touched upon, experiences such as depression and anxiety are social (they have a social context, which sees such experiences as 'disorders' to be treated, and they often emerge in social situations of alienation or oppression); they are psychological (they involve certain kinds of emotions and thought processes); and they are biological (these feelings and habits of thought map on to certain neural pathways, chemical processes and physical sensations). The experience of mindful practice has been demonstrated to operate on a biological level (alterations in brain activity and bodily experience), a psychological level (the way we experience our thoughts and feelings shifts) and a social level (we relate to others and the world differently) (see Chapter 4). Although I have separated out these levels here to make the point, it is important to recognise that they are really inseparable: social contexts enable us to make sense of the world in some ways rather than others, and lay down patterns of thoughts and feelings in the form of neural connections and habitual bodily reactions through which we experience the world and act upon it in our relations with others.

The same can also be said for experiences which are usually understood on a purely bodily or biological level, such as those we are focusing on in this chapter: pain, sleep, eating and sex. For example, consider Tim Parks's experience of pelvic pain described in his book *Teach us to Sit Still* (2010). On a biological level, muscle tension was certainly involved in the development and maintenance of this experience, but that took place in the social context of a culture which views the body as a means to an end. In Tim's case this translated, psychologically, as treating his body as a machine to enable him to produce writing or to engage in sex, sport and so forth. During Tim's book we see how this relationship to his body, and the desire for a quick physical fix for any pain, actually exacerbates and maintains the pain he experiences. The social dominance of a purely biomedical understanding is, for Tim, part of the problem, but equally the social availability to him (because of the time, place, class and culture he lives in) of other approaches (such as meditation) enables another – biopsychosocial – way of addressing the pain.

As we will see, such biopsychosocial conceptualisations of bodily experiences are at the heart of mindful therapies for pain, as well as those that address problems with sleep, eating and sex. A key issue across all of these areas as well as in many of the experiences that we tend to label 'psychological' (covered in the previous four chapters) is our tendency to treat our bodies as objects or things. This is what Tim is doing when he views his body only as a tool to enable him to write, which requires fixing if it stops being able to do this. There is a similar sense in Gwyneth Lewis's (2002) autobiography of depression, *Sunbathing in the Rain*: she pushes her body to perform, produce and perfect, and eventually depression kicks in and floors her so that she has to stop.

Pause for reflection

Before continuing, think about the ways in which we are encouraged to treat our bodies as objects in wider culture. You might consider the following areas: appearance, eating, sleep/rest, illness, work, sex, emotional expression and physical activity. You may find it useful to flick through the magazines on sale in your local shop to see how bodies are treated in these.

As well as treating our bodies as machines for work, and denying them rest when they are tired or ill (as Tim and Gwyneth describe), most of us also try to make our bodies appear in a certain way to others (which may involve restricting or forcing food intake, pushing or avoiding certain forms of exercise, time-consuming decoration of the surface of the body, and wearing painful clothes). We may also try to make our bodies respond (sexually, emotionally, etc.) in the ways we feel they should (due to wider cultural messages about the 'right' amount/type of sex and physical contact, or the 'appropriateness' of various emotional responses) (Barker, 2012a).

An alternative to this, suggested by a non-dualistic approach, is to regard ourselves as embodied beings whereby it makes no sense to separate our bodies from our selves in such ways. Research suggests that most of us experience more embodied moments, often when we are not being observed, when we feel pleasurable sensations like a hot bath or the breeze on our face, or when we are enjoying our bodies in motion, for example (Del Busso & Reavey, 2011). This is something which we could cultivate. Mindful practices that are good for this include slow walking (see Chapter 6), stretching practices like yoga or qigong, or simply engaging in physical activities that we enjoy (running, climbing, dancing, etc.) in a mindful way (attending to the experience). We can also attempt to 'tune in' more to our bodies. The body sweep is a classic meditation practice for doing this.

Practice: Body sweep (adapted from Batchelor, 2001: 37)

You might like to try this practice lying comfortably on the floor. Close your eyes and breathe easily, spend a few minutes on each part of the body:

• First pay attention to sensations in and around your head: your scalp and face. Don't try to visualise, just observe what is there and how your head feels.

- Move your attention gently down to your neck and shoulders. Observe any sensations, even painful ones, without grasping at them or rejecting them.
- Move your awareness down your torso. Notice any internal sensations, and the feeling of your clothes against your skin.
- Shift focus to the arms and hands. Feel their contact with the floor.
- Expand your attention down to the pelvic area. Consider sensations there: where does buttock stop and floor start?
- Move on to your thighs and the knees, and then the lower part of the legs: the ankles and the feet. Notice how sensations shift from moment to moment.
- Finally, be aware of your whole body.
- What is the experience of being embodied? How does it feel physically? Recognise and appreciate your ability to feel and sense as you rest there.

After you get up, try to pay the same gentle attention to sensations as you move.

Like this practice, the mindful approach to bodily experiences such as pain, sleep, eating and sex involves gently attending to what is there, rather than trying to eradicate, or identify with, difficult experiences or sensations. So we do not try to eliminate pain, to force ourselves to fall asleep, to lose or gain weight, or to make ourselves have orgasms, for example. A paradox of mindfulness is that we may find that these things do happen when we cease our patterns of aversion and attachment towards certain bodily sensations or states: acceptance and commitment therapy (ACT, see Chapter 3) uses the analogy of Chinese fingercuffs, which grow tighter the more we try to pull them apart and looser when we stop pulling. Alternatively or additionally we may find that our relationship to pain, sleep, eating or sex is altered such that we feel differently about it and are able to 'swim against the stream' of wider social messages about how we should relate to these things (see Concluding Thoughts for more on this).

In the remainder of the chapter I will briefly overview mindful approaches to pain, sleep and eating before spending a little longer on sex, which has become a major area of concern (in wider culture and within therapy) in recent years. Of course many of the ideas and practices translate well across all of these experiences, and others.

Pain

Western mindful therapies emerged in the context of helping people in chronic pain (Kabat-Zinn, 1982). It is estimated that 20–30 per cent of adults in western countries experience this, and that it is often linked to experiences of depression (see Chapter 5). The exploration of mindfulness as a possible treatment came out of acknowledgement that even the strongest drugs only reduce pain by 30–40 per cent in fewer than 50 per cent of patients (Chiesa & Serretti, 2011), coupled with a recognition of a biopsychosocial cycle of chronic pain. According to Siegel (2004), research supports Tim Parks's experience that chronic pain involves a cycle of psychological stress, muscle tension, misinterpretation of symptoms and avoidance of activities which are viewed as potential exacerbators of pain. Siegel summarises evidence that something beyond a purely physical condition is involved: the back structures that have been associated with pain are present in many people who don't experience pain; 'successful' surgeries often have little impact; and people in cultures where 'back-breaking labour' is common report low rates of back pain, whilst there is evidence that work-related stress and psychological trauma do predict back pain. Siegel focuses on muscular-skeletal pain but argues that a very similar cycle operates in experiences like chronic headaches, fibromyalgia and gastrointestinal distress.

Siegel suggests that mindfulness interventions can operate on all stages of the pain cycle, after a thorough medical examination has been carried out (to avoid overlooking treatable diseases or injuries and to assure patients that these have been ruled out in order that they can accept another explanation[1]). First, mindfulness can facilitate the kind of biopsychosocial understanding that we've suggested because meditation experience can help us to realise the interweaving and inseparability of these aspects. This also involves challenging popular notions that pain without a clear physical cause is not real or means that someone is malingering. Second, it is possible in meditation to observe the muscles tensing when stressed and to practise alternative physical responses. Third, people in pain can recognise the way that identifying with pain exacerbates and solidifies it, compared to the approach of observing it arising, falling away and changing in quality over time. Bringing attention to the present moment, and experiencing the sensation rather than labelling it 'pain' and trying to escape it, can decrease the stress, anxiety and high arousal that leads to tension. Finally, mindfulness can help people to re-engage with activities that they have avoided which will actually strengthen the body: they can shift from avoiding the fear of these activities to befriending fear as they engage with them (see Chapter 6) (Siegel suggests starting with the easiest activities and working up to more challenging ones).

---

[1] Of course this is important in all of the areas covered in this chapter, and others, as pain, difficulty sleeping, loss of appetite, erectile problems, and low mood (for example) can all be indicators of certain diseases.

The outcome research on mindfulness-based interventions for chronic pain has been reviewed (Chiesa & Serretti, 2011), although it is mainly CBT-based forms of mindfulness that have been studied in this way (see Chapter 4). In terms of reduction of perceived pain, mindfulness interventions have been found to be beneficial compared to waiting lists, but not compared to control groups who did the same things (time together, group support) without the mindful meditation. However, mindfulness groups *were* better than control groups on acceptance and tolerance of pain as well as improvements in stress levels and quality of life, which is what we might expect given that the aim is not to decrease pain, as such, but to alter our relationship with it and with our bodies. There are also some studies that do find links between people's degree of mindfulness and decreased pain perception (e.g. McCracken, Gauntlett-Gilbert, & Vowles, 2007) and evidence that even brief mindful training in an experimental setting decreases perception of acute pain (Zeidan, Gordon, Merchant & Goolkasian, 2008), so this is clearly an area that requires further investigation. It seems likely that the extent to which people engage with mindfulness in their daily lives (outside training sessions and after they have been completed) is important.

Sleep

Just as the goal of eradicating pain can increase the anxiety and arousal which increases muscle tension and pain itself, so – as most of us have probably experienced – the goal of falling asleep increases anxiety and arousal, making sleep the last thing that we are capable of doing. This kind of cycle is common in insomnia (whether of the kind where people struggle to get to sleep in the first place, or the kind where they wake up and can't get back to sleep).

Mindful approaches to sleep disturbance simply suggest mindful practice as an alternative to lying awake thinking anxiously about the fact that we are not sleeping. In this way it is similar to Frankl's ([1946] 2004) 'paradoxical intentionality', which advocates the opposite of what we usually do (attempting to stay awake rather than to fall asleep).

With clients it is worth framing this in relation to research which suggests that we often don't need as much sleep as we generally assume that we do; that resting can often be as beneficial as sleep; and that meditation, in particular, may have many of the same restorative qualities as sleep. We can also encourage clients to reflect on their own previous experience where they will likely have observed that they can function on a night or two of little sleep, and that the next day is rarely as difficult as they fear it will be during the night. Opinion varies over whether it is more helpful to get out of bed in order to practise (as conventional sleep disorder treatment recommends) or to remain there. Personally I have found both to be beneficial (see Figure 9.1 for an example of getting up) and the best strategy may also depend on whether a person sleeps alone or not.

It may, at least, be worth sitting up in bed to meditate rather than remaining lying down: I find that it is easy to remain in a semi-asleep loop of anxiety when lying down, which sitting and meditating can get me out of. Breathing, body sweep and listening meditations can all be good practices in this situation (whichever works best for the individual). The important thing is that worried thoughts about sleep are allowed to come and go rather than being grasped and proliferated.

As with pain, reviews of the evidence, which have focused on mindfulness based stress reduction (MBSR) so far, do not clearly demonstrate that mindfulness *training* improves sleep quality or duration compared to other approaches, but they do find that increased *practice* of mindfulness techniques decreases worry about lack of sleep and improves sleep (Winbush, Goss, & Kreitzer, 2007).

Beyond specific practices for insomnia, people who practise mindfulness may notice more clearly what activities relax them and wake them

Figure 9.1   Mindful sleep

up, thus helping them to develop night-time rituals that work for them, perhaps including meditation as the last thing before sleep.

Mindful interventions have also been found to be helpful for people who are struggling with experiences of chronic fatigue (Rimes & Wingrove, 2011), and some report beneficial impacts on their experience of dreaming. For example, Tibetan dream yoga practices can be used, which involve returning into (bad) dreams through meditative imagination and 'purifying' or 'mastering' them (Tulku, 2000). Working with clients, such meditations can usefully be integrated with the way in which your modality generally works with dreams.

Eating

Eating is a topic that requires a full biopsychosocial understanding, given the powerful and contradictory messages which people receive about it in western culture today. What might, on the surface, seem like a purely physical act of fuelling the body and taking in nutrients is actually a complex activity that is drenched in personal and social meaning. In our individual histories we may learn that food can be a reward for good behaviour, a punishment when we're forced to eat foods we don't like, a means of soothing when we are troubled, or something to be avoided in order to make us better people. Socially, there a rules around what substances can and can't be eaten, around the timing and size of meals, and around who eats together.

One currently omnipresent societal message is that there is a certain body shape that should be aspired to, and that intake of food, as well as physical activity, is our passport to achieving this (and all of the personal and relationship happiness that is bound up with it; Barker, 2012a). The strong message that being thin and/or toned is good exists alongside equally powerful commercial incentives to eat more food (just watch the adverts on television of 'beautiful' people tucking into fast food and soft drinks). All of this impacts on the habits that we develop around eating. We might question the rather arbitrary division of some people into categories of 'eating disordered' when so many people's eating and physical activity habits are problematic, although sometimes less obviously so.

From a non-dualistic perspective, a mindful approach to someone who is struggling with eating, in whatever way, would start by investigating the multiple meanings around eating that exist for the individual client, rather than assuming that starving or binging means the same thing to all people. It is important to understand the ways in which their body, background and cultural context have combined to develop the individual relationship they currently have with food. We might find, for example, that controlling food becomes important when every-thing else feels out of control, or that it is a form of self-punishment, self-soothing or emotion regulation. It may be that the shaping of the body is a way of rebelling against societal forces or specific people, or of maintaining a young or non-gendered body in a world where grow-ing up and being seen as a man or woman come loaded with expecta-tions and responsibilities.

When grounded in such an understanding, mindful therapy can then focus on reconnecting people with their bodies, rather than maintain-ing false splits between the body and the self whereby the body can be viewed as something separate to control, starve, fill, perfect and so on. As we've seen, there are various meditation practices which help people to see how they are inseparable from their bodies. In addition to these, by cultivating attention we can notice when we eat, what we eat and how we eat, and – as with other patterns – we can open up possibilities for shifting these. One classic mindful practice that may be undertaken is to eat a raisin or tangerine slowly and mindfully, tuning into the whole experience in the same way that we do in other mindful prac-tices. There are also approaches to 'overeating' that focus specifically on building self-compassion as a key to treating our selves and bodies more kindly and less critically (Goss, 2011).

Reviews of existing research on mindful therapies for 'eating disorders' have focused on standard forms of third-wave cognitive-behavioural therapy (CBT) (see Chapter 3). Evidence has been found to support their effectiveness (Wanden-Berghe, Sanz-Valero, & Wanden-Berghe, 2010), as well as a suggestion that learning mindful approaches early in life might prevent eating problems in young women who are a particularly at-risk group (Proulx, 2008).

Sex

Perhaps even more than food, sex is currently subject to huge societal pressures, as well as highly contradictory messages. We live in a sex-saturated culture where mythologised versions of 'perfect' sex are used to sell products (Loy, 2008), a certain version of successful sex is per-petuated in mainstream media, and porn is readily available. This gives us one set of messages about the importance of having 'great sex' regu-larly and what this should involve. At the same time, people are increasingly concerned about being sexually 'normal', and anxious if their bodies and desires do not conform by enabling them to have – and to be excited by – the kind of sex which is presented to them (Barker,

2011b). Again we see the patterns of attachment and aversion, craving and avoidance, that Buddhism highlights, played out as people simultaneously look to sex and sexual relationships to fulfil them in all kinds of ways, and experience high levels of anxiety over their sexual desires, functioning and practices. In this way we can see current concerns about sex and love 'addiction' (see Chapter 7) and sexual 'dysfunction' as rooted in the same patterns.

Pause for reflection

What is the dominant cultural view of sex in which our clients are operating? What forms of sex and sexual relationships are we encouraged to aspire to? Which are disallowed? What might a mindful approach to sex therapy look like in this context?

Conventional sex therapy is in danger of reinforcing the very patterns of craving and aversion highlighted above, by reflecting and perpetuating certain understandings of sex. The major manuals of psychiatric disorders distinguish 'functional' from 'dysfunctional' forms of sex, and also have a history of pathologising certain sexualities despite there being no evidence linking them to psychological difficulties (historically this includes homosexuality, and still includes kinky, or sadomasochistic, practices; Richards & Barker, 2013). The forms of 'sexual dysfunction' that exist are based on a model whereby sexual experience involves desire, arousal and orgasm following penis-in-vagina penetration. There is an industry of pharmaceuticals and therapies designed to fix low desire, problems achieving erection or penetration, or difficulties achieving orgasm. A non-dualistic mindful approach would question both the physical focus of such an approach which fails to also take account of the psychosocial meanings of sex, which are as individual and complex as those surrounding food. It would also challenge the goal-directed focus that aims at a certain endpoint rather than attending to the experience.

There has been a more positive history, in sex therapy, of encouraging practices, such as sensate focus, which take the emphasis away from penetration and orgasm to focus on the here-and-now experience (Goldmeier & Mears, 2010). Clients are often encouraged to stop trying to have sex and instead to go back to learning about what their body, and that of their partner, finds pleasurable with touch, massage and so forth. Mindful ideas and practices could be useful here in helping people to tune in to their bodies and to be present to their sensations, cultivating the kind of attention that would be useful to bring to sex (Brotto, Krychman & Jacobson, 2008). However, sex therapy often sneaks back in an overall goal of penis-in-vagina penetration and/or orgasm (Barker, 2011b). Some even suggest that mindfulness could enable people to have penis-in-vagina sex when not aroused, or when finding it painful (due to openness to all sensations). This is deeply problematic. A much better ground rule for sex therapy in a world of sexual pressure is to create a culture of consent wherein nobody has sex that they don't want to have.

We should be very wary of using mindfulness as an add-on technique to conventional sex therapy rather than developing a ground-up therapy which is rooted in mindful understandings of experience. From such a perspective we would avoid fixing what sex should involve and separating it off from other parts of life to be treated differently. We would also avoid fixing certain people according to their sexual practices. Instead, we would focus on reconnecting people with their bodies rather than treating them as machines that need to perform in certain ways; helping them tune in to their desires rather than grasping some and trying to avoid others; and making ethical decisions about how they relate to these. For example, we might help them to consider which ones they can consensually practise with other enthusiastic people or enjoy in fantasy, and which they find concerning and may want to sit with and understand more before acting upon them in any way.

Just as we saw that mindful practice could be useful for the therapeutic encounter because it cultivates attention and empathy (see Chapter 2), cultivation of mindfulness is useful for the sexual encounter, whether that involves having online sex, cuddling a partner, being spanked, engaging in solo-sex or taking part in a threesome. Through mindfulness, people can become more attuned to themselves and to their sensations, more present to the experience and more empathic towards any others they are with, as well as to themselves.

Case study: Louis

Louis is a man in his late twenties who comes for therapy because he is worried by the amount of time that he spends looking at pornography online. Lately he has even found himself using his work computer for this purpose and he fears being caught by his boss at work, or by his partner, Claire, at home who thinks that he is online gaming. Exploring this with Louis you find that he both enjoys and is frightened by the way that he can totally zone out looking at porn, feeling that he is away from the stress of his life in an exciting search for images or videos that will be the ultimate turn-on. He is embarrassed about the content of the porn and says that he tries not to think about it the rest of the time because he's worried about what it might mean about him that he sometimes likes looking at other men, or relates to a person being dominated in porn images. He also worries that it is affecting his sex life with Claire, which he doesn't enjoy and tries to avoid.

Think about

- How might a mindful approach understand Louis's issues (e.g. in relation to craving and fixing)?
- How would mindful therapy work with Louis differently to conventional sex therapy in relation to the aims of therapy and the process?
- What mindful practices might it be useful to suggest to Louis if he is interested in working in this way?

One way forward

Mindful ideas could usefully open up a middle way for Louis between the strategies he currently uses: either grasping hold of sex when looking at porn, or attempting to avoid it at other times. It could be useful to consider how it would be for him to hold sex more gently. For example, could he allow himself to engage with porn in a more attentive way, experiencing it more deeply rather than losing himself in flicking from image to image? Could he let himself reflect on sex at other times rather than hiding it away for fear of what he might find? Is it possible to sit with desire without trying to sate it, and to sit with anxiety without trying to quell it?

Such an approach can often lead to greater understanding and a sense of being in control rather than controlled, opening up the possibility of taking more responsibility for one's actions. Louis might feel better able to make decisions about what he does and doesn't want to look at, instead of feeling uncontrollably drawn into it and then ashamed afterwards. Also, instead of identifying with what he's doing sexually ('it must mean I'm this kind of person'), he may be able to tune in to the various desires he has, treating himself more compassionately, and considering ethically which he might like to act upon or not. Hopefully this will open up the possibility of both him and his partner sharing their desires with each other (see Barker, 2012a). Also exploring sex in the context of the whole of his life, rather than separating it out, could provide a fuller picture of what it is that he is escaping from when looking at porn (see Chapter 7).

Mindful practices could be helpful here in cultivating the kind of attention that Louis could then bring to all his sexual encounters in pornography and with his partner. Specifically bodily practices might help him to attend to all aspects of his experience, instead of separating off his mind. It might also enable him

(Continued)

(Continued)

to think about the people he is viewing, and his partner, as full human beings. Relational mindful practices might be useful in encouraging both verbal and physical communication between partners, if Claire wants to engage with this (see Chapter 10). They might also try using books of sexual practices that draw on mindful and tantra ideas[2].

Summary and conclusions

In this chapter (see below) we've seen that a mindful approach to the body involves taking a non-dualistic biopsychosocial perspective that includes understanding the sociocultural context, individual meanings and physical experiences, and how these are interwoven.

Mindful therapy often involves reconnecting these artificially separated aspects of being. Meditation in particular can help us to recognise that we are embodied beings and that societal norms and ideals operate through our bodies, thoughts and feelings. Bodily practices such as movement meditations, body sweeps, attentive eating and meditating on sensations can cultivate an attention to the body that is useful for specifically bodily issues, such as those around pain, eating and sex.

Focusing on sex, we have seen that the current prevalence of sex-related problems can be located in both a separation of people from their sexual feelings and a way of relating to sex which is rooted in craving. An alternative mindful approach focuses on tuning in to the body and sexual feelings, and on compassionate communication with sexual partners, which we will explore further in the next chapter.

In addition to those we have covered here, it may be that our clients are already involved in their own bodily practices. Many people who engage seriously in physical pursuits such as dancing, climbing, cycling, strength training, martial arts or swimming find that mindful ideas and practices are already familiar to them (McNamara, 2012). For example, there are resonances between mindfulness and the concept of 'flow' which is often applied to sports (Csíkszentmihályi, 1991), and there are similar paradoxes that good 'performance' cannot be forced, and that an embodied – rather than separated – way of being is required. With such clients it is likely to be useful to draw their existing understandings and

---

[2]Many such books may be off-putting in terms of the language used, and the focus on certain sexual practices and identities rather than the full range. A more down-to-earth book is Carrellas (2007).

practices into making sense of their experience and/or explaining mindful approaches. For example, I've found it useful for people struggling with sex to bring the kind of attention and present-ness they engage with in their sport to the sexual encounter. It can be a useful exercise to get people to richly describe experiences when their activity is going well/badly to help them to recognise mindful qualities. For those who do not engage in such activities already, engagement with them may prove just as useful as formal meditation.

In his chapter (see below), Siegel reflects that many people who turn to mindfulness in desperation due to experiences of chronic pain or insomnia find that there is a 'silver lining' of discovering a practice and way of relating to the world which is useful far beyond the issue they were having.

Further reading

There is a very good summary of the use of mindfulness interventions with pain, which is also relevant to many of the other issues covered in this chapter, in:
Siegel, R. D. (2004). Psychophysiological disorders: Embracing pain. In C. K. Germer, R. D. Siegel, & P. R. Fulton (Eds.). *Mindfulness and psychotherapy*. (pp. 173–196). New York, NY: Guilford Press.

The following website presents one mindful approach to pain: http://breathworks-mindfulness.org.uk.
The founder of breathworks has also written a helpful book:
Burch, V. (2008). *Living well with pain and illness: The mindful way to free yourself from suffering*. London: Piatkus.

You can read more about various mindful approaches to sex (and relationships) in this special issue:
Brotto, L., & Barker, M. (2013). Mindfulness Special Issue of *Sexual and Relationship Therapy, 28* (1–2).

There is guidance for working with clients of different sexualities and genders in:
Richards, C., & Barker, M. (2013). *Sexuality and gender for counsellors, psychologists and health professionals: A practical guide*. London: Sage.

A list of further references addressing bodies from a mindful perspective can be found at: http://socialmindfulness.wordpress.com/references/social-engagement/bodies.

TEN Relationships

Aims

This chapter aims to:

- consider a mindful understanding of relationship difficulties, locating them in the separation of self and others and a craving approach to relationships,
- introduce mindful ideas and practices for individual clients struggling with relationships (particularly around self and other compassion and understanding),
- introduce the potentials of mindful practices in interaction for relationship therapy (such as insight dialogue and interbeing practices),
- explore mindfulness beyond the individual and dyad and how it may be integrated with systemic therapies and sociocultural approaches.

A key aspect of the mindful approach to relationships is the non-dualist aspect of this perspective. Just as we separate ourselves from our bodies in order to approach them in the craving way that creates suffering (see Chapter 9), so relationship suffering can be located in our separation of ourselves from others. For this reason mindful approaches to relationship struggles emphasise ways of reconnecting ourselves with others and recognising how problematic such separations are.

A mindful understanding of relationship difficulties

For most of this chapter we will concentrate on romantic relationships as these have been the focus of relationship counselling and therapy. However, as we go through we will see that the separating out of romantic partnerships as a special kind of relationship could well be another reason for the particularly high levels of suffering in this area[1]. We will begin to question therapies and mindfulness approaches which take the importance of 'the couple' at face value. We will also seek further enquiry into the cultural assumptions that valorise a certain kind of love and explore therapeutic approaches which explicitly address this.

Pause for reflection

Before we begin, think about the ways in which romantic relationships are currently viewed in our society. Consider depictions in mainstream media (e.g. pop songs, advertisements, television programmes and films). What are we looking for from a romantic relationship? What is it meant to be like? How do we view those who do not have such a relationship?

Western Buddhist authors David Loy (2008) and Martine Batchelor (2007) both speak of the craving nature of our current view of love. Loy points out that the myth of romantic love is a relatively recent phenomenon, which has become bound up with personal happiness and fulfilment: we look to relationships to make us feel complete and to provide a permanent state of 'happily ever after'.

These authors mention two common patterns that follow from this. In one, the inevitable disillusionment that comes when the intense romance and physical connection of the early days of 'falling in love' cannot be sustained means that we assume it can't have been right and so separate off to try again, becoming caught in an endless search for 'The One' perfect person. In the other pattern, we stay together and collude in presenting a mask of perfection to the outside world (which perpetuates the myth for other people) whilst privately struggling with the fact that the relationship isn't meeting our perhaps unrealistic expectations. We might sink into a kind of resigned disillusionment with the relationship, or enter a conflictual cycle where we swing between feelings of love when we are connecting well, and panic and anger when we are not. Some people may remain in damaging relationships

---

[1]Relationship problems are perhaps the issues that are most commonly presented to counsellors and therapists other than the 'common mental health problems' of depression and anxiety (which are, themselves, often linked to relationship problems of course). There is much social concern over high rates of separation, infidelity and abuse in couples, and the wider impact of this.

because romantic feelings convince us that this must be the 'right' person, or because we fear there won't be anybody else for us.

One of the therapists and authors who has explored romantic relationships most extensively from a Buddhist perspective is John Welwood (1996). Like Batchelor and Loy, he locates our craving approach to relationships – and the suffering inherent in this – in the way in which we relate to ourselves. We look to romantic relationships to fulfil us primarily because of the sense we have that we are fundamentally lacking. We crave[2] that love will prove to us that we are okay whilst also being certain that, on some level, we really are not.

This is a perspective which is consistent with all the main therapeutic approaches (related to the synthesis I offered in Chapter 2). There is a common view in these approaches that as we grow up we learn both how we should and shouldn't be, and that the problems we experience are rooted in this. Whether we conceptualise it through the lens of core beliefs, conditions of worth or ego and superego, there is a sense that we internalise messages from the people and norms circulating around us about what it is for us to be good or bad. Perhaps we learn that it is good to take care of others, to be desirable or to be the best. Maybe we learn that it is bad to lose control, to be arrogant or to depend on somebody else. We then attempt to ensure that we consistently present to the world a self with all the 'good' qualities, but remain haunted by the potential that the 'bad' qualities will bubble up. This is the lurking fear we have that we are really fundamentally flawed, lacking or imperfect, and that this will be exposed if we do not police ourselves constantly. This way of thinking is exacerbated by our current culture of self-monitoring, comparison to others, and striving for success (Gergen, 2009).

The implication of this for relationships is that we enter them with both a yearning to be validated and a dread of being exposed. The early days of love offer the intoxicating possibility that maybe we really are all the 'good' things that we try to be and none of the 'bad', because that is what our partner reflects back at us. No wonder that we (individually and culturally) idealise and obsess over this period when we are seen as utterly delightful and wonderful and find the same qualities in somebody else.

But, of course, as relationships continue our partners cannot consistently reflect back only what we want to see and nothing that we don't want. And even if they did, we would come to distrust them because we ourselves have a nagging certainty that we are really lacking and flawed compared to some ideal of perfection. Problems come when we

---

[2]See Chapter 1 for the place of craving in the Buddhist understanding of suffering.

and our partners desperately attempt to keep hiding the sides of ourselves that we believe to be so bad, at the same time as living alongside each other day after day, which means that these sides of us will inevitably be revealed.

This view of relationships is consistent with recent scholarship that locates relationship – and other – problems in our own vulnerability about the aspects of ourselves that we believe to be unacceptable, and the deep shame that we feel about that[3]. This research also highlights the fact that we find it desperately difficult to admit that we are wrong (Schultz, 2010) or that we have made a mistake (Tavris & Aronson, 2008), meaning that we shunt all the blame onto other people.

In common with those researching shame and being wrong, Welwood (1996) offers a radical alternative to our current approach. Instead of desiring that partners will validate us as we want to be seen, and desperately defending ourselves or fleeing when they don't, we could view intimate relationships as a perfect place for learning about our areas of vulnerability, overcoming the shame surrounding them, letting go of confining identities, and opening up the potential for new ways of relating to ourselves and others. This constitutes a more mindful approach where we attend to our experience in relationships, noticing the habitual patterns that emerge within and between us, and being open about these rather than trying to avoid them or over-identifying with them.

This is a very challenging shift in perception as it requires that we are courageous enough to both confront the sides of ourselves that we are deeply uncomfortable with and to risk revealing them to others. It involves learning a completely different response to conflict and suffering in relationships. In this we embrace such times and use them as opportunities to examine ourselves, rather than avoiding them and responding as we habitually do by defending ourselves and focusing on what is problematic about the other person (leaning into experience, see Chapter 6). Beyond this, as we will see, the approach invites a shift from a dualistic view of ourselves and others as fixed and separate to a mindful perspective of people as in-process and interconnected.

This understanding has important implications for relationship therapy. As Welwood points out, standard problem-solving approaches to improving communication, managing conflict or making sex better, for example, are in danger of suggesting that there are external solutions that will fix any problems, rather than recognising the disconnected

---

[3]The work of Brené Brown on shame and vulnerability has captured the public imagination through her widely viewed TED talks (see www.brenebrown.com/videos) (Brown, 2008).

relationships with ourselves which are involved and the opportunities that relationship difficulties offer for learning to relate to ourselves and others differently.

Individual mindful practices for relationship struggles

Before we go on to explore the implications of this way of understanding relationships for working with individuals and couples in a mindful way, let's consider an example which illustrates the common ways of relating that I have introduced and which can help us to consider what a mindful approach to relationships might involve.

Case study: Ben and Nasima

Ben and Nasima are a couple in their late thirties who have been together for five years. They met at the restaurant where Ben works. He was impressed by the confident woman eating alone and asked her for a date. Nasima liked the way he made her laugh, and accepted. When Ben moved in to Nasima's flat he enjoyed supporting somebody who was so passionate about her work, cooking for her and listening to her day. However, now Nasima is going for a partnership at her law firm he complains that she gives little time to him and prioritises her work over their relationship. Nasima finds Ben too demanding and wishes he would take over more of the household chores whilst she is so busy. Both are disappointed by their dwindling sex life which was such a great part of their early relationship and wonder what has gone wrong.

Think about

- How would your current approach to therapy work with Ben and Nasima? Consider how you would work with each of them if they came as individual clients, and also how you might work with them in couple therapy if you practise in that way.
- From what we have covered so far about mindful approaches to relationships, how might you conceptualise Ben and Nasima's problems?
- What could mindful therapy with Ben and Nasima look like? What individual and/or couple practices might you engage them in?

One way forward

A first step with Nasima and Ben might be to normalise their experience by explaining that, although people tend to hide it, living with somebody else is an extremely challenging thing to do and inevitably brings up these kinds of tensions. We might then offer the idea that we look to partners to validate how we like to be seen, but fear them seeing what we feel vulnerable about[4]. It seems that Nasima loved Ben seeing her as a powerful woman with an important role, and Ben loved Nasima seeing him as a nurturing person who could support her and keep her smiling.

The challenge now is to step out of a cycle of blame to acknowledge what it is that they each fear that the other person is seeing. Individual practices (like meditation or journal writing) might be helpful in attending to the feelings and thoughts that come up when they conflict, rather than avoiding them by pushing them onto the other person or pretending that they weren't there. We might also consider specific practices to build compassion and understanding for the other person (see Chapters 2 and 3).

We'll return to this example in the next section when we consider what mindful relationship therapy might look like, and examine mindful practices that we can bring into interactions with others.

All of the mindful and meditative practices that we have explored in this book are relevant to relationships because, in enabling a different understanding of ourselves, they also foster a different understanding of others. We have seen (in Chapter 5) how mindfulness can stop us from seeing ourselves as fixed (e.g. as good or bad) and reveal that we are both multifaceted and constantly changing. If we understand ourselves in this way there is less need for somebody else to validate us, and less fear that somebody will see our flaws, because we know that how others see us does not define us. Also we recognise that our perceived flaws are not all that we are, or all that we will ever be, and that the very things we regard as flaws in one context may be strengths in another if we can hold them more gently.

In accepting this about ourselves we have to assume that it is also the case for other people, and this means we may be less likely to insist that somebody else meets all our expectations constantly, or remains exactly as they were when we met, for example. We will also be less likely to polarise them as all good when things are going well and all bad when we are in conflict, or to blame them for our own struggles. Indeed, the small amount of research on mindfulness and relationships

---

[4] I find the A. A. Milne story of Piglet and the heffalump to be a helpful metaphor for this. Because of his own vulnerability, Piglet sees Pooh with a jar stuck on his head as a monstrous heffalump; when he recognises that his own fear got in the way he can realise that Pooh also is stuck and so help him. See http:// rewritingtherules.wordpress.com/2012/01/06/heffalumps-and-conflicts.

has found that mindfulness is associated with better relationship quality, mediated by the way emotions are expressed and discussed (Wachs & Cordova, 2007).

As well as the positive impact of self-related mindfulness practices, we have seen in this book that there are several practices that explicitly address our relationships with others, such as the loving-kindness and compassion meditations we experienced in Chapters 1 and 2. Another (writing) practice which I find particularly valuable in situations of relationship conflict is to invite people to describe in rich detail a conflict, first purely from their perspective, and then purely from what they imagine to be the other person's perspective (see Barker, 2010a, 2012a).

As previously mentioned, though, a mindful approach to relationships invites us to go further than building compassion for ourselves and for others as separate beings. It invites us to recognise that this very separation of self and other is part of the problem. We might get a sense of this in meditations that reflect upon who we are and where our 'self' is located (such as those we considered in Chapter 3).

A meditation that I have personally found most helpful for breaking down boundaries between self and other is tonglen practice, which is described in detail in the writings of Pema Chödrön (1994). The Tibetan word 'tonglen' means 'sending and taking'. In tonglen practice we exchange ourselves for others, attempting to take in their pain and suffering, and send out the genuine wish that they will be relieved from suffering. In Chödrön's books it is suggested that we meditate by 'taking in' on the in breath, and 'sending out' on the out breath. However, I personally find that this way of practising tonglen feels rather artificial and doesn't give enough time for really connecting with the tough experience. Here I suggest an adapted form of tonglen which I have found helpful myself, but of course you may find that the breathing form, or other forms, work better for you or for your clients.

Practice: Adapted tonglen

First, call up a sense of stillness and openness. Draw upon your previous experience – of meditation or everyday life – when you have had a moment of calm and spaciousness, not identifying with anything and allowing whatever arises to come. Briefly draw upon that experience – like flashing a torch onto it – to remind yourself of the possibility for such openness. You can't hold onto this experience but you can touch on it briefly to prepare you for the rest of the practice.

Next, go into the experience of pain and suffering that you are focusing on. I have found it useful to do this in one of two ways. Either I take the opportunity when I am feeling bad myself to really experience that feeling, or I deliberately focus on somebody else who I am finding difficult and try to imagine the experience that they are having, drawing on experiences that I've had in the past when I have behaved similarly, or felt how they are likely to be feeling right now.

Whichever you do, try to feel the full richness of the experience. What is its texture? Its colour? What are your bodily sensations? Instead of the usual strategy of avoiding it or identifying with it, try to sit with it and experience it as it is. For example, you might tune in to an anger that you are feeling or sensing from a partner, experiencing how it squeezes you such that there is no room for anything else. It might be hot and boiling and dark red, drawing your brow and mouth into tight cruel lines. You feel its desire to spit out like forks of lightning destroying everything it hits. Still you sit with it spaciously, open to the fullness of the experience.

Then allow the experience to connect you to the other person (either the one who you are blaming for causing you to feel this way, or the one whose feelings you are imagining). Experience how you are brought together by this human experience of fear, shame, anger, insecurity or envy. Different things might trigger it for them, and it will likely have a different meaning for them, which you need to respect, but something in the overall quality of the suffering brings us together. You are suffering now as they have suffered in the past and will in the future. They are suffering now as you have suffered in the past and will in the future. We are united by suffering.

Reaching this point you can move from focusing on the difficult feelings to concentrating on relief and compassion (wishing these upon yourself and others). If you're finding it hard to be compassionate towards yourself, you can connect with your compassion for the other person who feels this way in order to bring that gentleness to yourself. If you're finding it hard to wish relief for the person who has bothered you so, you can remember how much pain you felt when you were in that situation and wish the kindness which you would have liked yourself on them now. If compassion to either person is hard, you can imagine a child, or a favourite fictional character or a friend, in that experience of suffering, given that it connects us all. You might send out a specific set of feelings or good wishes to counter the specific pain you've focused on, or a more general peace and steadiness, whatever works.

Chödrön (2002) describes those who train in such practices as 'warriors' because of the bravery required to deliberately enter painful situations in order to alleviate suffering rather than trying to escape pain or avoid uncertainty. She argues that tonglen for others ventilates our usual narrowed view on ourselves, freeing us from our tight grip on our self in a way that relieves our own suffering. If we do this practice whenever we and/or another is struggling, it becomes impossible to know whether we are practising for our own benefit or for others, and the distinctions between self and other begin to break down (see the end of Chapter 8 for more on some of the complexities of breaking down such distinctions).

Relational mindfulness practices for dyads

John Welwood's books (1996, 2006) provide some useful guidance for how we might work with relationship difficulties in both individual and relationship therapy.

Like conventional relationship therapy (Crowe & Ridley, 2000), when working with partners together there is a ground rule of 'no fault listening': the clients are invited to commit to listening to each other's descriptions of what it is like for them, and to try to express their experiences *as their* experiences rather than as something caused by the other person (Rosenberg, 2003).

Welwood invites partners into what he calls a 'fourfold truth' that in each conflict there is truth and distortion on both sides. 'Truths' are the genuine feelings and valid concerns that each person has, and 'distortions' are the ways in which we are shifting blame onto the other person and seeing them as bad. So for the case study we considered earlier, Ben's truth might be feeling neglected by Nasima, and his distortion might be viewing her as cold and detached, rather than recognising that she is pulling away due to work pressure. Nasima's truth might be feeling unsupported, and her distortion might be believing that Ben doesn't think it is okay for her to be ambitious.

Welwood provides many examples of working with individuals and couples in therapy to get at the vulnerability behind their relationship struggles and to communicate these to each other. Personally I find it useful to alternate individual sessions with each partner with sessions with both partners together (or all of them in the case of polyamorous relationships). This means that each person can first explore their part of the situation without their partner/s looking on, when that has become difficult. With Ben and Nasima, a conversation together, after such individual explorations, might go something like this.

Case study: Ben and Nasima (continued)

Therapist: Ben, how is it for you when you and Nasima fight?
Ben: She completely dismisses me. Everything is all about her.
Therapist: Can you focus on your experience rather than what Nasima does or doesn't do?

Ben:	Okay [pause]. I'm just not important. When we got together I was like a kind of rock for Nasima: a strong, safe place for her to come back to. And sex was part of it, she always wanted me so much physically whenever she came through the door.
Therapist:	You don't feel needed or wanted now?
Ben:	No.
Therapist:	What's it like to acknowledge that?
Ben:	Not good. I don't like this feeling.
Therapist:	Can you stay with it?
Ben:	I'll try [long pause]. It feels very lonely, actually. Like I don't matter to anyone. Maybe I just don't have anything to offer? I feel like giving up. I think that's why I've stopped doing the things I used to do.
Therapist:	Nasima, can you tell Ben what it's like for you to hear this?
Nasima:	[puts her hand on Ben's knee]. It's a big relief, actually. I thought you'd stopped doing that stuff because you stopped feeling that way about me.
Ben:	Not at all.
Nasima:	I hadn't realised you were feeling so bad about yourself.
Therapist:	And can you say what it is about for you? Like Ben did?
Nasima:	[pause] I think when I was growing up it wasn't really okay to be successful. I mean my parents were pleased when I got good grades, but also there was a sense, you know, of getting above yourself. With Ben it was like the more I did well, the more impressed he was. Just the opposite.
Therapist:	And now?
Nasima:	I'm scared it really isn't okay. When we fight I get this feeling like what I'm doing – going for partner – is ridiculous and arrogant, and that Ben is seeing right through me to that. That he'd rather be with someone more traditional and feminine and all that.
Ben:	I love what you're doing. I just want to be more of a part of it again.

Pause for reflection

Thinking back to what we covered about the counselling relationship in Chapter 2, do you think that it is possible for people to be mindful in the way that they relate to each other, for example in conversations or other interactions? If so, what might this look like?

As well as facilitating a kind of mindful, compassionate exchange between partners within relationship therapy, there have been attempts to develop relational mindful practices where a dyad work together to explicitly practise mindfulness in relation[5]. So far the main practice for cultivating mindfulness in conversation is Gregory Kramer's (2007) insight dialogue, which forms an integral part of the interpersonal mindfulness programme (bringing insight dialogue together with an adaptation of mindfulness-based stress reduction).

Practice: Insight dialogue (adapted from Kramer, 2007)

The stages of insight dialogue are:

Pause:	Remind yourself to pause, slow down, and try to step out of your habitual responses and thoughts, creating a spacc to be different in this encounter.
Relax:	Calm your body and mind, accepting whatever thoughts, feelings and sensations are present in this moment.
Open:	Extend this mindful and compassionate awareness beyond your body and self to the external world around you, including the person you are going to interact with. Spaciously open to them and whatever might arise in your conversation.
Trust emergence:	Come to the interaction without an agenda, try to ride the moment and let experiences arise and fall rather than forcing it or controlling it.
Listen deeply:	Mindfully attend to what the other person is saying and other aspects of the interaction, and commit to learning from it.
Speak the truth:	When you speak, commit to the simple truth of your own experience and articulate that to the other person, tuning into your experience and then speaking it.

We can practise these stages in conversations with one another. One way to keep reminding ourselves to pause, relax and open is to ring a bell a few times during the conversation.

Try having a 10-minute conversation with a friend on any topic (Kramer recommends relevant topics such as compassion, ageing, the desire for approval or home/work roles). Have a third person ring a bell at intervals (or set an alarm or meditation application to do that for you). Each time the

---

[5]I've focused on insight dialogue here, but other authors have put forward various activities and practices from different mindfulness therapies and Buddhist perspectives. Clients may find the following books useful: Walser & Westrip (2009), Kasl (1999, 2001).

bell rings, stop talking: pause, relax yourself, and think about whether you were still being present to the other person and listening, or whether your own agendas and habitual responses had crept in. When you are ready, start up again.

After the conversation, reflect on the experience together, considering how you might bring this way of being into other interactions and relationships.

We could facilitate such insight dialogues between our clients in relationship therapy or group therapy, as well as engaging with it ourselves as part of our counselling training.

Relational mindfulness beyond the dyad

In addition to insight dialogue, Janet Surrey (2005), who brings together relational psychotherapy with mindfulness, lists further dialogue exercises which might be useful in encouraging mindful interaction and breaking down boundaries between self and other in workshops or group therapy contexts. For example, we can experiment with attuning our breathing to that of another person (or animal) with our eyes shut; we can sit facing another person and use gently shared eye contact as an object of meditative attention; and we can practise the kinds of loving-kindness or compassion meditations outlined earlier in the book directly whilst meeting the eyes of another person and focusing the meditation on them.

These can all be useful activities to open up discussion of interconnection and relationship in group contexts. However, we must also be mindful of the meanings that such activities may have for different people and groups. For example, the look of another person can feel very different depending on gender (e.g. in cultures where women are regarded as desirable objects to be looked at) and cultural norms of eye contact (in some cultures it is considered more respectful to maintain eye contact, in others respect is signified by looking away). Exercises involving physical touch (such as hugging meditation[6]) might feel more comfortable for some people than others (depending on whether such touch has been experienced positively and/or negatively in the past). We shouldn't avoid touch, or insist upon it, on the basis of our own cultural and community norms. We need to discuss such issues in the

---

[6]See http://interbeing.org.uk/manual.

context of informed consent before encouraging people to participate in such exercises. It will be useful to think about our personal meanings beforehand and to agree a 'safeword'[7] or signal people can use if a practice becomes too distressing.

In group or family therapy, practitioners may also find it useful to draw on some of the interbeing practices advocated by Thich Nhat Hanh for groups and communities. *The Community of Interbeing Manual of Practice* (COI, no date) lists several group practices whereby people can undertake to connect more with each other and the world around them. However, on a more basic level, we could employ their guidelines for discussion in group therapy, perhaps starting and ending sessions with breathing/listening meditations (see Introduction and Chapter 8), and following these ground rules during the discussions:

> When someone is ready to speak, she nods to the rest of the group. Her right to speak is acknowledged by the others present, who nod in the same way. No one can interrupt the speaker. She is allowed as much time as she needs, and everyone else practises deep listening. When she has finished speaking she nods again and the others acknowledge this with a nod back[8].

If you want, you can add an object so that each speaker goes to the centre and takes an item to hold whilst they are talking, and returns it when they have finished.

Systemic therapists (Vossler, 2010) might find such practices particularly helpful since they share a very similar conceptualisation to the mindful approach in that they view the self as inevitably in relation. People's problems are located in relationships and dynamics between people rather than in their internal experience, and therefore the family or other grouping is worked with in therapy rather than the individual. Engaging mindfully with such systems may help to reveal the 'dances' between people that develop and sustain pain and suffering, as well as loosening such patterns when they have become stuck.

Social constructionist approaches, integral to systemic therapy, have also recently engaged with Buddhist perspectives to propose a 'relational being' perspective (Kwee, 2010). This is a valuable alternative to the way in which we culturally tend to regard people as 'bounded

---

[7]See http://en.wikipedia.org/wiki/Safeword.

[8]Adapted from 'Beginning anew' from http://interbeing.org.uk/manual. The community of interbeing use a bow with palms pressed together, but a nod may be more culturally familiar to those who are not involved in Buddhism or other religions.

selves' which are singular and separate from others. The metaphor of the 'net of Indra'[9] is often used, wherein each being is regarded as a jewelled node of a web which reflects all others. Under such an understanding, a key goal of both therapy and mindful practice is to reveal such interconnectedness and to enable a shift from the valorisation of a separate, autonomous or successful self to the ways in which we are all interwoven in webs of connections (see Figure 10.1).

Summary and conclusions

In this chapter we have seen that mindfulness locates relational suffering in a craving approach to other people where we treat them as objects to fulfil something in ourselves, or to reflect us back in ways in which we wish to be seen. Compassion and loving-kindness practices can challenge a fixed view of others and encourage us to relate to them in their full complexity, whilst meditations on the breath, the

Figure 10.1   Interconnections

---

[9]See http://en.wikipedia.org/wiki/Indra's_net.

body and the outside world can loosen the fixed, bounded view of the self which requires such validation from others and fears their disapproval and judgement.

Such understandings can be applied to relationship therapy where we can usefully explore how each person does, and does not, want to be seen by their partner/s. We can also see the role these fixed identities, and areas of shame and vulnerability, are playing in their relationships and conflicts. Imaginative exercises in understanding conflict from another's perspective, such as tonglen practice, can also help to loosen fixed and objectifying perceptions of partners, reminding us that we are all fluid and multiple relational beings.

Practices such as those explored here from insight dialogue, relational mindfulness and interbeing can help us to cultivate mindfulness explicitly in dialogue with others (in dyads or groups), and these can be usefully brought into relationship, family and group therapy contexts.

Returning to where we started this chapter, we can see that this conceptualisation of the self as interconnected and relational, rather than static, separate and bounded, offers a challenge to both the location on the individual as the focal point of suffering, and to the privileging of the private romantic relationship as the key relationship in people's lives. It may well be useful to explore with clients the ways in which they view romantic relationships compared to other relationships, the messages they have received about these, and the expectations these involve[10].

Ideas of interconnection provide a significant challenge to mainstream therapy which tends to locate the cause of suffering within the person, which regards counsellor and client as entirely separate, and which sees individual – rather than social – change as the way forward. It is these kinds of challenge that we turn to in the final chapter of the book, where we consider what a socially engaged form of mindful therapy might look like.

Further reading

I have written a book about relationships that integrates mindful approaches with other perspectives for a general audience. The book develops several of the themes touched upon in this, and the previous, chapter. This may be useful to read yourself, and to recommend to clients:

---

[10]My book, *Rewriting the rules*, goes through each aspect of relationships to explore dominant cultural messages about it, why we might question these, and how they might shift to a more mindful approach which embraces uncertainty.

Barker, M. (2012). *Rewriting the rules: An integrative guide to love, sex and relationships.* London: Routledge.

There is guidance for practitioners specifically for working with people in monogamous and non-monogamous relationships in:
Richards, C. & Barker, M. (2013). *Sexuality and gender for counsellors, psychologists and health professionals: A practical guide.* London: Sage.

You can read more about John Welwood's ideas in his books, including:
Welwood, J. (2006). *Perfect love imperfect relationships.* Boston, MA: Trumpeter.

You can find out more about Welwood's writing and ideas on his website: www.johnwelwood.com.
There is a nice introduction to Gregory Kramer's insight dialogue in this chapter:
Kramer, G., Meleo-Meyer, F., & Turner, M. L (2008). Cultivating mindfulness in relationship. In S. F. Hick, & T. Bien (Eds.). *Mindfulness and the therapeutic relationship.* (pp. 195–214). New York, NY: Guilford Press.

You can find out more about Kramer's writing and relational Buddhism on the metta website: www.metta.org.
A list of further references addressing relationships from a mindful perspective can be found at: http://socialmindfulness.wordpress.com/references/social-engagement/relationships.
The Social Mindfulness website also includes links to the websites of Pema Chödrön, the community of interbeing (whose manual might well be useful for group therapists particularly), and Kenneth Gergen's Taos institute.

ELEVEN Concluding thoughts

At the start of this book I introduced you to the idea that being mindful is about bringing this way of being to everything we do, rather than just being something that we practise on the meditation cushion and then forget about. I invited you to read this book mindfully and promised that I would likewise attempt to write it in a mindful way.

I don't know about you, but just like my experience of meditation practice, I have found this to be a challenge. Sometimes I have definitely engaged with the writing in a mindful way: connecting attentively with the work of others and sincerely attempting to synthesise this in helpful ways, and to communicate it as clearly and engagingly as possible. Other times I have written while distracted by other things, caught myself taking short-cuts or struggling to engage with the material, or tried to rush towards completion. It is all a useful reminder that being mindful is a great aspiration, but not a way of being that we can generally sustain all day every day. It is useful to continue to practise being mindful in order to cultivate the path, rather than with the aim of some perfect endpoint of 'mindfulness', and we try not to beat ourselves up each time we find ourselves falling back into habitual patterns.

In these final concluding thoughts I will briefly overview what I consider to be the key points covered in the book, particularly pulling out important things to be aware of when we bring mindful understandings and practices into our counselling and therapy. I will then summarise some of the ideas in this book which may not be present in other texts on mindfulness and psychotherapy in case you are interested in pursuing the social mindfulness lines of thought that I have introduced throughout.

Overview of the book

Being mindful involves giving open, curious attention to the way that things are, rather than attempting to avoid or grasp hold of any aspect of experience. In this way it differs from common patterns of going on autopilot; responding in mindless, habitual ways; getting caught up in cravings; or engaging in experiential avoidance. The book tried to draw fairly equally on three main sources of information about mindfulness: Buddhist writing, mindful forms of therapy, and research.

We have seen how mindfulness comes from Buddhist philosophy, which regards suffering as rooted in our attempts to get and maintain what we want (attachment) and to avoid and eradicate what we don't want (aversion). Mindful practices are about cultivating a different way of being through meditation and through noticing ourselves and our experiences in a gentle, curious way. Many have argued that mindfulness is intrinsically linked to other aspects of Buddhist philosophy, such as compassion, wisdom and commitment to ethical action.

Buddhist understandings and practices have been adapted to western contexts through processes of secularisation (stripping out some of the religious elements) and psychologisation (integrating the ideas with western psychologies and psychotherapies). For example, most western counselling highlights the way in which patterns laid down in our past become solidified through repetition in ways that limit us. Mindfully attending to our responses can reveal such patterns and open up alternative possibilities. As therapists we can engage with mindfulness through teaching it to clients, through practising it ourselves, and/or through cultivating mindful therapeutic relationships. Mindful understandings and practices have been integrated with cognitive-behavioural, humanistic and psychodynamic approaches, but it is important to be aware of some of the tensions involved in such integration.

Throughout the book we have encountered various mindful practices. These include:

- Breathing (Introduction).
- Loving-kindness, engaging in everyday tasks mindfully, and the three-minute breathing space (Chapter 1).
- Compassion and equanimity (Chapter 2).
- Thought meditations and mindful approaches to the self (Chapter 3).
- Mindful enquiry (Chapter 4).
- Shikano memory meditation (Chapter 5).
- Slow-walking and vedana feeling tones (Chapter 6).
- Urge surfing (Chapter 7).
- Meditation on sounds or visual stimulus (Chapter 8).

- Body sweep (Chapter 9).
- Tonglen and insight dialogue (Chapter 10).

Whilst suffering from all the usual difficulties of evaluating the effectiveness of therapies, and the additional problems inherent in trying to pin down and agree upon exactly what mindfulness is, research so far suggests that mindful one-to-one and group therapies are helpful in addressing most of the common issues which people present to counsellors and psychotherapists. We have explored, in detail, the mindful ideas and practices that might be helpful when working with depression, anxiety, addictions, 'psychotic' experiences, problems with eating, sleeping, pain and sex, and relationship difficulties.

Throughout our exploration of different issues we have highlighted some of the limitations of mindful therapy as well as some of the ways in which mindful practices may need to be adapted to different individuals, issues and groups.

Things to be aware of

We have seen that there is a balance to be struck between respect for the original Buddhist theories and practices that are being drawn upon and adaptation to new, often western, cultural contexts. It is important to think carefully about which aspects are intrinsic to mindfulness and which might be adapted using 'skilful means' to different cultures or individuals. We don't want to dilute or lose vital aspects, but we do need to find ways to make the ideas and practices accessible and explicable to clients (see Chapters 1, 2 and 3). We might, for example, consider the words that we use to describe and explain mindfulness, and the writers and thinkers who we draw upon. It is important to be respectful of clients' existing beliefs, practices and rituals, and to think about the aspects of mindfulness that will particularly speak to them (e.g. perhaps the neuroscientific or cognitive psychological aspects for some, and the more spiritual and creative elements for others).

One thing that has been emphasised throughout is that it is important not to slide into 'doing mindfulness' in self-perfecting and berating ways. Pema Chödrön (2001, pp. 89–90) reminds us how easy it is to engage in meditation and other trainings in ways which become 'one more way to feel that we never measure up'. This can happen, for example, if we aim to become perfectly mindful or to escape our sense that we are a bad person, or if we use 'being mindful' to avoid really engaging with the difficult stuff of our lives. Of this tendency she also says 'I'm not meaning to imply this is unusual. Welcome to the human race'! Equally she warns against the opposite scenario of using mindfulness to feel special and superior to other, less mindful, people. There is certainly a tendency for people who are rather evangelical about mindfulness to give off an air of superiority. This can particularly manifest itself in a kind of rather deliberately calm, compassionate manner, which can become quite passive-aggressive due to an avoidance of anything approaching anger or directness (see Chapter 6)[1]. We need to watch out if we find ourselves believing that we are more mindful than others, because this in itself suggests that we probably are not!

Drawing on a pluralistic approach to therapy, we've mentioned that different things work for different people at different times, so it is important not to be too rigid in the practices that we try to follow ourselves or that we recommend to clients. For example, we've seen how practices involving movement can be particularly good for anxiety, those involving sounds of visual stimulus might help with 'psychotic' experience, and perhaps writing practices can be useful for those who find externalising their thoughts and feelings to be helpful. Again, though, we shouldn't be too rigid in our assumptions of what works best, as this will vary between people as well.

One thing that has struck me recently is that sitting meditation emerged in a context where most people probably spent much of their daily lives on their feet and in forms of physical labour. In a current western context – where many people spend much of the day sitting down in offices and supermarket check-outs, watching television or surfing the net, and travelling and commuting on planes, trains and automobiles – it may be that more sitting is not quite what we need, and it is worth considering some of the more physically active forms of practice (see Chapters 6 and 9). Also, given that many people in western cultures spend lots of the time inside, we might want to consider outdoor practices (see Figure 11.1).

It can also be worth asking ourselves why we are drawn to particular practices. Given the mindful aim of leaning into difficult experiences, if we feel very comfortable sitting alone then we might need to supplement that with more challenging practices (e.g. mindful group interactions, or physical activities). However, for those of us who struggle to remain still and to be by ourselves, sitting meditation may be just what we need.

---

[1]For more on the tensions between being mindfully kind and mindfully honest, see http://socialmindfulness.wordpress.com/2011/09/15/mindfulness-and-social-engagement-communication.

Figure 11.1 Spacious meditation

Social mindfulness

This idea of how mindfulness fits into our current cultural context brings us on to the concept of social mindfulness, which has been introduced in several of the chapters. Whilst I hope that this book has synthesised much of what has been written (very well) elsewhere about mindful counselling and psychotherapy in a way that will be helpful to the beginner, I also hope that the book adds something new to the area at this critical point for taking stock of the convergence of Buddhism and psychotherapy (see Introduction). What I hope is specific to my writing is the emphasis on the social, and on thinking critically about our own assumptions and understandings. I believe that these things follow naturally from any kind of mindful engagement with counselling and psychotherapy, and with our lives in general.

Mindfulness actually emerged as part of a project of social reformation. In his philosophy, Siddhattha Gotama (the Buddha) was explicitly critiquing the hierarchical systems of power that were in operation in his society, notably caste systems wherein people inherited their birthrights and were fixed in this social position for the entirety of their lives. He challenged this idea, arguing that we become particular kinds of people through the actions we perform as we live (karma), whether wholesome or unwholesome.

As I suggested in Chapter 2, it is important to retain the project of mindfulness as social activism or radical politics because it seems highly likely that its current popularity is, at least in part, due to the fact that it counters many of the problematic ways of being that are inherent in current consumer capitalist, individualistic, neoliberal society. Notably we have considered how being mindful offers a different approach to the self-monitoring, self-judging, self-critical stance that we are encouraged to take by consumer culture and mainstream media which attempts to convince us that we are lacking in ways that it can fill. Instead of comparing ourselves unfavourably against others, constantly seeking to self-improve, trying to present 'successful' selves to the world (and criticising ourselves) we engage in radical acceptance of ourselves and others, deliberately facing up to our vulnerabilities and communicating them, as well as cultivating self-compassion and loving-kindness for all.

This is why, throughout the book, I have emphasised the need for a biopsychosocial understanding of mental health and human experience. Not only is this in line with the non-dualistic Buddhist way of understanding experience, but it also enables us to bring in the social aspect which is a vital component of suffering.

And herein lies the challenge of mindfulness for western psychotherapy. If we allow ourselves to fully engage with it, rather than simply using some of the practices as bolt-on techniques to our existing approaches[2], then we cannot fail to be altered by it, as therapists and as human beings. Here are just a few of the mindful challenges to conventional western psychotherapy that we have touched upon in this book:

- Non-dualistic understandings replace cause-and-effect relationships with the notion that things 'co-arise'. This challenges our views of mental health problems as simply caused, for example, by physiological problems, or early childhood experiences (see Chapter 4).
- Static conceptualisations of the self (such as fixed personality types, disorders or attachment styles) are challenged by the notion that the self is plural and always in a process of becoming (see Chapter 3).
- Mindful approaches warn against becoming identified with certain feelings or stuck in certain stories. This challenges the use of

---

[2]For more on the risks of this in secularised and psychologised mindfulness, see http://socialmindfulness.wordpress.com/2012/02/12/how-social-is-your-mindfulness.

diagnostic labels or universal explanations for particular difficulties, and suggests instead that we need to be open to the multiplicity of meaning and the various stories that are possible through the same set of life experiences (see Chapter 5).

- From a mindful perspective we are all interconnected and therefore we cannot think in 'us and them' ways about our clients (see Chapters 8 and 10).
- We need to be quite cautious of any therapeutic practices that encourage experiential avoidance (e.g. calming people rather than engaging with anxiety) or which implicitly give the impression that people need to change rather than accepting themselves as they are (e.g. correcting dysfunctional thoughts or fixing psychopathological behaviours) (see Chapter 3 for more on the dialectic between acceptance and change).
- The biopsychosocial, non-dualistic approach highlights the intrinsically interrelated nature of bio, psycho and social elements of experience. Therefore we need to be very wary of practices and understandings which completely internalise suffering rather than locating it in its social context.

This latter point is vital for western psychotherapy as there is a real danger that counselling, group therapy, self-help books and the like all reinforce the view that problems are internally caused and need fixing (by the individual themselves, with the help of experts). They generally all address the individual (e.g. rather than the dyad, the family, the group, the community or the culture), and they tend to locate problems and treatments in the internal, rather than the external, world. There is a particular danger in the one-to-one therapy context: in revealing their own pain and vulnerability to somebody who reveals nothing about themselves (for good reasons regarding boundaries), there is a risk that clients will be even more drawn into painful comparisons of their flawed self against some imaginary ideal of perfection. If we are not careful we can easily exacerbate the self-monitoring, self-perfecting way of being that is so much part of current suffering, rather than reducing it[3].

An important and often-quoted passage of the teachings of the Buddha goes like this:

Do not believe in anything simply because you have heard it.

Do not believe in traditions because they have been handed down for many generations.

---

[3]This ties in with critiques of western psychotherapy from writers such as Foucault, Laing, Furedi, Masson, and Smail. See http://rewritingtherules.word press.com/2011/10/16/mental-health-beyond-the-1-in-4/#more-531.

Do not believe in anything because it is spoken and rumoured by many.

Do not believe in anything simply because it is found written in your religious books.

Do not believe in anything merely on the authority of your teachers and elders.

But after observation and analysis, when you find that anything agrees with reason, and is conducive to the good and benefit of one and all,

Then accept it and live to it.[4]

Full mindful engagement calls upon us to think critically such that we can see what we are taking for granted and start to 'swim against the stream' (S. Batchelor, 2010: 125) of our habitual ways of thinking and behaving. This involves noticing the ways in which culturally dominant and socially accepted understandings and practices flow through us, and opens up the possibility of doing things differently.

This leads us to a final point, that if current social and cultural messages are a major element of the suffering that we – and our clients – are experiencing, if mindfulness calls upon us to think critically and to swim against the stream, and if there are some reasons to be cautious of the ways in which conventional psychotherapy alone may exacerbate rather than ameliorate distress, is the mindful therapist called upon to engage on a social, as well as an individual level?

My own answer to this question is 'yes'. I believe that mindful theory and practice, and mindful therapy with our clients, all point towards the importance of changing elements of society as well as helping the individuals who live in it as it currently stands. I agree with many who have argued that ethical action is intrinsically linked to mindfulness, and that we cannot have the one without the other (see Grossman, 2010).

It seems clear that the current ways in which we are encouraged to treat ourselves and others is a major part of the problem of human suffering, and that social engagement needs to be part of the solution. In our own worlds of therapy this means turning the critical lens back on our own practices and theories, and those of our teachers and overseeing bodies. On a wider level we might get involved, for example, in social activism, community projects around mental health, political change and putting out alternative messages about various forms of distress in the form of books, leaflets and blogs, for example. Of course the dialectic between acceptance and change is an important one to keep in mind here, as is the importance of knowing when we need to engage and when we need to retreat and compassionately

---

[4]Kalama Sutta, as quoted in Schipper (2012: 203).

replenish our energies and get support ourselves[5]. But to be mindful we need to be aware, and that includes ourselves and our society as well as our clients.

Further reading

You can read more in the ongoing social mindfulness project on the Social Mindfulness blog. Here you can also find information about related projects, definitions of terms and further references: http://socialmindfulness.wordpress.com.

My own attempts at combining individual mindful approaches to relationships with ourselves and others, with calls for social change, can be found in my book:

Barker, M. (2012). *Rewriting the rules: An integrative guide to love, sex and relationships*. London: Routledge.

and at my blog: www.rewriting-the-rules.com.

---

[5]For more on the importance of both internal practice and social engagement, see http://socialmindfulness.wordpress.com/2011/09/14/mindfulness-a-strategy-for-social-engagement/#more-40.

Bibliography

Adams, K. (1990). *Journal to the self*. New York, NY: Grand Central Publishing.

Alexander, B. (2010). *The globalization of addiction*. Oxford: Oxford University Press.

Analayo (2003). *Satipatthana: The direct path to realization*. Birmingham: Windhorse.

Archer, M. S. (2003). *Structure, agency and the internal conversation*. Cambridge: Cambridge University Press.

Bach, P. A., Gaudiano, B., Pankey, J., Herbert, J. D., & Hayes, S. C. (2006). Acceptance, mindfulness, values, and psychosis: Applying acceptance and commitment therapy (ACT) to the chronically mentally ill. In R. A. Baer (Ed.), *Mindfulness-based treatment approaches: Clinician's guide to evidence base and applications*. (pp. 93–116). San Diego, CA: Elsevier Academic.

Baer, R. A. (2011). Measuring mindfulness. *Contemporary Buddhism, 12* (1), 241–261.

Baer, R. A., Smith, G. T., Hopkins, J., Krietmeyer, J., & Toney, L. (2006). Using self-report assessment methods to explore facets of mindfulness. *Assessment, 13*, 27–45.

Barker, M. (2010a). Self-care and relationship conflict. *Sexual and Relationship Therapy, 25* (1), 37–47.

Barker, M. (2010b). Sociocultural issues. In M. Barker, A. Vossler, & D. Langdridge (Eds.), *Understanding counselling and psychotherapy*. (pp.211–233). London: Sage.

Barker, M. (2011a). Mindfulness: It ain't what you do it's the way that you do it. Accessed 25/1/12 from: http://socialmindfulness.wordpress.com/2011/04/03/mindfulness-it-aint-what-you-do-its-the-way-that-you-do-it/.

Barker, M. (2011b). Existential sex therapy. *Sexual and Relationship Therapy, 26* (1), 33–47.

Barker, M. (2012a). *Rewriting the rules: An integrative guide to sex, love and relationships*. London: Routledge.

Barker, M. (2012b). *Tuning out, turning in – Turning out, tuning in*. Accessed 10/6/12 from: http://socialmindfulness.wordpress.com/2012/05/17/tuning-out-turning-in-turning-out-tuning-in/.

Barker, M., & Heckert, J. (2011). Privilege & oppression, conflict & compassion. *The Sociological Imagination*. Accessed 14/6/12 from: http://sociological imagination.org/archives/6520.

Barker, M., Vossler, A., & Langdridge, D. (2010). *Understanding counselling & psychotherapy*. London: Sage.

Barkham, M., & Barker, M. (2010). Outcome research. In M. Barker, A. Vossler, & D. Langdridge, (Eds.), *Understanding counselling and psychotherapy*. (pp.281–305). London: Sage.

Barnes, R., Moss, D., & Stanley, S. (in prep). 'Shy' stories for the mindful: Making space for alternative theory, research and practice of mindfulness-based mental health care interventions.

Batchelor, M. (2001). *Meditation for life*. London: Frances Lincoln.

Batchelor, M. (2007). *Let go: A Buddhist guide to breaking free of habits*. Somerville, MA: Wisdom.

Batchelor, M. (2010). *The spirit of the Buddha*. New Haven, CT: Yale University Press.

Batchelor, M. (2011). Meditation and mindfulness. *Contemporary Buddhism*, *12* (1), 157–164.

Batchelor, S. (1983). *Alone with others: An existential approach to Buddhism*. New York, NY: Grove Press.

Batchelor, S. (1997). *Buddhism without beliefs*. London: Bloomsbury.

Batchelor, S. (2010). *Confession of a Buddhist atheist*. New York, NY: Spiegel & Grau.

Batten, S. V., Orsillo, S. M., & Walser, R. D. (2005). Acceptance and mindfulness-based approaches to the treatment of posttraumatic stress disorder. In S. M. Orsillo, & L. Roemer (Eds.). *Acceptance and mindfulness-based approaches to anxiety*. (pp. 241–269). Boston, MA: Springer.

Bazzano, M. (2009). The Buddha as a fully functioning person: Toward a person-centered perspective on mindfulness. *Person-Centered & Experiential Psychotherapies*, *10* (2), 116–128.

BBC (2012). *The science of silence*. Accessed 31/5/12 from: http://news.bbc.co.uk/today/hi/today/newsid_9671000/9671158.stm.

Bein, A. (2008). *The Zen of helping: Spiritual practices for mindful and open-hearted practice*. Hoboken, NJ: Wiley.

Bentall, R. (2009). *Doctoring the mind*. London: Allen Lane.

Bien, T. (2006). *Mindful therapy: A guide for therapists and helping professionals*. Boston, MA: Wisdom Publications.

Bien, T., & Bien, B. (2002). *Mindful recovery: A spiritual path to healing from addiction*. New York, NY: Wiley.

Bishop, S. R., Lau, M., Shapiro, S., Carlson, L., Anderson, N. D., Carmody, J., Segal, Z. V., Abbey, S., Speca, M., Velting, D., & Devins, G. (2004). Mindfulness: A proposed operational definition. *Clinical Psychology: Science and Practice*, *11*, 230–241.

Bodhi, B. (2011). What does mindfulness really mean? A canonical perspective. *Contemporary Buddhism*, *12* (1), 19–39.

Bowen, S., Chawla, N., & Marlatt, G. A. (2010). *Mindfulness-based relapse prevention: A clinician's guide.* New York, NY: Guilford Press.

Brantley, J. (2007). *Calming your anxious mind.* Oakland, CA: New Harbinger.

Brazier, D. (1995). *Zen therapy: A Buddhist approach to psychotherapy.* London: Robinson.

Brazier, D. (2001). *Zen therapy.* London: Robinson.

BBC (2012). *The science of silence.* Accessed from http://news.bbc.co.uk/today/hi/today/newsid_9671000/9671158.stm on 31/5/12.

Brotto, L., & Barker, M. (Eds.). (in press). Mindful sexual and relationship therapy. *Sexual and Relationship Therapy.*

Brotto, L. A., Krychman, M., & Jacobson, P. (2008). Eastern approaches for enhancing women's sexuality: Mindfulness, acupuncture, and yoga. *Journal of Sexual Medicine, 5,* 2741–2748.

Brown, B. (2008). *I thought it was just me (but it isn't).* New York, NY: Gotham.

Buber, M. (1958). *I and thou.* Edinburgh: Clark.

Burch, V. (2008). *Living well with pain and illness: The mindful way to free yourself from suffering.* London: Piatkus.

Carey, N. (2012). *The epigenetics revolution.* London:.

Carrellas, B. (2007). *Urban tantra.* Berkeley, CA: Celestial Arts.

Chadwick, P. (2006). *Person-based cognitive therapy for distressing psychosis.* Hoboken, NJ: Wiley Blackwell.

Chadwick, P., Hughes, S., Russel, D., Russel, I., & Dagnan, D. (2009). Mindfulness groups for distressing voices and paranoia: A replication and randomized feasibility trial. *Behavioural and Cognitive Psychotherapy, 37,* 403–412.

Chadwick, P., Newman Taylor, K., & Abba, N. (2005). Mindfulness groups for people with psychosis. *Behavioural and cognitive psychotherapy, 33,* 351–359.

Chieasa, A., & Serretti, A. (2009). Mindfulness-based stress reduction for stress management in healthy people: A review and meta-analysis. *The Journal of Alternative and Complementary Medicine, 15*(5), 593–600.

Chiesa, A., & Serretti, A. (2010). A systematic review of neurobiological and clinical features of mindfulness meditation. *Psychological Medicine, 40,* 1239–1252.

Chiesa, A., & Serretti, A. (2011). Mindfulness-based interventions for chronic pain: A systematic review of the evidence. *The Journal of Alternative and Complementary Medicine, 17* (1), 83–93.

Chödrön, P. (1994). *The places that scare you: A guide to fearlessness.* London: HarperCollins.

Chödrön, P. (2001). *The wisdom of no escape: How to love yourself and your world.* London: HarperCollins.

Chödrön, P. (2002). *Comfortable with uncertainty.* London: Shambala.

Christopher, J. C., & Maris, J. A. (2010). Integrating mindfulness as self-care into counselling and psychotherapy training. *Counselling and Psychotherapy Research, 10* (2), 114–125.

Claessens, M. (2009). Mindfulness and existential therapy. *Existential Analysis, 20* (1), 109–119.

Cohen, E. (2010). From the Bhodi tree, to the analyst's couch, then into the MRI scanner: The psychologisation of Buddhism. *Annual Review of Critical Psychology, 8,* 97–119.

Coltart, N. (1998). Slouching towards Buddhism: in conversation with Anthony Molino. In A. Molino (Ed.). *The couch and the tree.* (pp. 170–182). New York, NY: North Point Press.

COI (no date) *The Community of Interbeing Manual of Practice.* UK: Community of Interbeing. Available online at: http://interbeing.org.uk/manual.

Cooper, M. (2008). *Essential research findings in counselling and psychotherapy: The facts are friendly.* London: Sage.

Cooper, M., & McLeod, J. (2011). *Pluralistic counselling and psychotherapy.* London: Sage.

Corstens, D., Longden, E., & May, R. (2012). Talking with voices: Exploring what is expressed by the voices people hear. *Psychosis, 4* (2), 95–104.

Crane, R. (2009). *Mindfulness-based cognitive therapy.* London: Routledge.

Crowe, M., & Ridley, J. (2000). *Therapy with couples: A behavioural-systems approach to couple relationship and sexual problems.* Oxford: Blackwell.

Csíkszentmihályi, M. (1991). *Flow.* London: HarperPerennial.

das Nair, R., & Butler, C. (2012). *Intersectionality, sexuality and psychological therapies.* Hoboken, NJ: Wiley-Blackwell.

Davidson, R. J. (2012). *The emotional life of your brain.* London: Hodder & Stoughton.

Davidson, R. J., Kabat-Zinn, J., Schumacher, J., Rosenkranz, M., Muller, D., Santorelli, S. F., Urbanowski, F., Harrington, A., Bonus, K., & Sheridan, J. F. (2003). Alterations in brain and immune function produced by mindfulness meditation. *Psychosomatic Medicine, 65,* 564–570.

Davis, L., & Kurzban, S. (2012). Mindfulness-based treatment for people with severe mental illness: A literature review. *American Journal of Psychiatric Rehabilitation, 15* (2), 202–232.

de Botton, A. (2004). *Status anxiety.* London: Penguin.

Del Busso, L., & Reavey, P. (2011). Moving beyond the surface: A post-structuralist phenomenology of young women's embodied experiences in everyday life. *Psychology & Sexuality.* Published online DOI 10.1086/19419899.2011.589866.

Depraz, N., Varela, F., & Vermersch, P. (2003). *On becoming aware: A pragmatics of experiencing.* Amsterdam: Benjamins.

Dreyfuss, G. (2011). Is mindfulness present-centred and non-judgemental? A discussion of the cognitive dimensions of mindfulness. *Contemporary Buddhism, 12* (1), 41–54.

Dunn, B., Hartigan, J., & Mikulas, W. (1999). Concentration and mindfulness meditations: Unique forms of consciousness? *Applied Psychophysiology and Biofeedback, 24,* 147–165.

Dunne, J. (2011). Toward an understanding of non-dual mindfulness. *Contemporary Buddhism, 12* (1), 71–88.

Epstein, M. (2001). *Psychotherapy without the self: A Buddhist perspective.* New Haven, CT: Yale University Press.

Epstein, M. (2005). *Open to desire: The truth about what the Buddha taught.* New York, NY: Gotham.

Etherington, K. (2004). *Becoming a reflexive researcher: Using our selves in research.* London: Jessica Kingsley.

Favazzo, A. R. (1996). *Bodies under siege: Self-mutilation and body modification in culture and psychiatry.* Baltimore, MD: Johns Hopkins University Press.

Flaxman, P. E., Blackledge, J. T., & Bond, F. W. (2011). *Acceptance and commitment therapy.* London: Routledge.

Fox, N. (2012). *The body.* Cambridge: Polity Press.

Frankl, V. ([1946] 2004). *Man's search for meaning.* London: Rider.

Freud, S. ([1912] 1961). Recommendations to physicians practising psychoanalysis. In J. Strachley (Ed. and Trans.). *The standard edition of the complete psychological works of Sigmund Freud* (Vol. 21). London: Hogarth Press.

Fromm, E., Suzuki, D. T., & Martino, R. de (1970). *Zen Buddhism and psychoanalysis.* London: HarperCollins.

Fulton, P. R. (2005). Mindfulness as clinical training. In C. K. Germer, R. D. Siegel, & P. R. Fulton (Eds.). *Mindfulness and psychotherapy.* (pp. 55–72). New York, NY: Guilford Press.

Fulton, P. R. (2008). Anatta: Self, non-self and the therapist. In S. F. Hick, & T. Bien (Eds.). *Mindfulness and the therapeutic relationship.* (pp. 55–71). New York, NY: Guilford Press.

Gehart, D., & McCollum, E. E. (2008). Inviting therapeutic presence. In S. F. Hick, & T. Bien (Eds.). *Mindfulness and the therapeutic relationship.* (pp. 176–194). New York, NY: Guilford Press.

Gendlin, E. T. (2003). *Focusing: How to gain direct access to your body's knowledge.* London: Random House.

Gergen, K. (2009). *Relational being: Beyond self and community.* Oxford: Oxford University Press.

Germer, C. K. (2005a). Mindfulness. In C. K. Germer, R. D. Siegel, & P. R. Fulton (Eds.). *Mindfulness and* psychotherapy. (pp. 3–27). New York, NY: Guilford Press.

Germer, C. K. (2005b). Teaching mindfulness in therapy. In C. K. Germer, R. D. Siegel, & P. R. Fulton (Eds.). *Mindfulness and psychotherapy.* (pp. 113–129). New York, NY: Guilford Press.

Germer, C. K. (2005c). Anxiety disorders: Befriending fear. In C. K. Germer, R. D. Siegel, & P. R. Fulton (Eds.). *Mindfulness and psychotherapy.* (pp. 152–172). New York, NY: Guilford Press. p.154–5.

Germer, C. K. (2009). *The mindful path to self-compassion.* New York, NY: Guilford Press.

Germer, C. K., Siegel, R. D., & Fulton, P. R. (Eds.). (2005). *Mindfulness and psychotherapy*. New York, NY: Guilford Press.

Gethin, R. (2011). On some definitions of mindfulness. *Contemporary Buddhism, 12* (1), 263–279.

Gibbons, S. ([1932] 2006). *Cold comfort farm*. London: Penguin.

Gilbert, P. (2010a). *The compassionate mind*. London: Constable.

Gilbert, P. (2010b). *Compassion focused therapy*. London: Routledge.

Goldberg, N. (1998). *Writing down the bones*. Boston, MA: Shambhala.

Goldmeier, D., & Mears, A. J. (2010). Meditation: A review of its use in Western medicine and, in particular, its role in the management of sexual dysfunction. *Current Psychiatry Review, 6* (1).

Goleman, D. (2003). *Destructive emotions and how we can overcome them: A dialogue with the Dalai Lama*. London: Bloomsbury.

Goss, K. (2011). *The compassionate mind approach to beating overeating using compassion focused therapy*. London: Robinson.

Grossman, P. (2010). Mindfulness for psychologists: Paying kind attention to the perceptible. *Mindfulness, 1,* 87–97.

Grossman, P., & Van Dam, N. T. (2011). Mindfulness, by any other name ...: Trials and tribulation of Sati in Western psychology and science. *Contemporary Buddhism, 12* (1), 219–239.

Gumley, A., Brachler, C., Laithwaite, H., MacBeth, A., & Gilbert, P. (2010) A compassion focused model of recovery after psychosis. *International Journal of Cognitive Therapy, 3* (2), 186–201.

Hagen, S. (1997). *Buddhism plain and simple*. London: Penguin.

Halifax, J. (2009). *Being with dying: Cultivating compassion and fearlessness in the presence of death*. London: Shambhala.

Hannan, S. E., & Tolin, D. F. (2005). Mindfulness- and acceptance-based behavior for obsessive-compulsive disorder. In S. M. Orsillo, & L. Roemer (Eds.). *Acceptance and mindfulness-based approaches to anxiety.* (pp. 271–299). Boston, MA: Springer.

Hayes, S. (2005). *Get out of your mind and into your life: The new acceptance and commitment therapy*. Oakland, CA: New Harbinger.

Hayes, S. C., Follette, V. M., & Linehan, M. M. (Eds.). (2004). *Mindfulness and acceptance: Expanding the cognitive-behavioural tradition*. New York, NY: Guilford Press.

Hayes, S. C., Strosahl, K. D., & Wilson, K. G. (1999). *Acceptance and commitment therapy*. New York, NY: Guilford Press.

Heaversage, J., & Halliwell, E. (2012). *The mindful manifesto*. Carlsbad, CA: Hay House.

Herbert, J. D., & Cardaciotto, L. (2005). An acceptance and mindfulness-based perspective on social anxiety disorder. In S. M. Orsillo, & L. Roemer (Eds.). *Acceptance and mindfulness-based approaches to anxiety.* (pp. 189–212). Boston, MA: Springer.

Hick, S. F. (2008). Cultivating therapeutic relationships: The role of mindfulness. In S. F. Hick, & Y. Bien (Eds.). *Mindfulness and the therapeutic relationship.* (pp.3–18). New York, NY: Guilford Press.

Hick, S. F., & Bien, T. (Eds.). (2008). *Mindfulness and the therapeutic relationship*. New York, NY: Guilford Press.

Hickey, W. S. (2010). Meditation as medicine: A critique. *Cross currents*, June, 168–184.

Hofmann, S. G., Sawyer, A. T., Witt, A. A., & Oh, D. (2010). The effect of mindfulness-based therapy on anxiety and depression: A meta-analytic review. *Journal of Counselling and Clinical Psychology, 78* (2), 169–183.

Hölzel, B. K., Lazar, S. W., Gard, T., Schuman-Olivier, Z., Vago, D. R., & Ott, U. (2011). How does mindfulness meditation work? Proposing mechanisms of action from a conceptual and neural perspective. *Perspectives on Psychological Science, 6* (6), 537–559.

Horney, K. (1987). *Final lectures*. (pp.20–21). New York, NY: Norton.

Jacobs-Stewart, T. (2010). *Mindfulness and the 12 steps: Living recovery in the present moment*. Center City, MN: Hazelden.

James, O. (2007). *Affluenza*. London: Vermilion.

Jeffers, S. ([1987] 2007). *Feel the fear and do it anyway*. London: Vermilion.

Johnson, D. P., Penn, D. L, Frederickson, B. L., Meyer, P. S., Kring, A. M., & Brantley, M. (2009). Loving-kindness meditation to enhance recovery from negative symptoms of schizophrenia. *Journal of Clinical Psychology: In Session, 65* (5), 499–509.

Johnstone, L. (2000). *Users and abusers of psychiatry*. London: Routledge.

Kabat-Zinn, J. (1982). An outpatient program in behavioral medicine for chronic pain patients based on the practice of mindfulness meditation: Theoretical considerations and preliminary results. *General Hospital Psychiatry, 4* (1), 33–47.

Kabat-Zinn, J. (1994). *Wherever you go, there you are: Mindfulness meditation for everyday life*. London: Piatkus.

Kabat-Zinn, J. (1996). *Full catastrophe living: How to cope with stress, pain and illness using mindfulness meditation*. London: Piatkus.

Kabat-Zinn, J. (2011). Some reflections on the origins of MBSR, skillful means, and the trouble with maps. *Contemporary Buddhism, 12* (1), 281–306.

Kahneman, D. (2012). *Thinking fast and slow*. London: Penguin.

Kasamatsu, A., & Hirai, T. (1966). An electroencephalographic study on the Zen meditation (zazen). *Journal of the American Institute of Hypnosis, 14* (3), 107–114.

Kasl, C. S. (1999). *If the Buddha dated*. New York, NY: Compass.

Kasl, C. S. (2001) *If the Buddha married*. New York, NY: Compass.

Kawai, H, (1996). *Buddhism and the art of psychotherapy*. Austin, TA: Texas A&M University Press.

Keane, H. (2002). *What's wrong with addiction?* Melbourne: Melbourne University Press.

Keown, D. (1996). *Buddhism: A very short introduction*. Oxford: Oxford University Press.

Kornfield, J., Dass, R., & Miyuki, M. (1979). Psychological adjustment is not liberation. In A. Molino (Ed.). (1999). *The couch and the tree: Dialogues in psychoanalysis and Buddhism*. (pp. 96–106). London: Constable.

Koshikawa, F., Kuboki, A., & Ishii, Y. (2006). Shikanho: A Zen-based cognitive-behavioural approach. In M. Kwee, K. J. Gergen, & F. Koshikawa (Eds.). *Horizons in Buddhist psychology*. (pp. 185–195). Chagrin Falls, OH: Taos Institute Publications.

Kramer, G. (2007). *Insight dialogue*. Boston, MA: Shambhala.

Kramer, G., Meleo-Meyer, F., & Turner, M. L. (2008). Cultivating mindfulness in relationship. In S. F. Hick, & T. Bien (Eds.). *Mindfulness and the therapeutic relationship*. (pp. 195–214). New York, NY: Guilford Press.

Kwee, M. G. T. (Ed.). (2010). *New horizons in Buddhist psychology: Relational Buddhism for collaborative practitioners*. Chagrin Falls, OH: Taos Institute Publications.

Langdridge, D. (2013). *Existential counselling and psychotherapy*. London: Sage.

Langer, E. J. (1989). *Mindfulness*. Reading, MA: Perseus.

Langer, E. J. (2009). *Counter clockwise: Mindful health and the power of possibility*. London: Hodder & Stoughton.

Lazar, S. W. (2005). Mindfulness research. In C. K. Germer, R. D. Siegel, & P. R. Fulton (Eds.). *Mindfulness and psychotherapy*. (pp. 220–238). New York, NY: Guilford Press.

Levitt, J. T., & Karekla, M. (2005). Integrating acceptance and mindfulness with cognitive behavioural treatment for panic disorder. In S. M. Orsillo, & L. Roemer (Eds.). *Acceptance and mindfulness-based approaches to anxiety*. (pp. 165–188). Boston, MA: Springer.

Lewis, G. (2002). *Sunbathing in the rain*. London: HarperCollins.

Loy, D. (1996). *Lack and transcendence: The problem of death and life in psychotherapy, existentialism and Buddhism*. New York, NY: Humanity.

Loy, D. (2008). *Money, sex, war, karma: Notes for a Buddhist revolution*. Boston, MA: Wisdom.

Mace, C. (2008). *Mindfulness and mental health*. New York, NY: Routledge.

Maex, E. (2011). The Buddhist roots of mindfulness training: A practitioners view. *Contemporary Buddhism, 12* (1), 165–175.

Magid, B. (2008). *Ending the pursuit of happiness*. Boston, MA: Wisdom.

Marlatt, G. A., & Donovan, D. A. (Eds.). (2008). *Relapse prevention: Maintenance strategies in the treatment of addictive behaviors*. New York, NY: Guilford Press.

Marlatt, G. A., Bowen, S., Chawla, N., & Witkiewitz, K. (2008). Mindfulness-based relapse prevention for substance abusers. In S. F. Hick, & T. Bien (Eds.). *Mindfulness and the therapeutic relationship*. (pp. 107–121). New York, NY: Guilford Press.

Marlatt, G. A., Witkiewitz, K., Dillworth, T. M., Bowen, S., Parks, G. A., Macpherson, L. M., Lonczak, H. S., Larimer, M. E., Simpson, T., Blume, A. W., & Crutcher, R. (2004). Vipassana meditation as a treatment for alcohol and drug use disorders. In S. Hayes, V. M. Follette, & M. M. Linehan (Eds.). *Mindfulness and acceptance: Expanding the cognitive-behavioural tradition*. New York, NY: Guilford Press.

Maté, G. (2008). *In the realm of hungry ghosts: Close encounters with addiction.* Toronto: Random House.

May, R. (2007). Working outside the diagnostic frame. *The Psychologist, 20* (5), 300–301.

McCracken, L. M., Gauntlett-Gilbert, J., & Vowles, K. E. (2007). The role of mindfulness in a contextual cognitive-behavioral analysis of chronic pain-related suffering and disability, *Pain, 131,* 63–69.

McLeod, J. (2010). Process research. In M. Barker, A. Vossler, & D. Langdridge, (Eds.). *Understanding counselling and psychotherapy.* (pp.307–326). London: Sage.

McNamara, R. (2012). *Strengthening the body-mind.* Accessed 14/3/12 from: www.buddhistgeeks.com/2012/03/bg-249-strengthening-the-body-mind/.

Mearns, D., & Cooper, M. (2005). *Working at relational depth in counselling and psychotherapy.* London: Sage.

Mills, N. (2010). Learning to become centred and grounded and let the voices come and go. In I. Clarke (Ed.). *Psychosis and spirituality: Consolidating the new paradigm.* Hoboken, NJ: Wiley Blackwell.

Molino, A. (Ed.). (1999). *The couch and the tree: Dialogues in psychoanalysis and Buddhism.* London: Constable.

Moore, J., & Shoemark, A. (2010). Mindfulness and the person-centred approach. In J. Leonardi (Ed.). *The human being fully alive.* Ross-on-Wye: PCCS.

Morgan, S. P. (2005). Depression: Turning towards life. In C. K. Germer, R. D. Siegel, & P. R. Fulton (Eds.). *Mindfulness and psychotherapy.* (pp. 130–151). New York, NY: Guilford Press.

Morgan, W. D., & Morgan, S. (2005). Cultivating attention and empathy. In C. K. Germer, R. D. Siegel, & P. R. Fulton (Eds.). *Mindfulness and psychotherapy.* (pp. 73–90). New York, NY: Guilford Press.

Moss, D., & Barnes, R. (2008). Birdsong and footprints: Tangibility and intangibility in a mindfulness research project. *Reflective Practice, 9* (1), 11–22.

Murray C. J. L., & Lopez, A. D. (1996). *The global burden of disease: A comprehensive assessment of mortality, injuries and risk factors in 1990 and projected to 2000.* Cambridge, MA: Harvard School of Public Health and the World Health Organisation.

Naish, J. (2008). *Enough.* London: Hodder & Stoughton.

Nanda, J. (2006). Knowing it in the body – 'I Thou' in therapeutic encounter. *Existential Analysis, 17* (2), 343–358.

Nanda, J. (2005). A phenomenological enquiry into the effect of meditation on therapeutic practice. *Existential Analysis, 16* (2), 322–335.

Nanda, J. (2010). Embodied integration: Reflections on mindfulness based cognitive therapy (MBCT) and a case for mindfulness based existential therapy (MBET) – a single case illustration. *Existential Analysis, 21* (2), 331–350.

Neff, K. (2011). *Self-compassion.* London: Hodder & Stoughton.

Nhat Hanh, T. ([1975] 1991). *The miracle of mindfulness.* London: Rider.

Nhat Hanh, T. (2001). *Anger.* London: Rider.

NICE (National Institute for Health and Clinical Excellence) (2000). Depression: The treatment and management of depression in adults: NICE clinical guidelines 90. London: NICE. Accessed 21/1/12 from: www.nice.org.uk/nicemedia/live/12329/45888/45888.pdf.

Nugent, P., Moss, D., Barnes, R., & Wilks, J. (2011). Clear(ing) space: Mindfulness-based reflective practice. *Reflective Practice, 12* (1), 1–13.

Olendzki, A. (2011). The construction of mindfulness. *Contemporary Buddhism, 12* (1), 55–70.

Open University, The (2010). *Addictions (Book 3 of The science of the mind: investigating mental health)*. Milton Keynes: Open University Press.

Orsillo, S. M., & Roemer, L. (Eds.). (2005). *Acceptance and mindfulness-based approaches to anxiety.* Boston, MA: Springer.

Orsillo, S. M., & Roemer, L. (2011). *The mindful way through anxiety.* New York, NY: Guilford Press.

Owen, R. (2011). *Facing the storm: Using CBT, mindfulness and acceptance to build resilience when your world's falling apart.* London: Routledge.

Parks, T. (2010). *Teach us to sit still: A sceptic's search for health and healing.* London: Vintage.

Perkins Gilman, C. ([1892] 1998). *The yellow wallpaper.* Mineola, NY: Dover.

Pilgrim, D. (2010). The diagnosis of mental health problems. In M. Barker, A. Vossler, & D. Langdridge (Eds.). *Understanding counselling and psychotherapy.* (pp.21–43). London: Sage.

Pinto, A. (2009). Mindfulness and psychosis. In F. Didonna (Ed.). *Clinical handbook of mindfulness.* (pp. 339–368). Berlin: Springer.

Pirsig, R. M. (1976). *Zen and the art of motorcycle maintenance.* London: Corgi.

Proulx, K. (2008). Experience of women with bulimia nervosa in a mindfulness-based eating disorder treatment group. *Eating Disorders, 16,* 52–72.

Rhys-Davids, T. W. ([1810] 2007). *Buddhist suttas.* Whitefish, MT: Kessinger.

Rhys-Davids, T. W. ([1890] 1963). *The questions of King Milanda.* Mineola, NY: Dover.

Richards, C. (2010). 'Them and us' in mental health services. *The Psychologist, 23* (1), 40–41.

Richards, C. (2011). Are you sitting comfortably? *The Psychologist, 24* (12), 904–906.

Richards, C., & Barker, M. (2013). *Sexuality and gender for counsellors, psychologists and health professionals: A practical guide.* London: Sage.

Rimes, K. A., & Wingrove, J. (2011). Mindfulness-based cognitive therapy for people with chronic fatigue syndrome still experiencing excessive fatigue after cognitive behaviour therapy: A pilot randomised study. *Clinical Psychology and Psychotherapy,* published online DOI: 10.1002/cpp.793.

Robbins, L., David, D., & Nurco, D. (1974). How permanent was Vietnam drug addiction? *American Journal of Public Health, 64,* 38–43.

Rogers, C. R. (1957). The necessary and sufficient conditions of therapeutic personality change. *Journal of Consulting Psychology, 21,* 95–103.

Rogers, C. R. (1980). *A way of being.* Boston, MA: Houghton Mifflin.

Rosenberg, M. B. (2003). *Nonviolent communication: A language of life.* Encinitas, CA: PuddleDancer.

Safran, J. D. (Ed.). (2003). *Psychoanalysis and Buddhism: An unfolding dialogue.* Boston, MA: Wisdom.

Safran, J. D., & Reading, R. (2008). Mindfulness, metacommunication, and affect regulation in psychoanalytic treatment. In S. F. Hick, & T. Bien (Eds.). *Mindfulness and the therapeutic relationship.* (pp. 122–140). New York, NY: Guilford Press.

Salkovskis, P. (2010). Cognitive-behavioural therapy. In M. Barker, A. Vossler, & D. Langdridge (Eds.). *Understanding counselling and psychotherapy.* (pp. 145–166). London: Sage.

Salzberg, S. (2011). Mindfulness and loving kindness. *Contemporary Buddhism, 12* (1), 177–182.

Schipper, J. (2012). Towards a Buddhist sociology: Theories, methods, and possibilities. *American Sociology, 43,* 203–222.

Schultz, K. (2010). *Being wrong: Adventures in the margin of error.* London: Portabello.

Segal, Z. V., Williams, J. M. G., & Teasdale, J. D. (2002). *Mindfulness-based cognitive therapy for depression: A new approach to preventing relapse.* New York, NY: Guilford Press.

Shapiro, S. L., & Izett, C. D. (2008). Meditation: A universal tool for cultivating empathy. In S. F. Hick, & T. Bien (Eds.). *Mindfulness and the therapeutic relationship.* (pp. 161–175). New York, NY: Guilford Press.

Siegel, D. J. (2007). *The mindful brain: Reflection and attunement in the cultivation of well-being.* New York, NY: Norton.

Siegel, D. J. (2010). *The mindful therapist.* New York, NY: Norton.

Siegel, R. D. (2004). Psychophysiological disorders: Embracing pain. In C. K. Germer, R. D. Siegel, & P. R. Fulton (Eds.). *Mindfulness and psychotherapy.* (pp. 173–196). New York, NY: Guilford Press.

Spandler, H., & Stickley, T. (in press). No hope without compassion: The importance of compassion in recovery-focused mental health services. *Journal of Mental Health.*

Spinelli, E. (2005). *The interpreted world: An introduction to phenomenological psychology.* London: Sage.

Stanley, S. (2012a). Mindfulness: Towards a critical relational perspective. *Social and Personality Psychology Compass, 6* (9), 631–706.

Stanley, S. (2012b). *Psychoanalysis and Buddhism.* Accessed 29/4/12 from: http://socialmindfulness.wordpress.com/2012/03/14/psychoanalysis-and-buddhism.

Stanley, S. (2012c). From discourse to awareness: Rhetoric, mindfulness, and a psychology without foundations. *Theory & Psychology,* published online DOI: 10.1177/0959354312463261.

Stanley, S., Edwards, V., & Barker, M. (forthcoming). Swimming against the stream: Investigating psychosocial flows through mindful awareness. *Qualitative Research in Psychology.*

Stern, D. N. (2004). *The present moment in psychotherapy and everyday life.* New York, NY: Norton.

Surrey, J. (2005). Relational psychotherapy, relational mindfulness. In C. K. Germer, R. D. Siegel, & P. R. Fulton (Eds.). *Mindfulness and psychotherapy.* (pp. 91–110). New York, NY: Guilford Press.

Suzuki, D. T. ([1949] 1969). *An introduction to Zen Buddhism.* London: Rider.

Swales, M. A., & Heard, H. L. (2009). *Dialectical behaviour therapy.* London: Routledge.

Tavris, C., & Aronson, E. (2008). *Mistakes were made (but not by me).* London: Pinter & Martin.

Teasdale, J. D., & Chaskalson, M. (2011). How does mindfulness transform suffering? The nature and origin of dukkha. *Contemporary Buddhism, 12* (1), 89–102.

Toates, F. (2010). Understanding drug treatments: A biopsychosocial approach. In M. Barker, A. Vossler, & D. Langdridge (Eds.). *Understanding counselling and psychotherapy.* (pp.45–76). London: Sage.

Toates, F. (2011). *Biological psychology.* Harlow: Pearson Eduction.

Tulku, T. (2000). Lucid dreaming: Exerting the creativity of the unconscious. In G. Watson, S. Batchelor, & G. Claston (Eds.). *The psychology of awakening: Buddhism, science and our day-to-day lives.* York Beach, ME: Weister.

Valentine, E., & Sweet, P. (1999). Meditation and attention: A comparison of the effects of concentrative and mindfulness meditation on sustained attention. *Mental Health, Religion and Culture, 2* (1), 59–70.

Varela, F. J., Thompson, E., & Rosch, E. (1991). *The embodied mind: Cognitive science and human experience.* London: MIT Press.

Vossler, A. (2010). Systemic approaches. In M. Barker, A. Vossler, & D. Langdridge (Eds.). *Understanding counselling and psychotherapy.* London: Sage.

Wachs, K., & Cordova, J. V. (2007). Mindful relating: Exploring mindfulness and emotional repertoires in intimate relationships. *Journal of marital and family therapy, 33* (4), 464–481.

Walser, R. D., & Westrup, D. (2009). *The mindful couple.* Oakland, CA: New Harbinger.

Walsh, R. A. (2008). Mindfulness and empathy. In S. F. Hick, & T. Bien (Eds.). *Mindfulness and the therapeutic relationship.* (pp. 72–86). New York, NY: Guilford Press.

Wanden-Berghe, R. G., Sanz-Valero, J., & Wanden-Berghe, C. (2010). The application of mindfulness to eating disorders treatment: A systematic review. *Eating Disorders: The Journal of Treatment & Prevention, 19* (1), 34–48.

Watson, G. (2008). *Beyond happiness: Deepening the dialogue between Buddhism, psychotherapy and the mind sciences.* London: Karnac.

Welwood, J. (1996). *Love and awakening.* London: HarperCollins.

Welwood, J. (2006). *Perfect love imperfect relationships.* Boston, MA: Trumpeter.

Wetherell, M. (2012). *Affect and emotion: A new social science understanding.* London: Sage.

Williams, J. M. G., & Kabat-Zinn, J. (Eds.). (2011a). Special issue on mindfulness. *Contemporary Buddhism, 12* (1), 1–306.

Williams, J. M. G., & Kabat-Zinn, J. (2011b). Mindfulness: Diverse perspectives on its meaning, origins, and multiple applications at the intersection of science and Dharma. *Contemporary Buddhism, 12* (1), 1–18.

Williams, J. M., & Penman, D. (2011). *Mindfulness: A practical guide to finding peace in a frantic world.* London: Piatkus.

Williams, M., Teasdale, J., Segal, Z., & Kabat-Zinn, J. (2007). *The mindful way through depression.* New York, NY: Guilford Press.

Winbush, N. Y., Goss, C. R., & Kreitzer, M. J. (2007). The effects of mindfulness-based stress reduction on sleep disturbance: A systematic review. *Explore, 3* (6), 585–591.

World Health Organization (1973). *The international pilot study of schizophrenia.* World Health Organization: Geneva.

Yalom, I. D. (2001). *The gift of therapy.* London: Piatkus.

Young-Eisendrath, P., & Muramoto, S. (2002). *Awakening and insight: Zen Buddhism and psychotherapy.* New York, NY: Routledge.

Zeidan, F., Gordon, N. S., Merchant, J., & Goolkasian, P. (2008). The effects of brief mindfulness meditation training on experimentally induced pain. *The Journal of Pain, 11* (3), 199–209.

Index